A Brave Vessel

HOBSON WOODWARD

A Brave Vessel

The True Tale of the Castaways
Who Rescued Jamestown and Inspired
Shakespeare's *The Tempest*

VIKING

VIKING

Published by the Penguin Group
Penguin Group (USA) Inc., 375 Hudson Street,
New York, New York 10014, U.S.A.
Penguin Group (Canada), 90 Eglinton Avenue East, Suite 700, Toronto,
Ontario, Canada M4P 2Y3 (a division of Pearson Penguin Canada Inc.)
Penguin Books Ltd, 80 Strand, London WC2R 0RL, England
Penguin Ireland, 25 St. Stephen's Green, Dublin 2, Ireland
(a division of Penguin Books Ltd)
Penguin Books Australia Ltd, 250 Camberwell Road, Camberwell,
Victoria 3124, Australia (a division of Pearson Australia Group Pty Ltd)
Penguin Books India Pvt Ltd, 11 Community Centre,
Panchsheel Park, New Delhi–110 017, India
Penguin Group (NZ), 67 Apollo Drive, Rosedale, North Shore 0632,
New Zealand (a division of Pearson New Zealand Ltd)
Penguin Books (South Africa) (Pty) Ltd, 24 Sturdee Avenue,
Rosebank, Johannesburg 2196, South Africa

Penguin Books Ltd, Registered Offices: 80 Strand, London WC2R 0RL, England

First published in 2009 by Viking Penguin, a member of Penguin Group (USA) Inc.

1 3 5 7 9 10 8 6 4 2

Copyright © Hobson Woodward, 2009
All rights reserved

Map by Jeffrey L. Ward

LIBRARY OF CONGRESS CATALOGING IN PUBLICATION DATA
Woodward, Hobson.
A brave vessel : the true tale of the castaways who rescued Jamestown
and inspired Shakespeare's The tempest / Hobson Woodward.
p. cm.
Includes bibliographical references and index.
ISBN 978-0-670-02096-6
1. Jamestown (Va.)—History—17th century. 2. Sea Venture (Ship) 3. Shipwrecks—
Bermuda Islands—History—17th century. 4. Seafaring life—History—17th century.
5. Strachey, William, 1572?–1621. 6. Shakespeare, William, 1564–1616. Tempest. 7. Virginia—
History—Colonial period, ca. 1600–1775. 8. Bermuda Islands—History—17th century.
9. Great Britain—Colonies—America—History—17th century. I. Title.
F234.J3W65 2009
910.916348—DC22   2008051325

Printed in the United States of America
Set in Minion   Designed by Francesca Belanger

For Powell, Mary,
Beth, Sadie, and Sage

O, I have suffered
with those that I saw suffer—a brave vessel
(who had no doubt some noble creature in her)
dashed all to pieces.

—Miranda, *The Tempest*

PREFACE

To William Strachey the new play by William Shakespeare seemed oddly familiar. Watching *The Tempest* from a seat in the Blackfriars Theater on an autumn afternoon in 1611, Strachey was sure he recognized the luminous flight of the sprite Ariel about the masts of the *Tempest* ship. The scene was an eerie reminder of a rain-whipped night two years before, when St. Elmo's fire appeared on the masts of the vessel on which he rode. Strachey had written a letter home that described a "little round light like a faint star, trembling and streaming along with a sparkling blaze half the height upon the mainmast." Now here was Shakespeare's character onstage, a shimmering sprite who told of illuminating the *Tempest* ship in the same way—"on the topmast, the yards and bowsprit would I flame distinctly." The similarity seemed so strong, it was almost as if the playwright had read his letter and recast his very words as an enchanted idyll. As William Strachey would soon realize, William Shakespeare had done just that.

Most of the writings of William Strachey are long forgotten. Virtually all the sonnets and narratives he wrote between 1604 and 1612 met with indifference when he managed to put them in front of readers. His habit was to worry over every line, and his works were invariably labored—all of them, that is, but his tale of the sea voyage of 1609. Strachey told of the wreck of the *Sea Venture*, the flagship of a fleet carrying colonists to Jamestown in Virginia. That one account seizes the reader from the first sentence, carrying her through a drenching tempest, a shipwreck, and a harrowing adventure on an exotic isle. Perhaps not surprisingly, Strachey's evocative narrative was written without much thought in a wilderness hut for an audience of one. The woman who received his letter lent it to others, and those readers gave it to their friends, until it was eventually passed along to William Shakespeare.

The greatest writer of the English language was a bit of a literary pickpocket. Shakespeare was a voracious reader and extracted language and ideas from contemporary and classical literature alike. Such homage to the works of others was not only tolerated in Jacobean England, it was expected, and Shakespeare was a master. In his supremely creative mind, merely good language was made both accessible and profound for readers of his time and those of ages far beyond his own. The ability to select and transform language was one of Shakespeare's greatest gifts.

The use of William Strachey's narrative of the wreck of the *Sea Venture* as the framework of *The Tempest* is a prime example of Shakespeare's craft. In his nimble mind, the glow on the mast of the ship became the winsome Ariel. The enigmatic wild man Caliban was a descendant of a murderous sailor and Powhatan voyagers who were marooned with the English. Elements of the magician Prospero were developed out of Strachey's portrait of the leader of the shipwrecked company. Good-hearted Gonzalo had a silver-haired counterpart in the admiral who rode the *Sea Venture*. There are small details—a berry drink Strachey drank was poured into Caliban's cup, and a rock-dwelling bird the castaways stalked became the quarry of *Tempest* hunters. There are overarching themes, as well—the musings of Gonzalo about founding an ideal commonwealth on the *Tempest* isle are a crystallization of the contemporary debate about Britain's colonial ambitions. Strachey provided a true story of colonial exploration; Shakespeare applied his art and re-created it as a New World masterpiece.

The pages that follow tell the story of that collaboration between William Strachey and William Shakespeare, a joint project of which Strachey was unaware until he returned from the New World to find the reworking of his story on the London stage. Strachey was obscure, and his counterpart was one of the most famous men of his time. One lived through a hurricane and shipwreck on an uninhabited island; the other remolded the story of the voyage as a tempestuous tale with universal appeal. This book tells the story of those two writers, and the sea storm, black plague, rivalries, murder, love, mutiny, and war they experienced before they wrote their intertwined tale.

I first encountered the story of the literary intersection of William Strachey and William Shakespeare while reading about the life of Pocahontas. The Englishman whom Pocahontas would marry, John Rolfe, was aboard the *Sea Venture* and spent ten months as a castaway on Bermuda with Strachey. The reference I came across was brief, saying only that Strachey's narrative inspired Shakespeare's play. I was captivated nonetheless, and so began to read everything I could find about the voyage and the play, and—especially—the links between the two.

My foray into Virginia and *Tempest* history took me across the Atlantic, where I visited the libraries of London and Oxford and stood on the Thames riverbank where Strachey's ship departed for Jamestown. I saw Shakespeare's work on the stage of the rebuilt Globe Theater and wandered the sites of his London haunts. In Bermuda I searched for beach glass in the cove where the castaways launched one of their homemade ships and visited museums and archives to examine artifacts from 1609. Back in America I went to the Historic Jamestowne Archaearium museum to see artifacts of the settlement and inspect the bones of Bermuda birds eaten by the colonists. Nearby I saw Shakespeare's characters come alive again within the authentic walls of Virginia's replica Blackfriars Playhouse.

What I discovered in my travels was the incredible tale of shipwreck that I tell on the pages that follow. My studies reanimated the battering of the *Sea Venture* and the survival of the voyagers on a mid-Atlantic island, one of the great sea stories of Atlantic history. I recount findings of my own, including new clues about the presence of the two Powhatans on the *Sea Venture*. Most often, though, I gathered together the detective work of numerous researchers who over the last two centuries have unraveled a fascinating array of the connections between that *Sea Venture* tale and Shakespeare's *Tempest*. That remarkable web of correlations is revealed in the pages below. The men and women whose discoveries I report are credited in the endnotes that follow the text.

My goal in this book is to present for the first time the complete story of Strachey's remarkable account and Shakespeare's transformation of that narrative into his magical *Tempest*. The tale ends with the birth of a sprite, a monster, a magician, and a pair of chess-playing lovers. At its beginning is a true story of an aspiring writer who emerged from the shadow of a master to voyage to the New World, only to be overtaken by a wild tempest on a dark summer night in 1609.

CONTENTS

A Brave Vessel

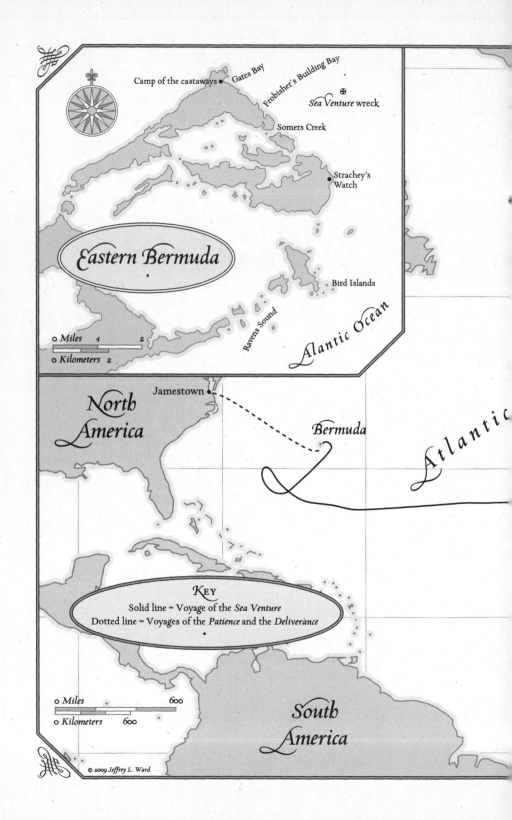

Camp of the castaways • • Gates Bay
Frobisher's Building Bay
⊕
Sea Venture wreck
Somers Creek

• Strachey's
Watch

Eastern Bermuda

Bird Islands

Ravens Sound

Alantic Ocean

o Miles 1 2
o Kilometers 2

Jamestown •

North America

Bermuda

Atlantic

KEY
Solid line = Voyage of the *Sea Venture*
Dotted line = Voyages of the *Patience* and the *Deliverance*

o Miles 600
o Kilometers 600

South America

© 2009 Jeffrey L. Ward

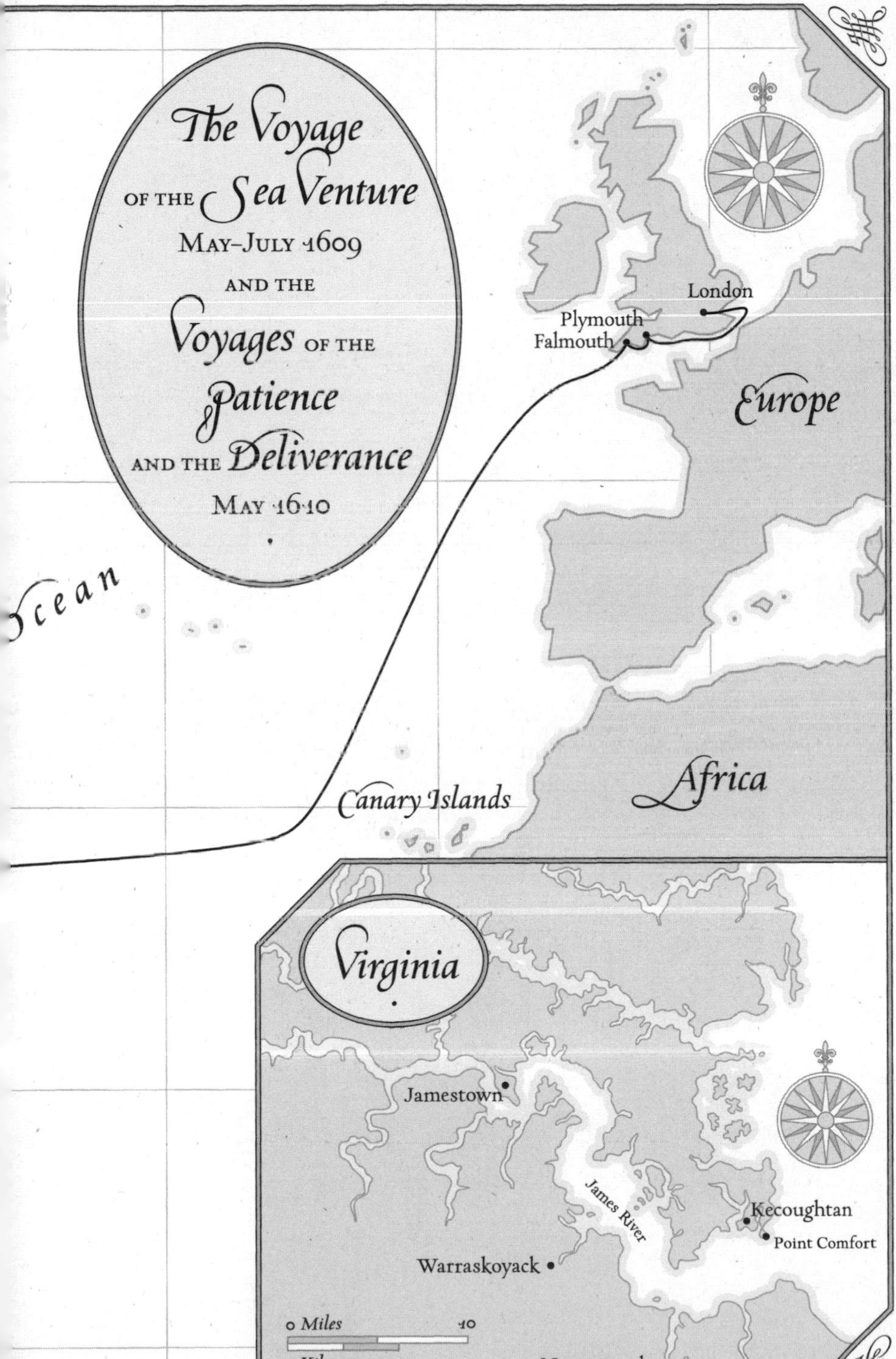

The Voyage
OF THE Sea Venture
MAY–JULY 1609
AND THE
Voyages OF THE
Patience
AND THE Deliverance
MAY 1610

Ocean

Europe

London
Plymouth
Falmouth

Africa

Canary Islands

Virginia

Jamestown

James River

Kecoughtan
Point Comfort

Warraskoyack

0 Miles   10
0 Kilometers 10

Nansemond

CHAPTER ONE

Poet of London

Thou hast howled away twelve winters.

—Prospero, *The Tempest*

Few read the markings of William Strachey's quill. The thirty-two-year-old from the English countryside had spent more than a decade in London trying to become a writer, but few beyond his immediate circle knew his name. That his initials were the same as the most successful literary man of his time, William Shakespeare, was an ironic coincidence. In many ways the two were similar—both came from modest stock, both were educated in classical literature, and both of them had wives and children living in distant villages—but in the most important respect they could not be more different. Few had ever heard of William Strachey, whereas William Shakespeare was renowned throughout the kingdom.

Now in 1604 the unknown William S. had an opportunity to be noticed. The playwright Ben Jonson had invited Strachey to contribute one of eight introductory sonnets to a new publication of his drama *Sejanus: His Fall*. The plays of Jonson were second in popularity only to those of Shakespeare, so the invitation was a true opportunity. Strachey's sonnet would circulate among the literary elite of the city. This was a major advance in his quest to become a writer, and he worked hard to make the verse his best work.

The family of William Strachey had not always been wealthy enough for the eldest son to lead a literary life in London. That only became possible when William's grandfather raised enough sheep and finished enough wool to become the richest man in his ancestral town of Saffron Walden. The new affluence had allowed William's father to go to school fifty miles away in London and to meet and marry the daughter of a city merchant. William the sonnet writer had spent a childhood divided between country and city, growing up in the household of a father whose goal was to attain a higher place in life. A month after grandfather William had died in 1587, father William had been granted a coat of arms by the College of Heralds, the first act of a newly liberated yeoman who longed to live the life of a gentleman. William the writer would emulate his father rather than his grandfather, maintaining minimal ties to the countryseat and pursuing a life in the city that his ancestors would have considered irresponsible.

Strachey the aspiring writer had attended Emmanuel College in Cambridge and Gray's Inn in London without earning a degree from either institution. At twenty-three he had married Frances Forster, the daughter of a prosperous Surrey family with political connections. Frances resided at her father's estate at Crowhurst while Strachey lived in London. Two children had been born over the previous decade—William Jr., delivered nine months after the marriage, and Edmund, still an infant. Strachey's wife and children were all in Crowhurst while he labored in London to produce the sonnet for Jonson's book, the work he was sure would be the first of many publications in his name.

The sonnet Strachey produced was a meditation on the life of the Roman soldier protagonist of Jonson's play. The metaphor he chose to illuminate Sejanus's rise and fall was a storm of thunder and lightning that produces fury but passes with little effect. The theme of "On Sejanus" was laid out in the final line—"nothing violent lasts." Strachey wrote of "swift lightning" and "ruinous blasts" of thunder. He then added a second metaphor, comparing both the lightning and Sejanus to a *vaunt-courier,* or a soldier in an advance guard who delivers an impressive first strike but ultimately falls to the enemy.

Upon publication of the book Strachey's theme proved disappointingly prophetic, as the work itself produced a momentary flash that soon faded. Friends complimented him, but the notice did little to change his prospects. As usual the only thing that seemed to advance his goal of gaining literary friends was spending money, and the money he spent was generally on the theater. While Strachey hoped to publish sonnets and travel narratives rather than plays, he loved the work of playwrights and the culture of London theaters. One of his strategic purchases was a share in the Children of the Revels, a troupe of children that performed in a converted room in the former Blackfriars monastery. Owning an interest in a theater company gave him credibility, but it also proved to be an expensive proposition. While he was entitled to a share of the profits, the investment ended up costing him money because he had to pay for food for the boy actors and theater repairs. Strachey had money, but it was growing short. As the eldest son among seven full siblings and five half-sisters, he had assumed control of the family holdings when his father died in 1598, selling much of the property immediately to distribute legacies to his brothers and sisters. Now six years later the inheritance was running thin.

Strachey had made many friends during his time in London, though he always wondered whether it was due to his generous spending habits. Poet John Donne was his closest companion. They were the same age and shared a love of verse and a thinly veiled anxiety about money, though Donne was more adept at both writing and cultivating patrons. There were others, too. At Gray's Inn, Strachey had associated with writer Thomas Campion, who would later call him "my old companion Strachey." Ben Jonson also professed himself a loyal friend. Strachey was also acquainted with Shakespeare, but the two were hardly close. Frankly it was not a very ample return on a dozen years and an inheritance spent in pursuit of literary success. Strachey was almost out of money, so something would have to change soon.

A break came two years after the publication of *Sejanus*, in 1606, when a cousin recommended Strachey for the position of secretary to the new ambassador to Turkey. Thomas Glover would soon depart for Constantinople and needed a reliable scribe. In August, Strachey departed with Glover's party aboard the *Royal Exchange*. After a stop in Algiers, the ship reached Constantinople in December. The Turkey assignment started well but would ultimately end badly. Glover was the former secretary of outgoing ambassador Henry Lello and had acquired the job by convincing officials to assign him the post even while Lello labored in Turkey. The two would-be ambassadors met in Constantinople, and during an ensuing power struggle Strachey sided with Lello and was abruptly fired. Cast in the streets of a foreign land without an income, the former secretary eventually returned to England with the deposed ambassador. When Strachey arrived back in London in June 1608, his first act was to borrow thirty pounds from Dutch moneylender Jasper Tien. He was home again, but poorer than ever and embittered by his overseas adventure. A friend told Glover in December that "one Strachey is making a book against you, which if it should be so, it peradventure may cost him both ears." Strachey never published his diatribe or suffered the punishment for libel, but he told everyone he knew that Glover was a scoundrel.

Upon his return from Turkey, Strachey was surprised by one development in literary London. He was amused to find that William Shakespeare had been impressed enough with his sonnet "On Sejanus" to use a version of one of its lines in his new play *King Lear*. Strachey discovered Lear himself comparing lightning to a *vaunt-courier*—the very term he had used in his sonnet. Strachey may have noticed, too, that three lines earlier Lear used a new word that voyagers had brought back from the West Indies. The word was *"hurricano,"* a term derived from the name of a Caribbean deity with a stormy disposition. Shakespeare, it seems, was as partial to storm imagery as the man from whom he borrowed the lightning line. Strachey was flattered to have even an uncredited line in a play by London's leading dramatist, but he realized that few in the audience would ever be aware of the debt. Strachey's unheralded debut on the London stage only made him long more keenly to write something in his own name that all England would want to read.

The Turkey debacle had not reduced Strachey's taste for adventure. For a while, though, he would content himself with reading travel narratives.

He loved the chronicles of New World explorers that appeared regularly in London bookshops. Richard Willes's classic *History of Travayle in the West and East Indies* was a favorite. One narrative Strachey may have read was an account by Antonio Pigafetta, a member of Ferdinand Magellan's crew and one of the few who survived the famous circumnavigation of the globe a century earlier. At the southern tip of Patagonia some people were lured aboard ship and captured, Pigafetta said, and "in time when they saw how they were deceived, they roared like bulls and cried upon their great devil Setebos to help them." The story was exotic and poignant at the same time.

Another popular travel book was Richard Hakluyt's *Principal Navigations, Voyages, Traffiques and Discoveries of the English Nation*. Among the stories in its pages was an incredible tale by an Englishman named Job Hartop, who had crossed the Atlantic on a Spanish ship. "When we came in the height of Bermuda," Hartop wrote, "we discovered a monster in the sea, who showed himself three times unto us from the middle upwards, in which parts he was proportioned like a man of the complexion of a mulatto or tawny Indian." What a peculiar story indeed—a monster with attributes of a fish and a New World man seen about an island far at sea.

Despite remaining in London, Strachey had an opportunity to see living individuals from the New World. Several indigenous people had been captured by early explorers and forced to come to the Old World, but a man named Namontack of Tsenacomoco was the first to cross the ocean from Virginia to England as an emissary of a New World nation. He had come in 1608 as a representative of Wahunsenacawh, known as "Powhatan" to the English, the leader of the people of Tsenacomoco who were collectively called Powhatans by the colonists. Wahunsenacawh ruled a confederation of thirty villages with a population of fifteen thousand to twenty thousand people that surrounded the place the English had occupied in 1607 and renamed Jamestown. John Smith, the most famous colonist of all, who at the time was already in Virginia, described Namontack as Wahunsenacawh's "trusty servant and one of a shrewd, subtle capacity." The Powhatan envoy had come into the English colony a few months earlier when colonial official Christopher Newport and Wahunsenacawh exchanged a pair of young men for the purpose of developing language interpreters. Thirteen-year-old Thomas Savage had been sent to live with the Powhatans, while Namontack had come to live with the English. Wahunsenacawh then agreed to allow his representative to travel to England with Newport, a visit the colonists hoped would generate interest and investment in the Jamestown enterprise.

Namontack became a celebrity during his time in London, in part because his English chaperones declared him to be Wahunsenacawh's son. The people who encountered the Powhatan envoy treated him as part diplomat and part sideshow marvel. Spanish ambassador Pedro de Zúñiga was perhaps unhappy that the man from Tsenacomoco was given diplomatic status. "This Newport brought a lad who they say is the son of an emperor of those lands," Zúñiga wrote in a dispatch home, "and they have coached him that when he sees the king he is not to take off his hat, and other things of this sort, so that I have been amused by the way they honor him, for I hold it for surer that he must be a very ordinary person."

When Strachey first saw Namontack, the physical appearance of the New World visitor was striking. Jamestown colonist Gabriel Archer noted that the traditional hairstyle of Powhatan men was a prominent feature. Hair was grown long on one side and knotted at the bottom. On the other side it was shaved close with sharpened shells to allow the unimpeded use of bowstrings. "Some have chains of long linked copper about their necks, and some chains of pearl," Archer said. "I found not a gray eye among them all. Their skin is tawny, not so born but with dyeing and painting themselves, in which they delight greatly." The Powhatan envoy may have worn a mix of English and Powhatan attire. Reverend William Crashaw was probably referring to Namontack when he spoke of a Virginian visitor who "had gone naked all his life till our men persuaded him to be clothed." Even obscured by English garb, the Powhatan elements of grooming and dress would have been visible to William Strachey.

Soon after Newport left London in July 1608 to return with Namon-tack to Tsenacomoco, the black plague began a sustained assault on London. Strachey had been home from Turkey for a month and was looking forward to resuming his life in London, money permitting, but he soon left the city for the countryside. The bulbous swellings of the lymph glands, the feverish sweats, the sores, and the involuntary spasms known as the danse macabre were familiar to all Londoners. A sure sign of the onset of a new epidemic were the beaked masks of the plague doctors. Anyone with enough money to leave the city fled to escape the contagion. Among them was William Strachey, who joined his family in Crowhurst.

Deprived of the theater and London friends during the plague winter of 1608 to 1609, Strachey read his travel books by the fireside while his sons played about him. Strachey also wrote letters to friends, including John Donne, a reliable companion who had tried to help him find a new position after he lost the Turkey post. In a letter to an influential acquaintance, Donne had called Strachey "my good friend" and blamed Glover for the unpleasant episode. "I dare boldly say that the greatest folly he ever committed was to submit himself and parts to so mean a master." No job had come of the referral, but Strachey appreciated the effort nevertheless.

Both Strachey and Donne were attempting to support their families on their writing alone. Donne had lately grown close to a patron known for her love of literature. The Countess of Bedford had been born Lucy Harrington, but gained a noble title when she married the third Earl of Bedford at the age of thirteen. The countess was extremely well situated in the court of King James as one of Queen Anna's Ladies of the Bedchamber. She regularly entertained poets and playwrights in her home and selected a few to receive regular stipends. Donne was her current favorite, so much so that she served as godmother to one of his children. In letters Donne called the countess "my Lady Bedford" and "the best lady." Strachey had joined his friend on some of his visits with the countess. Privately he entertained the idea that she might extend her patronage to him, though no offer had yet been made.

Also during the winter of 1608 to 1609, both Strachey and Donne observed the recruiting efforts of the Virginia Company of London as it prepared to launch the largest expedition ever sent to Jamestown. Indeed, because of the great amount of publicity material produced by the Virginia Company, it would be difficult not to be aware of its progress. A massive supply convoy was planned for the spring, and the company wanted hundreds of new settlers to sign on to join the two-year-old colony. The prospect of such a voyage was enticing to fortune hunters, rich and poor alike. For years Spanish ships had brought back treasure from the New World, and now for the first time England had established a permanent colony across the Atlantic. Here was a chance to join in what the pamphlets and printed announcements of the Virginia Company promised would be a lucrative venture. Spanish ambassador Zúñiga confirmed the success of the drive for money and recruits: "They have collected in twenty days an amount of money for this voyage that frightens me."

In the early months of 1609 the plague continued to kill with alarming rapidity. The epidemic had an equally devastating effect on the English economy. To anyone with an appetite for adventure, the Jamestown expedition offered both escape and economic promise. John Donne was the first of the two friends to make inquiries. He had been on voyages to Spain and the Azores in 1595 and 1597, and the idea of a new journey intrigued him. "News here is none at all but that John Dun seeks to be preferred to be secretary of Virginia," an official wrote in a letter to another on February 14, 1609. Donne turned out to have a fleeting enthusiasm for the venture. The secretary position was assigned to a man who was already in Jamestown, and the poet soon abandoned the idea of joining the expedition.

Strachey would prove more tenacious. As the winter went on, he became convinced that the Virginia voyage was an opportunity not to be missed. The promise of riches would answer his looming need for money. The financial security that awaited him across the ocean would be a great relief. Beyond that there was the chance to become a chronicler of England's explorations of the New World. An eager public read the Jamestown narratives that had been published to date. Travel accounts were something he could write easily and well if he were in Virginia, and here was an opportunity to go there. He would cross the ocean to a wild land and become a chronicler of the New World.

The post of secretary being filled, Strachey signed on as a planter. In that role he would be fed and clothed for the duration of the expedition in exchange for working on behalf of the colony. Simply agreeing to join yielded Strachey a share of stock in the Virginia Company valued at £12.10 (the equivalent of about $2,900 today). His status as an educated man of merit, in the judgment of company officials, was worth a second share. In return for his pledge to venture abroad he received a decorated stock certificate. No dividends were to be paid for seven years, at which time he was to receive two shares of all profits made during the period and two shares of all Virginia land under company control— expected to total five hundred acres per share. The immediate value of the expedition, however, would be exciting experiences to write about rather than money.

Strachey was delighted when he learned he would ride with the leaders of the expedition aboard the *Sea Venture*, the flagship of the fleet of nine vessels. The captain of the ship would be Christopher Newport, the man who had recently brought Namontack to England for a second time. The Powhatan emissary had returned to Tsenacomoco the first time with stories of "the kind reception and treatment he received in England." An intrigued Wahunsenacawh had sent him back across the sea again, this time accompanied by a companion named Machumps. Now, after a second London visit again chaperoned by Newport, the Powhatan visitors were preparing to return home on the *Sea Venture*. Strachey was pleased, since he would have many weeks aboard ship to learn to communicate with the Powhatans and begin to gather material for his chronicle.

Through the late winter and early spring of 1609, Strachey prepared to voyage to the New World. The departure date was delayed several times, but in early May it was clear the fleet would depart by the end of the

month. A couple of weeks in advance Strachey began to pack his trunk
at his father-in-law's estate in Crowhurst, where his family would live
during his absence. The articles he packed probably included the recommended supplies of a Jamestown settler: linen and silk shirts and
breeches, silk hose and gloves, leather and cloth jerkins to wear over his
shirts, silk gowns, cloaks, leather shoes, Castile soap, combs, orrisroot
and alum for deodorant, and a linen pouch of powdered rosemary wood
for a toothbrush. Strachey also carried clay pipes and tobacco and a sew-
ing kit of pins, needles, thread, thimbles, and scissors. Wool blankets
and a mattress bag stuffed with wool would serve as his bed.

An earlier colonist advised anyone planning a Virginia venture to
pack one more thing: "For the comfort of their souls let them bring
Bibles and other good books." Strachey did not need to be persuaded to
follow that advice. Along with paper, ink horn, quills, penknife, and sealing wax, Strachey placed at least two books in his trunk. He would bring
Richard Willes's *History of Travayle in the West and East Indies*, complete with its tale of the Bermuda sea monster. José de Acosta's *Naturall
and Morall Historie of the East and West Indies* also went in his trunk.
Those were the best books available on the New World, and Strachey
wanted to consult them when he encountered strange people, plants, and
animals. On the title page of *History of Travayle*, Strachey wrote his
name and the date, May 2, 1609, to identify it as his copy.

The wife and sons whom Strachey would leave behind helped gather
belongings from the chests and cupboards of the family's rooms. His wife,
Frances, and sons William, now thirteen, and Edmund, five, had become
used to his being away in London for months at a time and had centered
their lives at Crowhurst. They presumed that Strachey would not return
for years, but since he had been with them only occasionally in recent
times, the difference would be a matter of degree. During the plague Strachey had been with his family for an extended period and it had been good
for all of them. The opportunity to join the Virginia venture was a critical
one, however, and Strachey felt he needed to go. Frances and the children
would be fine.

The persistence of the plague confirmed Strachey's conviction that he had made the right decision. There was little prospect of earning money by writing while the epidemic continued. In May 1609, as the Jamestown fleet prepared to sail, the disease showed no signs of abating. "You all know God is angry," Reverend Daniel Price proclaimed in a London sermon that month. "Wrath is come out, the plague is begun, yea continued from year to year, rideth progress from country to country, executeth judgment upon high and low, and keepeth court at this time within this city." If the Virginia ships managed to leave the city without carrying the disease, all aboard would at least be free of that worry. "The sickness increases," a Londoner wrote to a friend on May 1. "The Virginians go forward the next week."

CHAPTER TWO

Aboard for Jamestown

Though fools at home condemn 'em.

—Antonio, *The Tempest*

S un broke through an overcast sky to illuminate the Virginia fleet as it rode the current of the Thames River on May 12, 1609. The port of Woolwich was a lively spot on any day, but on this one it was especially so as workers prepared for a transatlantic voyage. Aromas of river mud, canvas, and sweat were in the air as workers moved trunks from carts to rowboats for transfer to the moored ships. Seven vessels were bound from London to the English colony of Jamestown—the *Sea Venture*, the *Diamond*, the *Falcon*, the *Blessing*, the *Unity*, the *Lion*, and an unnamed ketch.

William Strachey traveled a day's carriage ride from Crowhurst to Woolwich, a town of docks and warehouses ten miles downriver from England's largest city. In his first view of the fleet, the *Sea Venture* stood out. The newly constructed flagship had a blunt stern and a pointed bow adorned with a figurehead. At a hundred feet and three hundred tons, the ship was the largest of a fleet that would eventually number nine vessels and carry five hundred colonists and a hundred and sixty mariners across the Atlantic. The most prominent people of the expedition would ride on the *Sea Venture*, and Strachey would be among them. It was a Friday afternoon, and on Monday the fleet would depart for the New World.

The British colony of Jamestown had been established two years earlier. The English had been slow to get into the colonial business, but watching the Spanish and Portuguese fleets return laden with treasure had been too much to resist. In May 1607 three vessels had landed just over a hundred colonists on a Virginia riverbank. Early reports had reinforced the perception that the settlement had the potential to yield treasure. Officials who received them were only too happy to share the rosy descriptions, though privately they admitted they were probably too good to be true. "We are fallen upon a land that promises more than the land of promise," one official wrote in 1607. "Instead of milk we find pearl, and gold instead of honey." Convoys known as the First and Second Supplies had carried additional settlers to Jamestown. Despite the good reports, though, the influx was hardly keeping pace with the mortality rate. Neither of the first two fleets approached the size of this one, the Third Supply. The Virginia Company hoped this new infusion of people and provisions would fortify their outpost in the New World.

In the spring of 1609 the Virginia Company was at the height of its recruiting power as a result of a revision of its charter. King James had agreed to shift the company from royal to private control, giving the Virginia Company sole command of the enterprise and providing the king deniability if the Spanish objected, since they also claimed Virginia. The royal treasury would still receive a large share of any profits—20 percent of gold and silver and 6 percent of other minerals. An additional effect of the new charter was to increase Britain's territorial claim in America from ten thousand square miles to more than a million. The revision also altered the way in which the colony would be run. During the first two years a colonial council governed Jamestown, but the roundtable method had produced only strife in the wilds of America. Now leadership would be vested in a single governor, Thomas West, Lord Delaware. Delaware was unable to go abroad immediately, however, so Thomas Gates was named interim governor and put in charge until Delaware could launch another expedition a few months later.

To ensure that the Third Supply reached its quota of colonists, the Virginia Company published several promotional pamphlets in the months before it departed. Jamestown was depicted as a verdant land of welcoming people. In one such pamphlet, *Nova Britannia*, London alderman

Robert Johnson ignored confidential reports from Virginia that told of food shortages and infighting. Instead he described the colony on the James River as an "earthly paradise" in which the first settlers were "ravished with the admirable sweetness of the stream and with the pleasant land trending along on either side." Even though in reality the settlers and the Powhatans were killing each other with alarming frequency, Johnson reported that the people of Virginia were "generally very loving and gentle, and do entertain and relieve our people with great kindness." To further allay the concerns of potential colonists, Johnson assured his readers that the ocean voyage to the New World was not to be feared: "Most winds that blow are apt and fit for us, and none can hinder us."

Two main arguments convinced voyagers to go to Jamestown. The most important was that recruits would share in any profit made in the New World. The suggestion that precious metals would be found had been freely made in the early days of the colony, and the impression persisted even though such claims had been largely eliminated from the company's most recent promotional literature. While officials were careful not to say so publicly, the grand hopes of the first colonists for gleaming treasure had been all but abandoned by the time the Gates fleet was preparing to leave England. During the first two years of settlement the Virginia Company had been rewarded with a return of only "petty commodities and hope of more." Promoters had begun to suggest that if gold and silver were not to be had, perhaps the flow of commodities could be enhanced until it was not so petty.

The most obvious raw material America offered was lumber, of which deforested England had little. The virgin forests of Virginia promised masts for ships and planks for houses. The wood could also be used as fuel to make secondary products like pitch, soap, turpentine, and glass. Virginia plants might yield oils, dyes, medicines, perfumes, wines, and textiles. There were fish and furs as well. Mines held the potential of iron and copper. Johnson in *Nova Britannia* listed a score of products imported from eastern Europe and the Mediterranean that could instead be produced by England in Virginia. If this was accomplished, he wrote, England might rightly expect "this little northern corner of the world to be in short time the richest storehouse and staple for merchandise in all Europe."

There was another economic goal of the Virginia explorers, but by 1609 it too was a fading prospect. The Virginia Company hoped to find a river passage through the continent of North America to the spice markets of India and China. If a passage could be found and controlled, the investors would become very rich indeed. Those prospects seemed to be enhanced by early reports from the Powhatans—undoubtedly garbled in translation—that a great body of water lay west of Jamestown. A possible explanation is that their trade networks extended north to the Great Lakes or south to the Gulf of Mexico. English exploration of the rivers so far had led only to narrowing channels and impassable rapids. While the hope of a route to the East Indies remained active, it too was becoming ever more distant as the Gates fleet prepared to sail.

The pamphlets of the Virginia Company quietly shifted their emphasis in another way also, from suggestions of easy fortunes to appeals about the glory of conquest. The settling of Jamestown, they said, was an opportunity to convert the Powhatans to Christianity. Ministers who favored the mission proclaimed from their pulpits that England had a duty to spread the Gospel to the New World. Reverend William Symonds was an enthusiastic backer of the Virginia experiment and had no problem attacking critics who saw the colonists as an invading force: "If these objectors had any brains in their head but those which are sick, they could easily find a difference between a bloody invasion and the planting of a peaceable colony in a waste country where the people do live but like deer in herds." Any opposition must be Catholic in origin, Symonds said. "Certainly our objector was hatched of some Popish egg."

Robert Johnson also answered detractors who saw the Virginia colonists as trespassers. "As for supplanting the savages, we have no such intent," he wrote. "Our intrusion into their possessions shall tend to their great good and no way to their hurt, unless as unbridled beasts they procure it to themselves." Johnson claimed that descendants of the Powhatans would thank the English for the gift of the European way of life. "Their children when they come to be saved will bless the day when first their fathers saw your faces," he told potential colonists. The message hinted at ominous consequences if the inhabitants of the New World resisted the imposition of a foreign culture.

Another commentator, Richard Hakluyt, used the metaphor of an artisan creating a fine work to explain how the voyagers would respond if the Powhatans refused to cooperate. "To handle them gently while gentle courses may be found to serve, it will be without comparison the best," Hakluyt wrote. "But if gentle polishing will not serve, the one shall not want hammerers and rough masons enough, I mean our old soldiers trained up in the Netherlands, to square and prepare them to our preachers' hands." Symonds also endorsed the use of guns and armor if the gifts of Christianity and Western civilization were not readily accepted. To argue otherwise, he said, was to argue that a parent should be denied the option of corporal punishment.

For as much ink as was devoted to the glory of converting the Powhatans, that element of the discussion had little practical application for most of the men and women who made the decision to go to the New World. They only paid true heed to the economic argument, the contention that riches were to be found and anyone with a stake in the enterprise would share in the wealth. To be sure, in the two years since the founding of Jamestown there had been plenty who dismissed the idea that Virginia held treasure, the most vocal being those who had no intention of ever leaving England. The critics did their speaking on street corners and in coffeehouses, however, rather than in printed pamphlets.

Virtually the only criticism that made it into print was the satire of the playwrights of London who regularly parodied the Virginia expeditions. Ben Jonson's 1605 *Eastward Hoe* lampooned the expectations of those preparing to go to Virginia. The character of Seagull echoed the wildest hopes of the Jamestown colonists. "Gold is more plentiful there than copper is with us, and for as much red copper as I can bring

I'll have thrice the weight in gold," he said. "Why, man, all their dripping pans and their chamber pots are pure gold, and all the chains with which they chain up their streets are massy gold; all the prisoners they take are fettered in gold; and for rubies and diamonds, they go forth on holidays and gather 'em by the seashore to hang on their children's coats and stick in their caps." Ironically, as plays like *Eastward Hoe* parodied dreams of Virginia treasure, they also raised the expectations of potential colonists. In a plague-ravaged city with little economic opportunity, the promise of the overseas expedition seemed an even better bet with the subtle nudgings of the stage players. Every one of the voyagers who rode the rowboats to the vessels of the Third Supply during the last weekend in port had heard the condemnations of the critics and the parodies of the wags. They had simply chosen to consider them in the best possible light.

William Strachey was one of the few colonists whose interest in the Powhatans was a major reason for voyaging to Virginia. His views about the need to impose Christianity upon them were just as vehement, but his real interest lay in recording details about the indigenous culture of the people he met. Strachey was as self-interested as the voyagers who still hoped to find gold and silver in Virginia. He intended to gather material for a book and return home to find fame as a New World chronicler. Strachey planned to learn all he could about the Powhatans' food, clothing, medicine, marriage customs, childhood rites, holidays, and burial practices. The treasure he expected to bring back was a journal of observation rather than pockets full of shiny nuggets.

The three men who would lead the expedition to Virginia were, according to one participant, "three most worthy honored gentlemen." Thomas Gates was the newly appointed acting governor of Virginia; George Somers was the admiral of the fleet and would command the ships at sea; and Christopher Newport was the vice admiral and captain of the *Sea Venture*. Somewhat inexplicably, all three would sail on the flagship. Apparently the comfort of traveling on the better appointed lead ship overrode any concern that the loss of the vessel would leave the colony bereft of its leaders. The decision would be one that Thomas Gates would have to answer for in the future. Exacerbating the possible consequences of the move, three sealed boxes with instructions for running the colony under the new charter were also carried on the flagship.

While the leaders would all ride on the *Sea Venture*, only Newport was on the ship when William Strachey arrived at Woolwich. Somers and Gates would come aboard when the ship put in to Plymouth, England, to take on supplies. At age forty-nine, Newport was a veteran privateer. His adventures began thirty years earlier when as a nineteen-year-old sailor he jumped ship in Brazil and made his way home on another vessel. John Smith called him "a mariner well practiced for the western parts of America," by which he meant the western Atlantic. Newport was celebrated in maritime circles for capturing the heavily laden Spanish treasure ship *Madre de Dios* in 1592, and for bringing home a live alligator for the king in 1605. Most of his accomplishments came after he lost his right arm in a skirmish with the Spanish in 1590. The vice admiral would be in charge of the *Sea Venture* at the pleasure of Somers, who outranked him.

Strachey had met few mariners during life in London and the English countryside. The sailors who would run the ships of the Third Supply were among the coarsest class of English society, and, as Smith said, their job demanded that they be tough when conditions turned stormy: "Men of all other professions in lightning, thunder, storms, and tempests with rain and snow may shelter themselves in dry houses by good fires and good cheer, but those are the chief times that seamen must stand to their tacklings and attend with all diligence their greatest labor upon the decks." While the mariners of the first transatlantic fleets were essential personnel at sea, they were only bystanders to the settlement of the New World. Their job was to deliver people and cargo to Virginia, pick up marketable goods collected and manufactured abroad, and carry them back to England.

The passengers who climbed aboard the *Sea Venture* were a varied group. The Virginia Company was pleased to tell prospective voyagers that "persons of rank and quality" like Strachey would be aboard the ships. John Smith was not so charitable in his assessment of the wealthy adventurers. The gents who had gone on the original voyage had not adjusted well to the wilderness setting. They soon missed "their accustomed dainties with feather beds and down pillows," he said, and once in Jamestown their only objective had become to commandeer ships and return to England.

Though Strachey would probably have denied it, he was just the type of adventurer Smith was criticizing. From his first days on the *Sea Venture* at Woolwich, Strachey was disdainful of the artisans and laborers who were also aboard. In his accounts he would write of "common people" whose actions were guided by "hot bloods." The rabble was invariably compared to the company's "gentlemen of quality and knowledge of virtue." Strachey would blame the problems of the expedition on "the idle, untoward, and wretched number" who would share the confines of the *Sea Venture* with "the better sort of the company."

The flagship would carry its share of the "wretched number." The Virginia Company was so in need of recruits that it allowed even penniless laborers to sign on. Just as Strachey had done, they could offer themselves as colonists and be awarded one share of Virginia Company stock simply for going to Jamestown. The laborers, however, were expected to do the heavy work of the colony while the gentlemen served as the leaders. Anyone agreeing to go without putting up cash was expected to "go in their persons to dwell there" and "thither to remain," though in reality many returned to England without forfeiting their shares. After seven years those in this class were to receive the same percentage of profits and land due to those who acquired shares through purchase. This practice made the Virginia expedition an opportunity available to anyone willing to voyage abroad, even the poorest laborers of London.

The Third Supply would also carry a mix of the tradesmen the Virginia Company had sought in its advertisements. The wide range of craftsmen solicited confirms that industry was expected to thrive at Jamestown. The Virginia Company was looking for druggists, gardeners, tile makers, fish processors, vine growers, soap makers, miners, sugarcane planters, pearl drillers, and charcoal makers, just to name a few. While the company hoped to attract established professionals, few experienced artisans could be convinced to abandon hard-won situations in England for the wilds of the New World. Most who joined were on the margins of their professions. Members of the livery companies of London—the unions of the day—were among the greatest supporters of the Virginia enterprise because the fleets cleared the city of unskilled pretenders to their crafts. Fifty-five companies provided funds for the upcoming expedition.

There were indeed many pretenders to the trades in London. A fundamental change in the English economic system—the fencing of farmland and the eviction of peasant farmers in favor of employees of landlords—was creating throngs of poor. Growing crowds from the countryside would soon increase the population of London from a hundred and fifty thousand to a quarter million. Robert Johnson even suggested that wealthy investors should look on the Virginia enterprise as a way to save money on the construction of English prisons: "Our land abounding with swarms of idle persons, which having no means of labor to relieve their misery, do likewise swarm in lewd and naughty practices, so that if we seek not some ways for their foreign employment we must provide shortly more prisons and corrections for their bad conditions." The Virginia Company was better than its word. As the sailing date of the Third Supply drew near and the quota of tradesmen remained unfilled, unemployed workers were accepted in place of experienced tradesmen. The blend of gentlemen, sailors, artisans, and laborers would prove a volatile mix.

CHAPTER THREE

Ocean Bound

Calm seas, auspicious gales.

—Prospero, *The Tempest*

Three days after William Strachey's arrival on board the *Sea Venture*, the vessels of the Jamestown fleet winched their anchors aboard, unfurled limited sail, and headed downstream with the current of the Thames. The cruise down the river, around the southeastern tip of England and along the coast of the English Channel, brought the fleet to Plymouth. The convoy passed the fish-curing houses at the entrance of the harbor and anchored to await going in turn to the quay for loading.

"From Woolwich the fifteenth of May, 1609, seven sail weighed anchor," Gabriel Archer reported, "and came to Plymouth the twentieth day, where Sir George Somers with two small vessels consorted with us. Here we took into the *Blessing* (being the ship wherein I went) six mares and two horses, and the fleet laid in some necessaries belonging to the action, in which business we spent till the second of June."

The port town on the Devon coast was well equipped to supply the fleet. A stone quay built in 1572 had proved its utility when British ships put in for provisions before going against the Spanish Armada in 1585. A freshwater stream was diverted to the town in 1591, providing a ready supply of water to fill the casks of outbound ships. Warehouses served by cranes lined Plymouth harbor and African slaves were among the shoremen who loaded ships. Here the vessels of the Jamestown fleet tied up and prepared to take on stores.

The *Swallow* and the *Virginia* joined the expedition at Plymouth and brought the fleet to a full complement of nine sail. The *Virginia* was a pinnace—a small sailing vessel designed for coastal waters—and had been constructed in 1607 at the Sagadahoc colony on the coast of present-day Maine, the second vessel ever built in English America. Meeting the fleet at Plymouth, too, was its admiral. A fellow colonist mistakenly judged the fifty-five-year-old George Somers to be "three score years of age at the least," presumably due to a white head of hair. One voyager reported him to be in possession of a "worthy and valiant mind." To another contemporary he was "a man very industrious and forward," and to Strachey he was "a gentleman of approved assuredness and ready knowledge in seafaring actions." Perhaps the best description of the admiral contrasted his demeanor on land and sea: "Sir George Somers was a lamb on the land, so patient that few could anger him, and (as if entering a ship he had assumed a new nature) a lion at sea, so passionate that few could please him."

The admiral of the Third Supply was born in 1554 in Lyme Regis on the Dorset coast and had more than a decade of West Indies experience. Somers came out of retirement to join the expedition. During the last five years he had spent enough time on land to serve as mayor of his native town and to occupy a seat in Parliament. He joined the fleet late because he had been detained in Dorset for the making of his will. On April 23, 1609, he declared in the will that he was "intending to pass the seas in a voyage towards the land called Virginia." In case of death he left his property to his wife Joan (who would stay behind) and, being childless, his nieces and nephews. One of those nephews was Matthew Somers, who would voyage to Virginia in the present convoy aboard the *Swallow*.

During the twelve days at Plymouth, the elite of the expedition may have stayed at a lodging house in a former monastery called the Mitre Inn and visited the house of the notoriously gregarious mayor. A contemporary observer gave the names of the officers of the fleet—Ratcliffe, King, Martin, Nellson, Adams, Wood, Pett, Webb, Moone, Philes, and Davies—and described them as "expert captains and very resolute gentlemen." Lower ranking crewmen and the artisan crowd slept on board the ships, but some of them surely made their way through the doors of the Rose & Crown Tavern and the Pope's Head Inn for beer and sack (white wine). The timing of the stopover worked well, since in early June the Plymouth fishing fleet was away at the Newfoundland banks. Few ships were in the harbor and plenty of workers were available to haul crates and operate pulleys and cranes.

The *Sea Venture* would carry one hundred and fifty-three people to the New World. On the flagship the personnel breakdown was about thirty-five mariners, with the other hundred and eighteen comprising gentlemen (and a few gentlewomen and children), servants, artisans, and peasants (also including a few family members). Only the total number and a few of the names are known, as no passenger list survives.

A servant woman named Elizabeth Persons was among those riding the flagship. Persons had left her family behind in England to travel to the New World in the employ of a Mistress Horton, one of the elite adventurers. As usual her chores would include tending to the needs of her employer, though in the unusual circumstances of the expedition her dealings with her would be less formal than usual. She would look after her clothing and luggage as best she could, fetch her water and other necessities from the general supply, and keep her sleeping area clean. The children on the vessel already tended to gravitate to the sides of young servants like Elizabeth, and would do so during the weeks ahead on the water.

John Rolfe, twenty-four, would also voyage on the *Sea Venture*. Rolfe would later marry Pocahontas as his second wife, but in 1609 his first wife (whose name is not known) was still living and would ride with him on the *Sea Venture*. Though the couple were probably not yet aware of it, they had conceived a child about two weeks before the fleet left Woolwich. Goodwife Rolfe would face both morning sickness and seasickness when the Third Supply set sail.

The expedition's minister, Reverend Richard Buck, twenty-seven, rode the *Sea Venture* as well. Buck was educated in the halls and courts of Caius College, Cambridge. A fellow minister called him accomplished and painstaking in his theology—"an able and painful preacher." Buck's time at sea would be taken up with writing sermons to be delivered daily and providing counseling to any colonist who was feeling anxious. A voyager named Stephen Hopkins, a vociferous shopkeeper from Hampshire who frequently quoted the Bible, spent a lot of time with Buck. Strachey called Hopkins "a fellow who had much knowledge in the scriptures and could reason well therein, whom our minister therefore chose to be his clerk to read the psalms and chapters upon Sundays at the assembly of the congregation under him."

Flint ballast from the Devon coast went first into the hold of the *Sea Venture*, to provide stability for the rough waters of the Atlantic. Large stones and scrap iron were placed in the bilge of the ship, then covered with gravel to provide a bed into which casks and crates could be nestled. The most important supplies in those containers were food and drink. The steward's room, bread room, and hold were all stocked from the Plymouth warehouses. Plenty of Newfoundland salt cod went onto the ship. Strachey listed additional edibles needed for such a voyage as "butter, cheese, biscuit, meal, oatmeal, aquavitae, oil, bacon, any kind of spice, or such like." John Smith went into greater detail, noting that transatlantic vessels carried ginger both dried and fresh, almonds, aged English and Dutch cheeses, wine from the Canary Islands, rashers of bacon, dried beef tongue, roast beef preserved in vinegar, minced mutton packed in butter, "the juice of lemons for the scurvy," and candied fruit in the form of "suckets" and "comfits."

Much of the food taken on in Plymouth was stored in earthenware containers made by potters in nearby Devonshire villages. Other utensils came from farther away: porcelain plates from China with painted images of hornless dragons; a calculating tool called a casting counter made in Nuremberg; ceramic Bartmann bottles molded by Germanic artisans with an image of a bearded man on each stem and the mottled coloration of tigerware; and Spanish olive jars filled with wine, wheat, and other foods. Foreign-made containers and implements were the exception, however. Most of the utensils were British-made: earthenware tankards, pewter spoons, knives, combs, thimbles, pins, padlocks, seals, and apothecary weights. The cookroom on such a ship, according to Smith, would have been stocked with all manner of eating and drinking vessels: "quarter cans, small cans, platters, spoons, lanterns, etc." A carpenter's chest would have been filled with "nails, clinches, rove and clinch nails, spikes, plates, rudder irons called pintels and gudgions, pump nails, scupper-nails and leather, saws, files, hatchets, and such like."

Live animals were among the more conspicuous supplies loaded aboard the ships. Venetian ambassador Marc Antonio Correr described the taking on of "many oxen and ponies" and "a number of stallions and other animals." A Dutchman wrote of animals as well, listing "some stallions and fourteen or fifteen mares, some young bulls and cows," a herd of "bucks and nanny goats," and "hogs as well." Most of the animals went aboard ships other than the *Sea Venture*, but hogs and heath sheep would ride on the flagship in stalls on the gun deck next to the passengers. The other live cargo on the flagship was a dog (probably a mastiff), a cat or two, and—unintentionally—a few dozen rats.

The *Sea Venture* also carried arms, more as a hedge against attacks by other Europeans than the Powhatans in Virginia. The ship carried twenty-four guns classed as falconets, minions, sakers, and demiculverines, which weighed between five hundred and thirty-four hundred pounds and fired cannonballs up to twelve pounds. A good quantity of matchlock pistols and muskets, small shot, swords, and daggers completed the vessel's arsenal.

Cape-merchant Thomas Whittingham oversaw the lading of the *Sea Venture*. Whittingham likely paid close attention to the placement of cargo in the hold, for the tilting of a ship to the starboard (right side) during loading was considered a bad omen. Conversely, a heel to larboard or landward was considered a sign of a fair sail. A sailors' manual of the day advised care in loading: "Some superstitious seamen, when they take in goods or victuals for a voyage, if by chance in stowing the provision she heel to the starboard, will say it is a sign of a long and bad voyage."

The passengers and crew who came from London had already marked out areas for sleeping and stowing belongings. The general choice of quarters was defined by tradition: sailors resided in the narrow confines of the bow in hammocks and bunks; officers and gentlemen occupied cabins at the stern. In the crowded conditions of the *Sea Venture*, temporary walled-in rooms in the rear portion of the enclosed gun deck probably augmented the permanent cabins. The common sort who had no room assignments slept on mattresses atop chests or on the gun deck floor.

John Rolfe tacked up curtains around the sleeping mattress he would share with his wife. The servant Elizabeth Persons selected a spot near the door of the cabin of her employer, Mistress Horton. Namontack and Machumps had little with them but their bows and arrows. They spent much of their time above on the open deck, but when below they kept to a cramped spot behind some crates. The reality was that for many of the voyagers the next few weeks would be spent in a small room with scores of strangers.

As May drew to a close, Governor Thomas Gates had still not arrived at Plymouth to join the expedition. The other leaders were growing concerned as the six hundred and sixty colonists and crew consumed the stores while the fleet sat in port. "The coming hither of Sir Thomas Gates is much desired to the end the ships may be speedily dispatched from hence," a Virginia Company official wrote from Plymouth to London. "Sir George Somers has been here these two days, and the ships, if weather serve—God willing—shall be ready this next day. Their people—God be thanked—are all in health and well."

Two things had delayed the expedition's leader in London. First, the revised charter of the Virginia Company was not signed until May 23, necessitating Gates's presence in Westminster Hall for that business. A week after the signing he was still in the city helping to organize the expedition that would follow in a few months. The governor finally finished his business on May 29 and immediately embarked to Plymouth to join the expedition he would lead to the New World.

Another turn of events was holding up the departure of the Third Supply. On April 9, 1609, Spain and the Netherlands signed a treaty ending fighting that had persisted despite a 1604 treaty between two other belligerents of the conflict, Spain and Great Britain. The end of the war prompted large numbers of British soldiers who had served as mercenaries in the Netherlands to come home, offering the Virginia Company a last-minute opportunity to fill its personnel quota for the expedition. The coincidence of the signing of the Dutch treaty and the launching of the expedition resulted in a larger-than-expected contingent of soldiers going to Virginia. The battle-tested men were familiar with the camp conditions they would find in the New World, but their presence would exacerbate the gulf between the elite gentlemen and the artisan class that was evident from the first days of the voyage.

One of the veterans of the Dutch battlefield was Gates himself, said by contemporaries to be "a grave, expert," and "very remarkable soldier." The leader of the Third Supply was born in about 1559 in Colyford, Devon. His overseas adventures began at age twenty-six, when he accompanied explorer Francis Drake to the Caribbean and South America to raid Spanish settlements. On the way home the fleet stopped at the Roanoke colony on the Virginia shore, providing Gates his first encounter with English colonial life. Gates also fought the Spanish on their home territory at Cadiz and was knighted for his efforts in 1596. He enlisted to fight in the Dutch wars in 1604, and four years later was granted leave to lead the present expedition to Jamestown.

Gates now at Plymouth and the ships laden with cargo and settlers, the expedition to Virginia began. Strachey reported that the departure from Plymouth was a nocturnal one on June 2. "Upon Friday late in the evening we broke ground out of the sound of Plymouth, our whole fleet then consisting of seven good ships and two pinnaces." The vessels encountered contrary breezes before they cleared the channel, however, and withdrew to another port to await better prospects. "Crossed by southwest winds, we put in to Falmouth," Gabriel Archer reported, "and there staying till the eighth of June, we then got out."

The initial destination was the latitude of the Canary Islands, where the captains of the fleet would gather on the flagship to chart their course across the Atlantic. Crewmen of the *Sea Venture* were divided into watches soon after they left port. Captains traditionally called all hands to the upper deck and masters and master's mates then took turns choosing sailors until the men were divided into two groups. Passengers on the *Sea Venture* who had never been to sea would then have listened with curiosity to the series of commands shouted by the master and mate as they put the ship to sea—as described by John Smith: "Yea, yea. Let fall your foresail. Tally, that is, haul off the sheets. Who is at the helm there? Coil your cables in small fakes. Haul the cat, a bitter, belay, loose fast your anchor with your shank painter. Stow the boat. Set the land, how it bears by the compass, that we may the better know thereby to keep our account and direct our course. Let fall your mainsail. Every man say his private prayers for a boon voyage."

It was June 8, 1609, and the *Sea Venture* was departing for the New World. The men, women, and children aboard watched the sails set on the companion ships and the bluffs of the Falmouth coast recede to a line on the horizon. As the English coastline fell away, many on board surely felt the weight of the decision to go. The passengers did indeed say many prayers as the land of their birth was lost to view. Those on shore also appealed to heaven for a safe voyage. An official of the Virginia Company wrote in his diary as the ships departed: "God bless them and guide them to His glory and our good."

For seven weeks the ships of the Jamestown fleet sailed in convoy. Strachey reported that the vessels "kept in friendly consort together, not a whole watch at any time losing the sight each of other." The fleet would not be quite as large as expected, however, as the pinnace *Virginia* proved out of condition for a transatlantic crossing. The vessel that had joined the fleet at Plymouth turned around after a week at sea. Eight craft would sail on to Jamestown.

One family was especially glad that the ships stayed within sight of each other. Gentleman William Pierce was traveling to Virginia on the *Sea Venture*, while his wife Joan and their ten-year-old daughter of the same name were making the voyage on the *Blessing*. The reason for the separation is not known, but perhaps only one space was available on the *Sea Venture* and William and Joan thought it important that he make connections with the leaders who would ride on the flagship. William took to hailing his wife and child when the *Blessing* rode close enough to see the people on deck.

The rhythms of shipboard life were soon adopted by all aboard. When mariners traditionally came off watch to the mess on such a voyage, John Smith said, the cook gave them "a quarter can of beer and a basket of bread to stay their stomachs till the kettle be boiled, that they may first go to prayer, then to supper." Meals consisted of "a dish of buttered rice with a little cinnamon, ginger, and sugar, a little minced meat, or roast beef, a few stewed prunes, a race of green ginger, a flapjack, a can of fresh water brewed with a little cinnamon, ginger, and sugar." For a main course the cook might prepare "a little poor John—or salt fish—with oil and mustard, or biscuit, butter, cheese, or oatmeal pottage on fish days; or, on flesh days, salt beef, pork, and peas with six shillings beer."

If the ships were becalmed at any point during such a voyage, Smith reported, "the men leap overboard to swim." Voyagers like Stephen Hopkins were the ones most likely to take to the water. Gentlemen were less apt to partake in a cool dip, but they might watch from the gallery balcony at the stern. A resort to the gallery would have provided an opportunity for William Strachey or John Rolfe to smoke tobacco in clay pipes with tiny bowls—a small amount was used because tobacco was an expensive commodity in 1609.

For the few passengers who preferred the ship's toilets to chamber pots, the onboard facilities were simply holes in the "head" deck that projected from the bow of the ship. The passengers accepted such things without complaint during the first days of the voyage. As time went on, the concessions in everyday living—certain to become even more pronounced in the forests of Virginia—began to seem more radical than they

did when they first went to sea. The fresh breezes on the open deck, however, made up for some of the compromises. As the weather warmed with
the fleet's progress south it was at times downright pleasant to sit on deck
and watch the other ships sail alongside.

The convoy made good progress during June and July. Colonist
George Percy, then in Jamestown, would report that the fleet heading in
his direction encountered "prosperous winds" during the first weeks at
sea. Those winds and the Portugal Current pushed the convoy at an average speed of 3.3 knots (3.8 mph), for an average daily distance of 70 nautical miles (80.5 statute miles). The speed of the ships was measured using
a line with a wooden float at the end, called a "chip log," that was thrown
into the sea from the stern balcony. The log line was allowed to play out
until the sand finished falling through an hourglass (or in this case a
half-minute glass), at which point the "knots" in the played-out line were
measured.

As the Jamestown ships neared the latitude of the Canary Islands
after two weeks on the water, they paused and the officers of the fleet
came over to the *Sea Venture* in skiffs to plot the course they would take
across the Atlantic. The route they chose would initially trace the traditional one, through the tropics at twenty-four degrees latitude. That would
put them in tropical climes, but it was a latitude reliably within the west-
bound circulation at the bottom of the Atlantic's vast clockwise wheel of
trade winds. Once across the mid-Atlantic, however, the fleet would veer
from the traditional passage. Instead of threading through the Caribbean, the vessels would turn north and traverse open water to Virginia.
Company officials recommended such a route to avoid the Spanish waters of the Caribbean.

During the meeting on the *Sea Venture*, the officers of the Gates
fleet selected a place at which the ships would rendezvous if they became separated. The decision was made to reunite at Barbuda in the
Caribbean. Sir Walter Raleigh had sighted the island twelve years earlier and no other European power claimed it, making it a relatively safe
place for a fleet of English vessels to meet in case of trouble. Barbuda's

location on the eastern fringe of the Caribbean chain meant ships going to it would be unlikely to encounter vessels of other European powers.

When the consultation on the *Sea Venture* was complete the officers returned to their ships and the fleet resumed the voyage. "We ran a southerly course for the Tropic of Cancer, where, having the sun within six or seven degrees right over our head in July, we bore away west," Gabriel Archer wrote. The ships now began what Archer described as "tracing through the Torrid Zone." The sailors strung sails as awnings to keep the sunshine from the pallid skin of the English passengers. An awning was essential for a ship passing through the tropics, according to a contemporary sailor's manual. "In all hot voyages this is of infinite use, both to keep men from the sun by day and the dews by night, which in some places are wonderful infectious." The tropics proved infectious, indeed, for the ships of the Jamestown fleet. Calenture or heatstroke killed thirty-two people on two of the ships, Archer wrote. There was a report of plague on the *Diamond*, he said, "but in the *Blessing* we had not any sick, albeit we had twenty women and children." Children in another vessel were not so lucky: "In the *Unity* were born two children at sea, but both died, being both boys." No disease broke out on the *Sea Venture*, but watching the splashes of bodies buried at sea from the other ships was a somber reminder that a combination of London plague and hot sun could be lethal.

In late July, after two months at sea and a week to go until landfall in Virginia, the voyage had proved to be a relatively easy one. The exotic nature of the New World had become clear as the temperate world of England gave way to blistering days and sweltering nights in the tropics. The weather had turned cooler, though, as the ships turned north before reaching the West Indies. The calm voyage muted any second-guessing among the passengers. In any case, there was no point in questioning the decision to leave home. As everyone in the fleet knew, there was no turning back now.

CHAPTER FOUR

Hurricane

Ride on the curled clouds.

—Ariel, *The Tempest*

The end of the serene sail of the *Sea Venture* came on the evening of Monday, July 24. A week from Jamestown in open water between the Caribbean and Bermuda, inky clouds and rising wind had the sailors working through the night to tie down everything on the ship in preparation for a storm. Canvas covers were lashed over wooden grates that provided ventilation to the gun deck. The guns were rolled back and tied in place and the gun ports closed, and the passengers secured their personal belongings. After a sleepless night on the ships of the Gates fleet, the morning of St. James Day, July 25, dawned with a frightful prospect.

Charcoal clouds overtook the ship, the winds rose sharply, and rain began to fall. Despite the worsening conditions, George Somers stationed himself outside on the high poop deck at the stern of the *Sea Venture*. There he shouted directions through a grate to the helmsman at the whipstaff below on the enclosed steerage deck—Jacobean ships were steered by a vertical staff rather than a wheel. Somers could tell this was no ordinary gale. The fleet was facing a kind of storm that few English mariners had seen but many had heard about since Europeans began crossing the Atlantic—a *hurricano* of the West Indies.

The storm that overtook the *Sea Venture* was born of winds off Africa in the tropical waters of the Equator. Gathering strength, it followed the trade winds (and the *Sea Venture*) across the Atlantic toward the Caribbean, veering north before encountering the West Indian island chain. The ship and the hurricane both turned north, but the *Sea Ven-*

ture was closer to the coast when it did so. They then followed converging tracks and met in open water halfway between the Caribbean and Bermuda. The circular storm caught the flagship with the counterclockwise winds of its northwestern edge, placing the ship at the ten o'clock position if the storm were a giant clock face. Thus, as William Strachey reported, the *Sea Venture* initially encountered northeast winds.

"A dreadful storm, and hideous, began to blow from out the northeast," Strachey said, "which swelling and roaring as it were by fits, some hours with more violence than others, at length did beat all light from heaven, which like a hell of darkness turned black upon us." Within an hour the fleet was scattered and each vessel was on its own. The *Diamond*, the *Falcon*, the *Blessing*, the *Unity*, the *Lion*, and the *Swallow* disappeared from the view of the *Sea Venture* watch. George Somers and his crew were now in a desperate struggle for the safety of all on board.

The ketch under the command of Michael Philes that was being towed by the flagship would sail on its own as well. The conditions were too dangerous for the tiny vessel and the much larger *Sea Venture* to remain tied together within striking distance of each other, and in the rough seas there was no way to transfer the people from the ketch to the ship. After signaling their intention with flags, the crewmen of the flagship cast off the towropes, and Philes and his complement of about thirty people were left to the mercy of the waves. There was a last look at the faces of the sailors on the bobbing ketch as they disappeared into the sheets of rain—never to be heard from again.

A sea storm of any kind, much less a hurricane, was a dreadful new experience for most of the colonists. Within an hour or two all the passengers on the *Sea Venture* feared they would die. Strachey, for one, could think of nothing but his own mortality. "It works upon the whole frame of the body and most loathsomely affects all the powers thereof," he wrote, "and the manner of the sickness it lays upon the body, being so insufferable, gives not the mind any free and quiet time to use her judgment and empire."

The gun deck where Strachey and the other passengers braced themselves was stifling, and the increasingly steep movements of the ship were alarming. Servant Elizabeth Persons huddled on her straw mattress as the ship pitched with a nauseating rhythm. Resorting to the rail when seasickness arose was impossible, and so chamber pots were used. Many of those then spilled with the pitching of the ship. The sleeping area with its hatches battened to keep the storm waters out quickly became a foul place. Elizabeth put her face down into her mattress, closed her eyes, and waited for the ordeal to end.

A typical Atlantic hurricane produces a trillion gallons of rain each day, and the hurricane of July 1609 was no exception. "The sea swelled above the clouds and gave battle unto heaven," Strachey said. "It could not be said to rain, the waters like whole rivers did flood the air." In Strachey's mind the winds and the waves became angry giants. "The glut of water (as if throttling the wind ere while) was no sooner a little emptied and qualified, but instantly the winds (as having gotten their mouths now free and at liberty) spoke more loud and grew more tumultuous and malignant. What shall I say? Winds and seas were as mad as fury and rage could make them."

Taking the flagship through a hurricane would test the mettle of George Somers. The admiral was faced with an immediate choice between the two options available to Jacobean mariners in heavy weather. The first was to run with the wind and "spoon afore," or keep the ship headed in the direction of the wind with little or no sail (later called "scudding"). This would put the vessel under the least stress, but steering would be difficult and the *Sea Venture* might be overwhelmed and sunk by a large wave breaking over the stern. The second option was to "weather coil," or turn the vessel around and let the waves hit the bow. The wind would then push the high stern structure as if it was a sail and the ship would ride backward.

Somers chose to spoon afore and ride the giant swells of the hurricane. To make use of the winds out of the northeast, he turned the ship and pointed it to the southwest toward the Caribbean. The waves would approach from behind and push the ship forward as they passed under-neath. If Somers sensed that the ship was at all weak, this was the safest option, but it was labor-intensive and any lapse in steering would likely mean doom. A series of helmsmen would take turns wrestling the whip-staff to positions called by the admiral. Silvester Jourdain, a passenger on the *Sea Venture*, recalled, "Sir George Somers sitting upon the poop of the ship (where he sat three days and three nights together, without meal's meat and little or no sleep) conning the ship to keep her as upright as he could (for otherwise she must needs instantly have foundered)."

While the storm was a horrific trial, at least it seemed that it could not get worse—and yet it did. On Tuesday morning the sailors discov-ered that the pitching *Sea Venture* was losing its oakum, the fiber caulk-ing between its planks that was covered with pitch to keep the sea out. A leak allowing a flow of water into the hold during a hurricane was a grave development indeed. The hot sun of the tropics may have softened the pitch covering the *Sea Venture*'s oakum and weakened the seals, or the pitching during the storm may have loosened them. Perhaps, too, the new flagship had not been properly sealed before the voyage.

"It pleased God to bring a greater affliction yet upon us," Strachey wrote. "For in the beginning of the storm we had received likewise a mighty leak. And the ship in every joint almost, having spewed out her oakum, before we were aware (a casualty more desperate than any other that a voyage by sea draws with it) was grown five feet suddenly deep with water above her ballast, and we almost drowned within whilst we sat looking when to perish from above."

Before the leak was discovered the confident work of the sailors had given the passengers reason to hope. The mariners' confidence vanished with the report that the ship was taking on water. The look on the faces of the sailors was enough to deepen the dread of the idle passengers. Death was almost certain—there was little question now. "This impart-ing no less terror than danger," Strachey said, "ran through the whole ship with much fright and amazement, startled and turned the blood, and took down the braves of the most hardy mariner of them all, insomuch as he that before happily felt not the sorrow of others, now began to sorrow for himself when he saw such a pond of water so suddenly broken in, and which he knew could not (without present avoiding) but instantly sink him."

Gates immediately ordered pumping and bailing to begin. At the same time, he dispatched his officers and men to search the ship for the source of incoming water. "There might be seen master, master's mate, boatswain, quartermaster, coopers, carpenters, and who not," Strachey said, "with candles in their hands, creeping along the ribs viewing the sides, searching every corner and listening in every place if they could hear the water run." Ceramic pots may have been pressed against the inside of the hull of the ship to magnify the sound of in-rushing water. The standard method for stopping leaks at sea was to smear them with a mixture of animal fat and ashes, according to the standard sailor's manual of the time. Stouter plugs were needed to fill larger gaps, the manual says, and "in some cases (when the leak is very great) pieces of raw beef, oatmeal bags, and the like stuff" would be pounded into the seams.

Since the situation on the *Sea Venture* was dire, the sailors used the most readily available time-tested method—stuffing strips of dried beef into the seams. Once moistened with seawater the beef expanded and formed an adequate temporary caulking. Each time a leak was discovered, the sailors wedged their candlesticks between higher boards of the ship and pounded a strip of beef into place. "Many a weeping leak was this way found and hastily stopped, and at length one in the gunner room made up with I know not how many pieces of beef," Strachey reported, "but all was to no purpose, the leak (if it were but one) which drunk in our greatest seas and took in our destruction fastest could not then be found, nor ever was, by any labor, counsel, or search."

The water already in the hold hampered the sailors' effort to stop the flow. Somers claimed it was nine feet deep when discovered, substantially more than the five of Strachey's estimate. The flood and the cargo made it impossible to search the most sensitive part of the ship, the bottom along the keel. That left pumping and bailing as the only option. One last attempt to find the leak was prompted by the pumping operation. Soggy masses of bread kept clogging the pumps, Strachey said, raising the possibility that the inflow was in the bread room. "The waters still increasing, and the pumps going, which at length choked with bringing up whole and continual biscuit (and indeed all we had, ten thousand weight), it was conceived as most likely that the leak might be sprung in the bread room, whereupon the carpenter went down and ripped up all the room, but could not find it so."

Many on the *Sea Venture* were near despair. "To me this leakage appeared as a wound given to men that were before dead," Strachey said. "The Lord knows I had as little hope as desire of life in the storm and in this it went beyond my will, because [it was] beyond my reason why we should labor to preserve life, yet we did, either because so dear are a few lingering hours of life in all mankind or that our Christian knowledge taught us how much we owed to the rites of nature, as bound, not to be false to ourselves or to neglect the means of our own preservation."

Teams of men—the dozen or so women and children on the ship did not work—were at the task of pumping and bailing from the hour the leak was discovered. At the beginning of the operation Somers briefly put another man on steering so that he could take a turn at the pumps. "The men might be seen to labor, I may well say, for life, and the better sort, even our governor and admiral themselves, not refusing their turn and to spell each the other to give example to other," Strachey said.

Colonist William Pierce worked with his fellows at the pumps and buckets. As much as he feared for his own safety, the fate of his wife and daughter on the *Blessing* was of greater concern. At the beginning of the storm he had stayed on deck until the sheets of rain obscured the view of the other ships. The *Blessing* had been lost to view on the surface of a wild sea. Now as Pierce passed buckets down the line he was wracked with worry for his wife and child. Whether they lived or were deep in the sea he knew not, and the uncertainty was sorrowful indeed.

There were three pumps on the *Sea Venture*, two below by the capstan (the winch used to raise the anchor) and one on the open half deck by the mainmast at the center of the ship. Water drawn from them flowed through pipes to scupper holes at the sides of the ship. Strachey reported that the pumpers maintained a pace of a thousand strokes per hour, the equivalent of one every three seconds. While the pumpers worked, bailers labored in lines from the water-filled hold to three open gun ports— apparently each of the three teams Gates created was responsible for a pump and a bailing line. The bailers managed a pace of twelve hundred buckets per hour, with each pail holding either six or eight gallons and weighing fifty or seventy pounds—a rate of one bucket dumped every nine seconds. Strachey estimated that the pumpers and bailers together removed sixty-four hundred gallons of water each hour (an amount that would, as he put it, fill twenty-five "tun" barrels). That would make just over a half million gallons of water removed from the ship during the storm.

"We kept one hundred men always working night and day," Somers reported. Jourdain recalled that during the "sharp and cruel storm" the men put forth an unceasing effort: "With the violent working of the seas our ship became so shaken, torn, and leaked, that she received so much water as covered two tiers of hogsheads above the ballast; that our men stood up to the middles with buckets, barricos, and kettles to bail out the water, and continually pumped for three days and three nights together without any intermission."

Not only did the men have little rest; they also had little to eat or drink. Food was inaccessible in the hold, and conditions made it impossible to light a fire in the cookroom. Besides, there was no time to eat. Since the *Sea Venture* was carrying an unintended load of tons of seawater, the leaders of the expedition ordered the ship lightened by the dumping of heavy material. The heaviest things to go over the side were half of the guns, which were unhitched from their mounts and pushed into the roiling sea. Personal items were also thrown over the side. "We much unrigged our ship," Strachey said, "threw overboard much luggage, many a trunk and chest (in which I suffered no mean loss), and staved many a butt of beer, hogshead of oil, cider, wine, and vinegar, and heaved away all our ordnance on the starboard side."

Through it all, everyone on the *Sea Venture* knew well that the vessel might sink at any time. Strachey said the pounding was violent and thunderous: "Sometimes strikes in our ship, amongst women and passengers not used to such hurly and discomforts, made us look one upon the other with troubled hearts and panting bosoms, our clamors drowned in the winds and the winds in thunder. Prayers might well be in the heart and lips, but drowned in the outcries of the officers; nothing heard that could give comfort, nothing seen that might encourage hope."

The pregnant Goodwife Rolfe was among the "women and passengers not used to such hurly and discomforts," whose mournful calls despaired of salvation. Sleepless, thirsty, seasick, and without hope, the agonizing hours of the storm passed with a cruel lethargy. Lacking the monotonous but mind-numbing activity of the men left the women with nothing to do but mull the fate that awaited them in the angry sea. Terrified, too, were Namontack and Machumps. Powhatans were accomplished small-craft mariners and they surely had been on rivers and in coastal seas many times. The Powhatans were also familiar with Atlantic hurricanes, but being at sea in the midst of one in a foreign vessel over which they had no control was a deeply frightening experience.

By the afternoon of Tuesday, July 25, the *Sea Venture* voyagers had fought the storm for nearly twenty-four hours. During that time the flagship had begun to follow the path it would take through the hurricane, ultimately tracing a backward-leaning *J*. At the time the storm hit, Virginia lay ahead to the northwest, the Caribbean was to the southwest, and Bermuda was to the northeast. When the flagship entered the swirl at the ten o'clock position, Somers veered from his Virginia-bound path to point the bow toward the Caribbean. As time passed he would trace a half circle (the bottom of the backward-leaning *J*) before ultimately being carried on a long straight line to the northeast toward Bermuda.

Through Tuesday as the ship followed its half-circle path it was drawn ever closer to the center of the hurricane. Then at dusk, the *Sea*

Venture passed through the eye. "For four and twenty hours the storm in a restless tumult had blown so exceedingly, as we could not apprehend in our imaginations any possibility of greater violence," Strachey wrote, "yet did we still find it, not only more terrible, but more constant, fury added to fury, and one storm urging a second more outrageous than the former." To the people on board the *Sea Venture*, the passage through the eye was a bizarre interlude between one intense storm and another of even more power.

In a description that probably referred to the passage over the haphazard waves of the eye, Strachey recalled that the *Sea Venture* "ran now (as do hoodwinked men) at all adventures, sometimes north and northeast, then north and by west, and in an instant again varying two or three points, and sometimes half the compass." After passing through the center, the vessel reentered the maelstrom and began riding with the hurricane toward the center of the Atlantic. A storm that would have passed over an anchored vessel and left it behind instead pushed the floating flagship along with it as it moved. Those on board consequently experienced extreme weather conditions for an unusually long time.

All through Tuesday and into the night Somers remained at his post on the stern deck. The heavy clouds made it impossible to use the sun or stars to chart the ship's position, and Somers steered in the dark by the feel of the ship as it rode the waves. The helmsman below at the whipstaff had it a little easier, as fellow sailors kept lanterns lit so he could see to move the steering pole to the positions ordered from above. Even in its horror the rhythm of the ship was lulling, at times almost enough to cause Somers to shut his eyes and sleep, but he did not. If he could just remain awake and steer the *Sea Venture* through the storm, they might make it to Virginia without further incident. The admiral settled in for a long stint at his post, unaware that even as he did so a foaming giant was looming behind him and preparing to strike.

CHAPTER FIVE

Rogue Wave

We all were sea-swallowed.

—Antonio, *The Tempest*

Georges Somers was the first to feel the wall of white water hit the *Sea Venture* from behind. He did not see it, since sailors were advised not to look back while spooning afore because the sight of waves rising higher than the ship was enough to make even the heartiest mariner forget his steering duties. All the previous waves had passed under the *Sea Venture* without incident, picking up the ship and sliding beneath it. This one was different, mounting higher than the others and catching the ship with its breaking crest. To put it in maritime language, when the wave washed over the stern the *Sea Venture* was "pooped."

The massive breaking swell hit the admiral and smashed him to the deck. For a moment he was underwater as tons of brine passed over him and cascaded onto the lower parts of the ship. Then he emerged sputtering and horribly unsure whether the *Sea Venture* had survived. Within seconds he determined that the vessel was still afloat, but facing a dire new threat. The flagship had passed through instead of over the highest portion of a wave. Though the ship emerged on the other side still on the surface of the sea, the seawater passing over it tore aside canvas hatch covers and poured into the enclosed decks below. For a moment the hull of the ship was underwater.

"So huge a sea broke upon the poop and quarter, upon us, as it covered our ship from stern to stem like a garment or a vast cloud," Strachey wrote. "It filled her brim-full for a while within, from the hatches up to the spardeck. The source or confluence of water was so violent, as it rushed and carried the helmsman from the helm and wrested the whipstaff out of his hand, which so flew from side to side that when he would have seized the same again it so tossed him from starboard to larboard as it was God's mercy it had not split him, it so beat him from his hold and so bruised him." The ship would probably have gone broadside to the waves and capsized had not another sailor wrestled the whipstaff under control.

As the water swept down into the gun deck, it hit Gates, Strachey, and others in the bailing lines, knocking Gates from a resting spot at the capstan. "It struck him from the place where he sat and groveled him and all us about him on our faces, beating together with our breaths all thoughts from our bosoms else than that we were now sinking," Strachey said. "For my part, I thought her already in the bottom of the sea." Despite the apparent futility of going topside, the people below scrambled to avoid being trapped in a sinking hull.

For a moment after the wave hit, the *Sea Venture* stood almost still. Since the wall of water had passed around the ship rather than underneath it, the ship did not mount the top of the swell and strike as the stern fell down the back of the wave. The pooped *Sea Venture* was momentarily stopped dead. In the halted ship Strachey recalled a classical account he once read about a parasitic tropical fish, called a remora, that survives by attaching itself to a shark with a suction mouth. Superstitious sailors believed the remora could also stick to a ship, grow to enormous size, and slow or stop its progress. "It so stunned the ship in her full pace," Strachey said, "that she stirred no more than if she had been caught in a net, or than as if the fabulous remora had stuck to her forecastle."

The image of the remora was fleeting and Strachey soon turned to other thoughts as the motion of the *Sea Venture* resumed. The people who made it up the ladders reported that the ship remained afloat and under control. The alarm abated and the direction of the traffic on the ladders reversed. The seawater on the gun deck drained through hatchways that led to the hold. While that made it possible to again move freely, the workers knew that the water in the hold was now higher than it had ever been. Yet they still lived, and the voyage would go on. The glassy-eyed men returned to their stations and began once again to pass the buckets and raise the levers of the pumps.

Through Wednesday and into Thursday the pumping and bailing continued, though the workers were near collapse. They knew, though, that if they stopped the ship would certainly sink. "There was not a passenger, gentleman or other, after he began to stir and labor but was able to relieve his fellow and make good his course," Strachey said. "And it is most true, such as in all their lifetimes had never done hour's work before (their minds now helping their bodies) were able twice forty-eight hours together to toil with the best."

Strachey's own fatigue was something he had never before experienced. His arms ached from passing the heavy buckets and his hands were raw. The adrenaline that initially charged his movements had long since drained from his veins and was replaced by an utter exhaustion. Still he pushed on with the work, more for the occupation of mind rather than from any real hope that death was not imminent in the hours to come.

As the ship was pushed northeast into the Atlantic with the hurricane, the wind and rain that had begun on Monday continued to lash the vessel. To the people on the *Sea Venture* the storm seemed endless. As Thursday night fell the voyagers were in a dark mood, but it was a mood that would be unexpectedly brightened at the darkest hour. Near midnight George Somers noticed an eerie luminescence in the rigging of the ship. Knowing that his fellows could do with a diversion, he called to them and pointed to the flitting radiance on the masts and yards. Strachey was among the off-duty bailers who ventured above.

"Upon the Thursday night," Strachey reported, "Sir George Somers being upon the watch had an apparition of a little round light like a faint star, trembling and streaming along with a sparkling blaze half the height upon the mainmast, and shooting sometimes from shroud to shroud, attempting to settle as it were upon any of the four shrouds, and for three or four hours together, or rather more, half the night it kept with us, running sometimes along the main yard to the very end, and then returning, at which, Sir George Somers called diverse about him, and showed them the same, who observed it with much wonder and carefulness."

Static electricity had built up on the rigging as the ship moved across the surface of the sea, so much so that the rigging was alight with the plasma energy known as St. Elmo's fire. The phenomenon is often a sign of an imminent lightning strike, but on the *Sea Venture* it proved only a benign distraction. The uneducated people on board were awed by it, Strachey said, but the experienced officers and learned gentlemen saw it only as a curiosity. The luminescence dissipated with the first gray of dawn. "Towards the morning watch they lost the sight of it and knew not what way it made," Strachey said. "The superstitious seamen make many constructions of this sea fire, which nevertheless is usual in storms."

In the dawn of Friday morning the marvel of St. Elmo's fire was gone. The *Sea Venture* voyagers were incredulous that the storm still raged around them after four days, but they stayed at their tasks. The flood in the hold continued to gain on the bailers and pumpers, and the leaders of the expedition began to consider other ways to lighten the ship. The step of last resort was contemplated but so far not done—some on the *Sea Venture*, Strachey reported, "purposed to have cut down the mainmast, the more to lighten her, for we were much spent, and our men so weary, as their strengths together failed them, with their hearts, having travailed now from Tuesday till Friday morning, day and night, without either sleep or food."

Despite the efforts of Somers and Gates to keep the men working, most were in despair. "It being now Friday, the fourth morning, it wanted little but that there had been a general determination to have shut up hatches and commending our sinful souls to God, committed the ship to the mercy of the sea," Strachey said. "Surely that night we must have done it, and that night had we then perished." Passenger Silvester Jourdain recalled that many of the off-duty pumpers and bailers were lying down in dark places on the ship. "They were so overwearied and their spirits so spent with long fasting and continuance of their labor that for the most part they were fallen asleep in corners and wheresoever they chanced first to sit or lie." Flasks were passed and final toasts were made. "Some of them having some good and comfortable waters in the ship fetched them and drunk one to the other taking their last leave one of the other, until their more joyful and happy meeting in a more blessed world."

On the late morning of Friday, July 28, 1609, not everyone on the *Sea Venture* was asleep, but George Somers was losing his ability to keep the men working. Though the pumping and bailing continued, many of the off-duty workers appeared unlikely to return for another shift. The work was keeping the ship afloat, but it was an unsustainable solution to the crisis. In the muted light of late morning, the never-ending storm continued to hammer the ship. If the removal of water was not continued through the afternoon and evening, the inflow and the pounding seas would sink the *Sea Venture* and the coming night would be the last.

Somers continued to scan the ocean, watching the waves but also looking for ships that might offer relief. He was exhausted, famished, and thirsty, but still he watched and called rudder adjustments to the helmsman below. On one of his sweeps, a movement far off caught his eye. At the crest of a swell he detected a flutter on the horizon to the west, slightly higher than the surface of the sea. The ship descended into a trough and he froze and waited for it to rise again. At the top he saw it again, and this time more clearly—above the waves, he was almost sure, he saw the tops of palm trees moving in the wind. He waited one more time as the ship dipped between swells. The consequences to morale of making a mistake would be devastating. They were far out in the Atlantic and sighting trees—while not impossible—was incredible. At the top of the next wave he saw them again and this time he was sure. Somers then let go a bellow that reached the ears of everyone on the ship, and he repeated his call, drawing out in a sustained holler the word "Land." To the people on the *Sea Venture* it was a miraculous sound.

"See the goodness and sweet introduction of better hope by our merciful God given unto us," Strachey said. "Sir George Somers, when no man dreamed of such happiness, had discovered and cried land." Jourdain also recalled the moment when Somers "most wishedly, happily descried land." The first call caught the pumpers and bailers staring into the smiling faces of their mates, and the second prompted a rush up the ladders so they might see for themselves. Only a few were able to immediately confirm the sighting, but after a moment or two most were able to catch a glimpse of the palm tops. "It being better surveyed, the very trees were seen to move with the wind upon the shoreside," Strachey said.

John Rolfe sought out and hugged his wife. They now might live and the child Goodwife Rolfe carried might yet be born. They had begun to count the remainder of their lives in hours rather than years. Now their family might survive—they themselves might yet live to escape this sloshing, stinking ship. They had become so dulled that they hardly dared hope they would again stand on land, and now hope permeated their minds.

Though it had been days since Somers was able to see the stars and calculate the location of the *Sea Venture*, he was quite certain that the ship was in the middle of the Atlantic rather than in the Caribbean or along the coast of America. That meant that the land was almost certainly Bermuda, an island (or, more precisely, an archipelago) discovered by Spaniard Juan Bermúdez in 1505 and shown on maps since 1511. The fact that the land was probably Bermuda did not inspire confidence, as it was known to be surrounded by shallows stretching far out to sea that were rightly considered the most dangerous waters of the Atlantic. Nevertheless, they had to attempt to bring the *Sea Venture* to shore. After a conference with Somers, Gates gave the order to bring the ship in.

Despite the newfound optimism of everyone on board, the mariners knew that they were far from safe. Getting passengers and crew from a distressed ship on a stormy sea through unmapped shallows to an unknown shore was a perilous undertaking. Under normal conditions Somers would have anchored the ship offshore and awaited calmer conditions to send in the longboat, but if he did that now the *Sea Venture* would sink in place. The best option was to run toward the land and ground the ship. If this worked, equipment and supplies would be salvageable. The danger was that the *Sea Venture* and its unplanned cargo of seawater could run aground, be pushed on its side, and break apart in the surf. If that happened, a few strong swimmers might fight the waves and make it to shore, but most of the exhausted voyagers would die.

At Somers's insistence, the pumpers and bailers went back to work to lighten the *Sea Venture* as much as possible for the run into land. The knowledge that their labors would soon be over produced a surge of activity. "Hearing news of land, wherewith they grew to be somewhat revived, being carried with will and desire beyond their strength, every man bustled up and gathered his strength and feeble spirits together to perform as much as their weak force would permit him."

As the ship turned and headed toward the island, a fortuitous event occurred. Perhaps the hurricane was finally veering away or maybe the vessel came within the lee of the island, but for whatever reason the wind slacked as the ship began its final run. To Jourdain the abrupt change had a divine quality. "It pleased God to work so strongly, as the water was stayed for that little time (which, as we all much feared, was the last period of our breathing)." Strachey was more matter-of-fact in his description of the drop in wind: "The morning now three-quarters spent, had won a little clearness from the days before." When the ship was a mile from shore Strachey noted it again, saying "we had somewhat smooth water." So far, things were going well.

As they moved toward the island, a sounding lead and line was used to measure the decreasing depth. "The boatswain sounding at the first found it thirteen fathoms; and when we stood a little in, seven fathoms; and presently heaving his lead the third time had ground at four fathoms." The *Sea Venture* had a draft of fifteen feet when it was not carrying a hold full of seawater. With the ocean depth at four fathoms (twenty-four feet), the mariners knew the ship would soon run aground. Somers clenched his teeth as he anticipated impact, and in a few minutes it came with a sickening grind. Now would come the true test of their luck. The sailors waited to see whether the ship would be pushed sideways in the surf, and to their great relief it held fast. As they had hoped, the *Sea Venture* remained wedged in an upright position. "Neither did our ship sink," Jourdain said, "but more fortunately in so great a misfortune, fell in between two rocks where she was fast lodged and locked for further budging."

The *Sea Venture* had run into the shallows blind, and the outcome could hardly have been better. Granted there was still three-quarters of a mile of rough water to cross in the small boats, but the people on the ship would gladly take their chances. The distressed ship had approached Bermuda from the east and grounded at the northeastern tip of the archipelago, off the shore of a medium-sized island. As the voyagers would discover later, the place where the *Sea Venture* came in was the only place on the entire coast that was deep enough to allow a large vessel to approach so close.

Not knowing how long the ship would remain upright, the sailors worked quickly to untie the *Sea Venture*'s longboat and skiff and put them over the side. Ladders were dropped and the boats were filled to capacity. The longboat held perhaps thirty people and the skiff about ten. The first contingent included Gates, a number of male passengers, and almost certainly the dozen or so women and children on the ship. Sailors manned the oars as the boats pulled away. The *Sea Venture* had come to rest "under a point that bore southeast from the northern point of the island," Strachey said, and it was just below that northern point that the two small boats would make landfall. After coasting north along a shore of jagged rocks the oarsmen reached a bay that would forever after carry the name of the governor. Strachey described it as "a goodly bay, upon which our governor did first leap ashore, and therefore called it (as aforesaid) Gates his Bay, which opened into the east, and into which the sea did ebb and flow, according to their tides."

The bay featured a pink sand crescent onto which the longboat and skiff managed to land without upsetting despite the heavy surf. The thirty or so passengers in the boats were left on shore and the ten or so sailors pushed off immediately to pick up more people from the ship. Unsteady on their feet but vastly relieved to be on solid earth, the landing party waded onto the beach. The palm leaves that had been sighted from the ship moved against a dark afternoon sky in the diminishing wind. A heavy growth of vegetation covered the base of the trees. The island was relatively flat. To the south the land rose to a rocky bluff of perhaps thirty feet, and to the north a point of jagged rocks extended a short way into the sea. There was no time to explore at the moment, though, and the voyagers set about collecting firewood in the wet underbrush. A circle of stones was laid on the beach above the high tide mark and wood was propped in the center to make a fire to guide in the returning boats and, perhaps, other ships at sea. Lighting the kindling proved difficult in the damp conditions, but presently a blaze was lit.

A short way into the woods the voyagers chose a campsite and laid a second circle of stones in the center. When it too was filled with wood, they brought an ember from the beach and the upland fire was alight by the time the second load of people arrived. Through the afternoon teams of sailors in the boats rowed at maximum effort, not knowing whether the Sea Venture would remain fast in its nook. The ship was three-quarters of a mile off the nearest land, but the campsite up the coast was almost a mile and a half over water from the grounded vessel. The five or so trips to clear the ship required at least seven miles of rowing by teams of sailors who had just endured four days of constant work in the midst of a hurricane. Dusk was falling as the last group came ashore. In accord with maritime tradition, Newport and Somers were the last off the ship. Incredibly, despite the dire situation of just a few hours earlier, no one on the Sea Venture had died or even suffered a serious injury during the storm. "By the mercy of God unto us," Strachey said, "making out our boats, we had ere night brought all our men, women, and children, about the number of one hundred and fifty, safe into the island."

The sailors kept the watch schedule they had followed on the ship and tended the fires through the night. Since the castaways could not hunt for food until first light, they lay in a circle around the fire under layers of palm fronds. The survivors of the *Sea Venture* had just come through the most exhausting experience of their lives. Despite growling stomachs they closed their eyes, huddled close to one another, and fell into a deep sleep.

CHAPTER SIX

Devil's Land

The still-vexed Bermudas.

—Ariel, *The Tempest*

On the morning of July 29, 1609, sunrise awoke William Strachey to the saturated colors of leaves waving in the fresh breeze of a departed hurricane. What he noticed immediately was the hot and humid air. Sand stuck to his damp face and hands as he raised himself from his sleeping place on the ground. All around him men, women, and children slumbered. The relief of being on land struck him anew as he rediscovered that he was safe after four terror-filled days.

Strachey stood up and walked to a small water barrel at the edge of the campsite and dipped a drink. Being able to quench his thirst was another refreshing change. Soon after arriving on the previous afternoon the first people in camp had dug a shallow well. Heavy rains had soaked the island and it was not necessary to dig deep to find what Strachey called "gushings and soft bubblings." Everyone in camp had quenched their thirst, and buckets and the barrel had been filled for the next day. Strachey noticed that the water in the well had already drained away during the night. The hole would have to be deepened or an alternative water source found.

After taking a moment in the woods Strachey walked down to the beach. A heavy surf broke on the sand and the sky was clear. He walked on to the point of rocks just north of the camp. From there he could see that the shore formed almost a square corner just north of the camp. The crescent beach where the boats were pulled up extended about eight hundred feet to the south before merging with a rocky shoreline. To the west the northern coast of the island ran as far as he could see. With the exception of the pinkish sand of the beach, the shoreline was sharp black rock. Foam covered the water as waves crashed down. Palms and cedars lined the shore in both directions.

The beach in front of the camp faced northeast toward England, three thousand miles across the Atlantic, while Virginia lay six hundred miles to the west. Bermuda is an archipelago consisting of one main island and many small ones. The castaways had come to rest at the extreme northeastern point of the archipelago, on the medium-sized island that would later become known as St. George's. The main land mass lay beyond the castaways' isle, beginning on the other side of a sheltered bay and extending ten miles to the west in the shape of a giant hook.

Strachey had read about Bermuda in his travel books. The castaways were the only humans there, as the island had never been reached by people from the New World. Europeans had known of Bermuda since 1505, but its dangerous shallows had kept ships at a distance, and it was never occupied. A few had shipwrecked and left their marks, but all had departed after brief stays. What was notable was Bermuda's reputation as a bewitched place. During the last minutes before the wreck, the sailors of the *Sea Venture* had lamented their fate even as they bailed and pumped to get the ship close to the island. The island, they said, was a place of strange nighttime noises and supernatural storms.

"We found it to be the dangerous and dreaded island, or rather islands, of the Bermuda," Strachey wrote. "Because they be so terrible to all that ever touched on them, and such tempests, thunders, and other fearful objects are seen and heard about them, that they be called commonly the Devil's Islands, and are feared and avoided of all sea travelers alive above any other place in the world. Yet it pleased our merciful God to make even this hideous and hated place both the place of our safety and the means of our deliverance."

Fellow *Sea Venture* passenger Silvester Jourdain would also write of the apprehension of the castaways. Seafarers avoided Bermuda "as they would shun the Devil himself," Jourdain wrote. "The islands of the Bermudas, as every man knows that has heard or read of them, were never inhabited by any Christian or heathen people, but ever esteemed and reputed a most prodigious and enchanted place, affording nothing but gusts, storms, and foul weather, which made every navigator and mariner to avoid them."

A call to gather brought Strachey back to camp. All were now awake, and the *Sea Venture* cook, Thomas Powell, was preparing what little food had been brought from the ship. The castaways had been told to prepare for a meeting with Governor Thomas Gates. Presently the castaways formed a half circle around Gates as he addressed the crowd. The mariners would row back to the ship and retrieve everything they could. As they did that, the passengers would form teams and spread out from the camp in search of food and water. Several leaders were chosen and the voyagers broke into groups and prepared to go in assigned directions.

Strachey joined a team of gentlemen who left the camp and pushed through the underbrush. In his speech Gates had not mentioned the sailors' stories of enchantment that virtually all the castaways had now heard, but his manner, the bright sunshine, and focused activity had dispelled the apprehensions of most for the moment. The sun rose higher and the day grew even hotter as the moist tropical air the hurricane pulled behind it settled over the island. While the searchers found no brooks or springs, they soon discovered a pond. They waded in and tasted the water and detected no salt. A lack of running water put the body of water in a category Strachey described as "fens, marshes, ditches, muddy pools." The water tasted good, though, and there was no hint of contamination. As a later settler would note, rainwater percolated through Bermuda's limestone to produce pond water that "drinks always sweet like milk." Strachey and his fellows headed back to camp to tell of their find and retrieve buckets to fill.

The sailors had already returned in the longboat and skiff with useful salvage. Live hogs and the few remaining undamaged containers of food and drink were the first things brought to shore. On the first run of the day the mariners had collected equipment that would be of immedi-ate use—guns for hunting, line and nets for fishing, and containers for water. The remainder of the space in the boats was filled with chests, chairs, cooking utensils, rope, and tools. "We saved all our lives and after-wards saved much of our goods, but all our bread was wet and lost," George Somers said. As the Virginia Company would later report, the salvage crews would eventually strip the ship and leave behind "nothing but bared ribs as a prey unto the ocean."

Fishing equipment from the *Sea Venture* was immediately prepared for use. A team headed by George Somers waded into the waters off the beach and found them filled with life. Within minutes of dropping lines they were pulling in fish by the dozen. Silvester Jourdain said the cast-aways found "many kind of fishes and so plentiful thereof that in half an hour he took so many great fishes with hooks as did suffice the whole company one day. And fish is there so abundant that if a man step into the water they will come round about him so that men were fain to get out for fear of biting. These fishes are very fat and sweet."

By midafternoon teams had beaten a path to the pond and filled ev-ery available container. Somers's men were bringing in scores of fish. The campsite, too, was taking form. The sailors brought in rope and canvas and the voyagers strung sails between trees to serve as awnings. Under one canvas roof near the fire a rude kitchen was set up. The well was dug deeper and was again supplying limited water. Separate privies for men and women were dug and equipped with benches at secluded spots out of sight of the camp.

Toward the end of the day a great fish feast commenced in the camp of the voyagers. Among the species eaten were many of those listed by early settlers as teeming in the island's waters—rockfish, hogfish, amber-fish, hedgehogfish, cunnyfish, old wives, snappers, groupers, cavallyes, mullets, mackerels, pilchers, and breams. Thomas Powell oversaw the cleaning of the exotic fish and the roasting of them on the campfire. As each came crackling from the flames it was laid on a plate or leaf and passed through the crowd. Deep draughts of fresh water followed. In a few hours the stomachs of the castaways were full.

Surveying the camp during the banquet of strange fish, the survivors of the *Sea Venture* looked around at a tiny village that was well appointed beyond all expectation. The sailors had already brought ashore all manner of goods from the ship, including mattresses and blankets, furniture, and chests filled with personal goods. To have these precious items at hand rather than at the bottom of the sea made their situation relatively comfortable. The castaways marveled at their good luck. Despite the desperate times of the hurricane, the *Sea Venture*'s passengers were indeed fortunate.

The history of the island as a supernatural land was always at the back of the castaways' minds, so much so that when they heard rustling in the brush during dinner some surely thought they were hearing one of Bermuda's fabled devils. The commotion in the underbrush did indeed turn out to be a monster, but a monstrous hog rather than a savage and deformed being. The famished domestic swine from the ship had been allowed to root about loose for food, and their presence had not gone unnoticed. "We had knowledge that there were wild hogs upon the island at first by our own swine preserved from the wreck and brought to shore, for they straying into the woods, a huge wild boar followed down to our quarter," Strachey said.

The presence of hogs on Bermuda was not a surprise to some among the shipwreck survivors. One of the books Strachey brought on the voyage included an account by Gonzalo Fernández de Oviedo of an unsuccessful attempt by Juan Bermúdez in 1511 to stock his namesake island with hogs as a mid-Atlantic larder for passing ships. Another Spaniard, Pedro Menéndez de Avilés, was apparently successful in a similar attempt in 1563. A Spanish captain who landed on the island in 1603 reported that hogs left by Avilés had prospered. Diego Ramirez found large herds when he paused to repair a damaged ship six years before the *Sea*

Venture wreck. The hogs had trod out wide paths to watering holes, and trees along the trails were worn where the animals rubbed their backs against the bark.

After dinner around the campfire the sailors devised a plan to capture the boar. The animal turned out to be remarkably unafraid of humans, Strachey said, and "at night was watched and taken in this sort. One of Sir George Somers's men went and lay among the swine, when the boar being come and groveled by the sows he put over his hand and rubbed the side gently of the boar, which then lay still, by which means he fastened a rope with a sliding knot to the hind leg and so took him and after him in this sort two or three more."

During the next two weeks many more hogs were taken and penned in enclosures at the camp. The Bermuda hogs were descendants of wild boars from the forests of Europe, a fierce breed that lacked the docility modern pigs have acquired through selective breeding. Living for generations on an island without predators had dulled their sense of danger, however, and the *Sea Venture* dog proved an efficient hunter. "Our people would go a-hunting with our ship dog," Strachey said, "and sometimes bring home thirty, sometimes fifty, boars, sows, and pigs in a week alive."

The fauna of Bermuda was proving useful, as was the flora. The leaves of the palmetto trees around the camp were the first plants used by the voyagers. The fan leaves spanned up to ten feet in width and breadth. Within two weeks of landing several castaways had constructed huts of wood frames covered with leaves. The individual structures provided privacy at family campsites around the main camp. "With these leaves we thatched our cabins," Strachey said. "So broad are the leaves, as an Italian *umbrello,* a man may well defend his whole body under one of them from the greatest storm rain that falls. For they being stiff and smooth as if so many flags were knit together the rain easily slideth off."

The palmetto palm tree also provided food. The castaways noticed that the wild hogs ate the berries that grew in clumps below the sprays of leaves. They tried them themselves and found them palatable. The base from which the leaves sprouted was found to be edible as well. Each tree yielded a twenty-pound head that could be eaten raw, grilled, or boiled. "Roasting the palmetto or soft top thereof, they had a taste like fried melons, and being sod they eat like cabbages," Strachey said.

Palmetto berries were not the only succulent treats awaiting the castaways. On exposed parts of the island the castaways found growing among the limestone boulders a cactus with an edible pear. Though one had to be careful getting past the spines of the hull, Strachey said, the reward was a center filled with maroon juice. "A kind of peas of the bigness and shape of a Katherine pear we found growing upon the rocks, full of many sharp subtle pricks (as a thistle) which we therefore called the prickle pear, the outside green but being opened of a deep murrey, full of juice like a mulberry and just of the same substance and taste. We both eat them raw and baked."

As the voyagers gathered food, they also explored the islands. What they found was a natural fortress that was as easy to defend as it was difficult to approach. Accompanying the discovery that Bermuda was a secure sanctuary, Strachey said, was the confirmation that it was "desolate and not inhabited." This was not a real surprise, either, given its distance from inhabited lands and its dangerous reputation. Still, in their first weeks after the shipwreck it dawned on the voyagers that they had discovered a well-stocked mid-Atlantic bastion that was theirs for the taking. An historian who wrote about the *Sea Venture* wreck in 1705 bluntly stated the main attraction of the place: "The best of it was, they found plenty of provisions in that island and no Indians to annoy them."

Yet for all its good points, Bermuda was not quite a paradise. While there were no rival humans to compete with the *Sea Venture* castaways, there were inhabitants of another kind to annoy them. "They were long and slender-leg spiders," Strachey said, "and whether venomous or no I know not, I believe not, since we should still find them amongst our linen in our chests and drinking cans but we never received any danger from them." Nathaniel Butler, who would come to Bermuda a few years later, would note that the spiders were so big that they would occasionally catch sparrows in their webs. "They are here of a most pleasing and beautiful aspect, all over as it were decked with silver, gold, and pearl," Butler said, "and their webs (woven in the summer upon trees) are found to be perfect silk."

Within days of the wreck the voyagers planted a garden near the camp using English seeds brought in from the *Sea Venture*. Sprouts appeared, Strachey said, but the plants grew no further. "Sir George Somers in the beginning of August squared out a garden by the quarter and sowed muskmelons, peas, onions, radishes, lettuce, and many English seeds and kitchen herbs. All which in some ten days did appear aboveground." Grubs killed the plants, he said. Butler later reported other pests. "The mosquitoes and flies also are somewhat over-busy, with a certain Indian bug called by a Spanish appellation a caca-roach, the which creeping into chests and boxes eat and defile with their dung (and hence their Spanish name) all they meet with." Summer flies were the closest things to devils on Bermuda, according to an anonymous account by another colonist of a few years later. "Whereas it is reported that this land of the Bermudas with the islands about it (which are many, at the least a hundred) are enchanted and kept with evil and wicked spirits, it is a most idle and false report. God grant that we have brought no wicked spirits with us or that there comes none after us, for we found none so ill as ourselves," he said. "No, nor any noisome thing or hurtful, more than a poor fly which tarries not above two or three months."

Even with spiders, cockroaches, mosquitoes, and flies, Bermuda was turning out to be as fine a refuge as anyone on the *Sea Venture* could have imagined. What was thought to be a land of devils and brimstone turned out to be a temperate and angelic place. "My opinion sincerely of this island is," Jourdain said, "that whereas it hath been and is still accounted the most dangerous, unfortunate, and most forlorn place of the world, it is in truth the richest, healthfulest, and pleasing land (the quantity and bigness thereof considered) and merely natural as ever man set foot upon."

"I hope to deliver the world from a foul and general error," Strachey wrote. "It being counted of most that they can be no habitation for men but rather given over to devils and wicked spirits, whereas indeed we find them now by experience to be as habitable and commodious as most countries of the same climate and situation, insomuch as if the entrance into them were as easy as the place itself is contenting it had long ere this been inhabited."

Discord among the castaways also made it clear that despite their good fortune the castaways' situation was less than perfect. On a hot summer day in August a grudge between two sailors flared into a wrestling match in the sand and fellow sailors formed a circle around the fighters. Before Governor Gates or his lieutenants arrived to stop the fight, Robert Waters picked up a shovel and struck his opponent Edward Samuel in the head, instantly killing him. When Gates determined that Samuel was dead, he ordered Waters held and Samuel's body buried some distance from the camp. Later in the day he held a tribunal before the assembled voyagers, and after hearing testimony he condemned Waters to be hanged the next morning. The prisoner was tied to a tree under guard within sight of the camp.

Waters's death sentence caused dissension within the *Sea Venture* company for the first time since it had formed in London twelve weeks earlier. Relations had been good during the sail, the fight with the hurricane, and the building of the Bermuda camp. Gates's decision to condemn Waters to death, however, immediately set him at odds with the mariners of the shipwrecked company. The *Sea Venture* sailors had never expected to be subjected to military control, even the mix of civilian and military authority afforded the governor of the Virginia colony. Their anticipated role had been solely as transport specialists who served at the pleasure of the highest-ranking marine officer. Now unexpectedly marooned in a foreign land they were begrudgingly subject to Gates's rule. That had been fine during the first two weeks, but now one of their own was condemned to die as the result of a fair fight. They couldn't watch their shipmate hanged. In the night while Waters's sentries slept they cut his bonds and took him to a hiding place in the forest.

Strachey learned of the escape with the rest of the camp when a sentry awoke and sounded the alarm. His loyalties and those of the other gentlemen of the company were fully with the governor. To Strachey, Waters's flight was a grave affront to authority. The conspirators who had cut him free, he said, demonstrated "disdain that justice should be showed upon a sailor, that one of their crew should be an example to others, not taking into consideration the unmanliness of the murder nor the horror of the sin."

Gates now faced the first open challenge to his authority as leader of the expedition. The split in the company displeased him and he knew that a killer lurking in the woods would have a corrosive effect on morale and discipline. The only way to bring the fugitive in, it seemed, was a major concession to the sailors. Certainly he wanted the matter resolved soon and in a definitive way. Gates sought the counsel of George Somers, who was well positioned to assist. As an educated and wealthy man, the gray-haired admiral had the trust of Gates despite his ties to the sailors. The two men met in a palmetto hut, and after a long talk emerged to announce a solution.

Strachey alone describes the final disposition of the case, and he does so in few words, perhaps because he was a consistent apologist for Gates and thought the outcome did not reflect well on the governor. Waters, Strachey said, "afterward by the mediation of Sir George Somers, upon many conditions, had his trial respited by our governor." Intervention by the admiral won a sentence reduction that was startling in its leniency—clemency with the only condition being a requirement of good behavior. When Waters returned to the camp to slaps on the back from his compatriots and wary looks from the gentlemen, it was clear to all that Gates had literally allowed a man to get away with murder. Either Somers was a master defender or Gates was an unusually malleable judge. The prevailing opinion of the castaways tended to the latter view. Gates had resolved the murder case, but it came at a high cost to his reputation.

In addition to exposing the leader of the *Sea Venture* company as a vacillating commander, the Waters case served to expose a division within the ranks of the castaways. Governor Gates and Admiral Somers were forced into adversarial roles neither wanted, and the effect of that split would persist. While the negotiation over Waters's fate was carried out in decorous terms, the talks placed the two leaders and their constituencies in blocs that cut along traditional lines of soldiers and sailors. The fistfight had pitted mariner against mariner, but its resolution had pitted Waters the sailor against Gates the soldier. Despite the outcome in the sailor's favor, under the leadership of Gates the mariners would continue to perceive themselves as an aggrieved party and would nurse that sense of grievance as time went on.

CHAPTER SEVEN

Angel's Garden

Had I plantation of this isle.

—Gonzalo, *The Tempest*

On hot August nights as the fire in the center of the castaways' camp turned to embers, the *Sea Venture* survivors may have heard what sounded like sprites in the dark. When all was quiet, the distinct calls of thousands of birds could be heard as they flew over the camp. Warblers, thrushes, swallows, plovers, and sandpipers were among the migrants passing over the island each night on long flights from the continent to lands far to the south. Some would rest on Bermuda, and during the day the castaways would occasionally see a flash of color in the brush. Among the migrants, too, were dragonflies that came from the Virginia coast to winter on the mid-Atlantic isle.

As William Strachey had during the weeks on the *Sea Venture*, he spent most of his time on Bermuda among the elite voyagers of the company—Thomas Gates, Reverend Richard Buck, Captain Newport, and Mistress Horton. Within this group Strachey joined in quietly disparaging the laborers and artisans of the company. The lesser sort, he said, were guilty of overharvesting palmetto trees for their berries and cabbagelike heads, even in places where there was no need to clear the land. "Many an ancient burger was therefore heaved at and fell not for his place but for his head, for our common people whose bellies never had ears made it no breach of charity in their hot bloods and tall stomachs to murder thousands of them."

Many of those whose "bellies never had ears" suffered diarrhea when they gorged on palmetto berries. Luckily, the castaways discovered that another native Bermuda plant offered a cure for the malady they called the flux. The bay grape bears clusters of edible berries among red-veined leaves. Strachey described the grape as "a round blue berry, much eaten by our own people—of a styptic quality and rough taste on the tongue like a sloe—to stay or bind the flux."

There was another use of the bounty of the palmetto tree that made trips to the privy a little easier to take, though perhaps no less frequent. The castaways missed having alcoholic drinks, and some of the more creative among them tried fermenting the produce of the island as a substitute. The palmetto tree yields a sap that when mixed with water makes a sugary drink. When fermented, it turns to a liquor that was a tolerable alternative to English beer. The settlers took to calling the palmetto drink "bibby" and indulged in it often.

The castaways made a second spirituous liquor from berries of another Bermuda tree. Cedars grew in large groves in the valleys, Strachey said, "the berries whereof our men seething, straining, and letting stand some three or four days made a kind of pleasant drink. These berries are of the same bigness and color of currants, full of little stones and very restringent or hard building." The berries were eaten raw as well. Jourdain added, "There are an infinite number of cedar trees (the fairest I think in the world) and those bring forth a very sweet berry and wholesome to eat."

Many other useful plants grew on the island, not all of them native. The Spanish had planted at least three crops that still grew in patches. Jourdain reported that the *Sea Venture* voyagers discovered good quality tobacco, and, while they are not mentioned in the chronicles, olives and pawpaws had been growing on the island for more than a decade. Jourdain also found another potential crop—native mulberries and a new variety of silkworm feeding on the leaves that he hoped might produce threads that could be made into cloth. The find was notable because English explorers were eager to develop a silk industry to replace expensive imports from Asia.

With the addition of plant foods the Bermuda larder was becoming ever more ample, though summer temperatures in the low eighties meant only a small supply of meat could be stored. The *Sea Venture* castaways had only limited opportunity to use the traditional preservation technique of salting. Among the casks rescued from the ship were two or three of brine that could be boiled down to make salt. Gates ordered a salt-boiling operation set up under a palmetto-leaf roof, and, according to Strachey, "kept three or four pots boiling and two or three men attending nothing else in a house (some little distance from his bay)." When the brine in the casks ran out, seawater was used, though because it had a lower salt content it required more boiling and more firewood—a full cord to produce 4.5 bushels of salt. The salt-house fire, a continuously burning signal fire on the beach, and the campfire made woodcutting and log carrying a steady occupation in the *Sea Venture* camp.

Castaway carpenters also cut cedar trees for use as lumber, an activity possible only because the grounding of the *Sea Venture* allowed the retrieval of tools from the ship. One of the books Strachey brought on the ship reported that the Spanish had already transported Bermuda cedar boards to their Caribbean colonies and found them useful, albeit prone to splitting and difficult to handle. Gonzalo Fernández de Oviedo wrote that the wood of the Bermuda cedar was resistant to shipworms when used in seagoing vessels. The largest cedars growing on the island were fifteen feet in circumference, though the woodcutters selected more manageable specimens in their forays for lumber.

In August two boat-building operations commenced. English carpenters constructed a flat-bottomed boat that Strachey compared to a Venetian gondola. The boat allowed the castaways to transport substantial cargoes across water. This was important because it allowed the hog hunters to more easily venture to the main island. Jourdain described Somers's returning with more than thirty live hogs on the wide bottom of the craft. The gondola was used for offshore fishing when heavy angling thinned near-shore stocks. Crustaceans and shellfish were collected and brought to camp in the boat as well. "We have taken also from under the broken rocks crayfishes oftentimes greater than any of our best English lobsters, and likewise abundance of crabs, oysters, and whelks," Strachey said. "True it is, for fish in every cove and creek were found, snails, and schools in that abundance as (I think) no island in the world may have greater store or better fish."

Among the fishermen who brought in the Bermuda catch were Namontack and Machumps. During the summer they dug out two canoes of Bermuda cedar. A single log was used to make each canoe, the center of the tree being slowly removed by burning with coals and scraping with shells and stones. A colonist who saw canoes in Virginia called them "a kind of boat they have made in the form of a hog's trough." The canoes added two more vessels to the *Sea Venture*'s miniature fleet of gondola, longboat, and skiff. Once the considerable task of hollowing out the first canoe was complete, the Powhatans were able to put their fishing skills to work. Namontack and Machumps fished both with fish-bone hooks and bow and arrow. A third method was to trap fish behind a weir staked across a tidal race. At high tide the fish would pass over the porous barrier of brush, then at low tide the barrier would break the surface and trap the catch behind it. Fishermen then used nets made of bark and animal sinew to collect the corralled fish. Powhatan weirs were "enclosures made of reeds and framed in the fashion of a labyrinth or maze set a fathom deep in the water," Strachey said, "with diverse chambers or beds out of which the entangled fish cannot return or get out."

While the gondola and canoes were useful for on-island activities, they did nothing to help the castaways leave Bermuda. No ships had appeared on the horizon by mid-August. Surely if those on the other ships of the Third Supply had survived the hurricane, they now thought the *Sea Venture* was at the bottom of the sea. The castaways on Bermuda were hundreds of miles from the point at which the flagship lost contact with the other vessels. The chance that they had made it to land would be considered so slight and the resources of Jamestown would be so scant that no rescue ship would be dispatched to look for them. The castaways would have to devise their own means of deliverance. To that end, Gates formulated a dual plan to transport the voyagers from their unintended sanctuary.

First the castaways would fit *Sea Venture*'s longboat with a cabin and sail and send it to Jamestown as soon as possible. Construction would also begin on a larger vessel, a pinnace capable of carrying half the stranded party. The new vessel would sail to Jamestown and send back the pinnace that was routinely left at the colony for use in coastal exploration. No large ships would be available because those of the *Sea Venture* fleet—if they made it through the storm—would have long since returned to England with the produce of Virginia.

Four carpenters were on Bermuda, the most accomplished of whom was Richard Frobisher. Strachey described him as "a painful and well-experienced shipwright and a skillful workman." Frobisher set up a work site in a small bay a half mile south of the main camp. The spot was thereafter referred to as Frobisher's Building Bay, or simply Building Bay. The first task was the fitting out of the longboat, which at twenty-one feet was little more than an oversized rowboat. The boat was hauled onto the beach and the carpenters began transforming it into a miniature sailing vessel. "We made up our longboat in fashion of a pinnace," Strachey reported, "fitting her with a little deck made of the hatches of our ruined ship, so close that no water could go in her, gave her sails and oars, and entreating with our master's mate Henry Ravens (who was supposed a sufficient pilot) we found him easily won to make over therewith as a bark of adviso for Virginia."

Gates wrote letters to the leaders of Jamestown and others to be forwarded to the Virginia Company in London. After two weeks or so of work the reconstruction was complete, and toward the end of August the tiny vessel was sailed the half mile up the coast to the camp for stocking. Ravens was pleased with the handling of the boat and said he was ready to put to sea. The longboat was packed with food and water, fishing equipment, clothes, bedding, and weapons. Then Ravens, according to Strachey, "the twenty-eighth of August being Monday, with six sailors and our cape-merchant Thomas Whittingham, departed from us out of Gates his Bay." Two days later the castaways were disappointed to see the tiny sail return to view off the north shore and the longboat come back to camp. Incredibly, even though the vessel drew only twenty inches, it could not clear the reefs to the north and west of Bermuda. The men rested two days, restocked the longboat, and departed to the east through the channel the *Sea Venture* had traversed on the way in. This time Ravens made it to sea, Strachey said, "promising if he lived and arrived safe there to return unto us the next new moon with the pinnace belonging to the colony there."

On the same day that Ravens left the first time—August 28—carpenters laid the keel of the new pinnace. The vessel would be built within wooden stocks just above the tidal zone in Building Bay. A boardwalk around the construction cradle ensured that the surf did not dampen the feet of the builders while they worked. Construction at the water's edge was necessary to make it possible to pull the completed pinnace off the stocks when the tide was highest. The keel was forty feet long and made from an oak beam scavenged from the *Sea Venture*. Construction likely progressed as described by John Smith in one of his two primers on nautical methods. "First lay the keel, the stem, and stern in a dry dock or upon the stocks and bind them with good knees, then lay all the floor timbers," Smith wrote. Only the most experienced shipwright should attempt to build a vessel, he said. "The lengths, breadths, depths, rakes, and burdens are so variable and different, that nothing but experience can possibly teach it." Fortunately the *Sea Venture* castaways had such an experienced wright in Richard Frobisher.

Strachey, who was a devoted disciple of Gates, told of the governor setting a good example for the workmen building the pinnace. Rather than simply order them to cut lumber for the construction project, Gates did some of the heaviest work himself in order to model how he expected his charges to act. "The governor dispensed with no travail of his body nor forbore any care or study of mind," Strachey said, "persuading as much and more an ill-qualified parcel of people by his own performance than by authority, thereby to hold them at their work, namely to fell, carry, and saw cedar fit for the carpenters' purpose."

The work proceeded well, but Gates's rescue plan did not please everyone in the castaway camp. Though the voyagers had been recruited by a promise of riches in Virginia, they had heard whispers of the bloody resistance of the Powhatans. Here they stood on an unclaimed island of plenty. Little time passed before it became clear to some that they could live on Bermuda in relative comfort until a passing vessel afforded an opportunity to present themselves in England as the founders of an island colony. Gates discouraged talk of such a plan, believing the obligation of all lay with the Virginia Company that had financed the fleet and to whom everyone on the island had pledged loyalty. Notwithstanding the appeal of Bermuda and the potential hardships of Jamestown, Gates contended that every person who rode the *Sea Venture* was bound by contract and reputation to go to Virginia. If he had not insisted that every possible means to do so be pursued, Strachey said, "I am persuaded we had most of us finished our days there, so willing were the major part of the common sort (especially when they found such a plenty of victuals) to settle a foundation of ever inhabiting there."

The desire to stay was so persistent among "the common sort" that at the beginning of September a second challenge to Gates's authority arose. The insubordination first manifested itself in a reluctance to work on the construction of the pinnace. "Some dangerous and secret discontents nourished amongst us had like to have been the parents of bloody issues and mischiefs," Strachey said. Sailors were the first to conspire, and they were then joined by landsmen. The argument that persuaded others to join was that "in Virginia nothing but wretchedness and labor must be expected with many wants," Strachey said, "there being neither that fish, flesh, nor fowl which here at ease and pleasure might be enjoyed."

The plot was betrayed to Gates on September 1 and six men—John Want, Christopher Carter, Francis Pearepoint, William Brian, William

Martin, and Richard Knowles—were brought before Gates for trial. The plan of the mutineers was to separate from the main group and establish homesteads for themselves on another of the islands of the Bermuda archipelago. They had hoped to draw into the conspiracy a carpenter named Nicholas Bennit, whom Strachey characterized as "a mutinous and dissembling imposter." Gates decided that the fittest sentence would be to banish them to a small island with just enough provisions to sustain themselves. "They were condemned to the same punishment which they would have chosen (but without smith or carpenter) and to an island far by itself they were carried and there left," Strachey said.

Earlier a murderer had walked free, and now mutineers were exiled instead of being hanged. For the second time Gates had exercised unusual restraint in punishing capital offenses. The governor's compassionate streak endeared him to some of the castaways, but to others it revealed him as unable or unwilling to impose a deserving sentence, or, once imposed, to carry it out. Only to the six banished mutineers did the punishment seem quite severe enough as the skiff pushed off from their island prison to return to the main camp.

In late September the weather turned wet and windy and the misery of the banished mutineers increased accordingly. The boats that brought the exiled men rations returned to camp with word that the six were quarrelsome and bored and tired of subsistence living. In his account of the end of the banishment, Strachey takes pains to demonstrate that the governor was justified in paroling the mutineers. "Our governor (not easy to admit any accusation and hard to remit an offence, but at all times sorry in the punishment of him in whom may appear either shame or contrition) was easily content to reacknowledge them again." The ostracized men were reunited with the company and the castaway party was whole again.

Namontack and Machumps probably shed the uncomfortable clothes of England when they reached Bermuda. In the woods again, they resumed the lives they had led in Tsenacomoco. The Bermuda episode was an unusual interlude of cooperation in the era of contact between English and Powhatan people. For the first time they had been thrown together in a land foreign to both. On the island the two Powhatans led relatively autonomous lives, setting up their own camp some distance from the main settlement. The hurricane had been a harrowing experience for them. Their lack of control over the boat and the terrified looks on the faces of the English had been hard to endure. Even this strange land was a welcome relief.

The Powhatans' first weeks on the island were likely spent in manufacture. The canoes were the most time-consuming project. They may have made arrows, but the wood on Bermuda was not right for bows, and so they would use the ones they had unless they came across trees as strong and flexible as the witch hazel or locust of Virginia. William Strachey was especially interested in learning about the Powhatans of Virginia, and he sometimes visited their fire and talked to them in a mix of English and Powhatan. On the visits the Powhatans and Englishman were wary of each other and concealed mild distaste for the opposite cultures. Much of the initial conversation was spent in learning words. They often resorted to hand signals, but nevertheless managed to converse on a wide range of subjects. Strachey hoped his journals would form the basis of his narrative of the New World, albeit one with an unexpected mid-Atlantic detour.

Initially Namontack and Machumps would have hunted birds in the woods near the camp. White-tailed deer were their main quarry at home, but the only large animals on the island were feral pigs, and so they became the prey. The canoes Namontack and Machumps hollowed out by their fire allowed them to roam throughout the archipelago. This they did freely, going to the main island, where there were large flocks of birds and herds of pigs. One canoe was left with the English for their use, and the two from Tsenacomoco took the other to distant hunting grounds. They would return in two or three days with a canoe laden with pigs, fish, and fowl. Much of the food would be given to the English, still leaving plenty for the Powhatans.

On one of the hunts away from the camp Namontack apparently came to an unexplained end. Machumps never admitted to knowing any details about the disappearance of his companion, if in fact he did know anything beyond Namontack's having never returned from a foray into the brush. All Machumps seems to have said was that Namontack disappeared. When Machumps returned to camp alone, the English apparently assumed that his companion was still away hunting. When Namontack had not come back for several days, Machumps's explanation seems to have been that his companion never showed up at a meeting place and a search revealed nothing of his fate.

An accident could certainly have befallen a man hunting in an unknown land. The Powhatan method of hunting demanded the rapid pursuit of wounded prey. Namontack may have sunk an arrow in a hog and taken up the chase across unfamiliar terrain. Perhaps he tripped on broken limestone and hit his head. Maybe he was hunting along the shore and slipped while traversing rocks. If he had fallen in the ocean and drowned his body could have been washed away. Another possibility is that the man from Tsenacomoco discovered one of Bermuda's two hundred limestone caves, the longest of which runs for more than a mile underground. Namontack may have come across a cavern entrance, gone inside, fallen, and died.

Such a scenario is apparently what Machumps expected the English to believe, either because he thought it true or he wanted an alibi. They were suspicious that he knew more than he told. The Englishmen's attempts to extract information across a significant language barrier proved ineffective. Their suspicions would remain unanswered. The English were not inclined to launch a search for a lost man of another culture, especially when resources were needed for hunting and finding a way off the island. In the absence of proof, Machumps was allowed to continue to live in his camp and contribute to the general larder, but the English now kept a close watch on his activities. After all, he might be a liar and a murderer.

As time passed the story of Machumps and Namontack was retold and embellished. Eventually Machumps would be cast as the perpetrator of a grisly murder. "Some such differences fell between them," John Smith would write years later, "that Machumps slew Namontack, and having made a hole to bury him, because it was too short, he cut off his legs and laid them by him, which murder he concealed." Sensationalized with gore it became a fantastic tale indeed, but one that seems exaggerated in light of Machumps's continued residency among the English. They may have suspected foul play, but if they could prove it—even by the low standard required in a cross-cultural case—they would not have hesitated to execute him.

CHAPTER EIGHT

New Life

'Twas a sweet marriage.
—Sebastian, *The Tempest*

Autumn days were noticeably cooler for the *Sea Venture* survivors. During October and November temperatures averaged in the high sixties and cold fronts crossed the island with clouds and rain. Day and night the fires burned on the beach, though there was no sign of a rescue ship sent by Henry Ravens. The coming of cool weather brought concern that if the stay on Bermuda stretched into winter, the bounty of the island might wane and hardships might increase. The prospect of a winter in exile caused the more pessimistic among the shipwreck survivors to be watchful for signs that the devil was afoot on the island, after all. Perhaps he would materialize in the rains and winds of the dead season.

The first voyager to hear a cahow in the autumn night might well have thought that evil spirits were at hand. The gull-sized seabirds (also known as Bermuda petrels) had frightened Spanish sailors who briefly touched on the island in October 1603. Diego Ramirez reported that when he anchored off Bermuda, "at dusk, such a shrieking and din filled the air that fear seized us." The sailors first attributed the noise to devils, Ramirez said, but after realizing that the banshees were plump fowl rather than hellish specters the men clubbed five hundred and brought them back to the ship for food.

Six years later the night calls were again heard on Bermuda as the cahows returned to the island to nest in late October and early November. The *Sea Venture* castaways, having lived on Bermuda three months, were apparently more reserved than the Spanish in their reaction. Hunters followed the growing flocks of cahows to what would become known as the Bird Islands to the south. "A kind of web-footed fowl there is," Strachey said, "of the bigness of an English green plover, or sea-mew, which all the summer we saw not, and in the darkest nights of November and December (for in the night they only feed) they would come forth, but not fly far from home, and hovering in the air and over the sea made a strange hollow and harsh howling."

The cahows nested in holes in the limestone soil of the islands, which prompted Strachey to compare them to rabbits living in dens in a stony field. "Their color is inclining to russet with white bellies (as are likewise the long feathers of their wings russet and white). These gather themselves together and breed in those islands which are high and so far alone into the sea that the wild hogs cannot swim over them, and there in the ground they have their burrows like conies in a warren and so brought in the loose mould though not so deep, which birds with a light bough in a dark night (as in our lowbelling) we caught. I have been at the taking of three hundred in an hour, and we might have laden our boats."

The traditional hunting technique of lowbelling, or hunting at night with torches to stupefy prey, proved an effective technique on Bermuda. Little effort was necessary after landing on the Bird Islands, however, as the birds seemed perfectly willing to come to the hunters. "Our men found a pretty way to take them," Strachey said, "which was by standing on the rocks or sands by the seaside and hollowing, laughing, and making the strangest outcry that possibly they could, with the noise whereof the birds would come flocking to that place and settle upon the very arms and head of him that so cried, and still creep nearer and nearer answering the noise themselves, by which our men would weigh them with their hand and which weighed heaviest they took for the best and let the others alone, and so our men would take twenty dozen in two hours of the chiefest of them, and they were a good and well relished fowl, fat and full as a partridge.

"There are thousands of these birds and two or three islands full of their burrows," Strachey said, "whither at any time (in two hours' warning) we could send our cock-boat and bring home as many as would serve the whole company, which birds for their blindness (for they see weakly in the day) and for their cry and hooting we call the sea owl. They will bite cruelly with their crooked bills."

The Bird Islands were one of many features the Englishmen named as they explored the island by foot and boat. In addition to naming Gates Bay where the expedition came ashore, the castaways designated the channel out to sea Somers Creek. A promontory on an island to the south the castaways passed on the cahow hunting trips also received a name. Strachey may have been the first to climb to its lookout point, as the castaways built a signal fire and shelter there and took to calling it Strachey's Watch. Somers duly marked all of these locations on a map he was making as he led hunting parties throughout the islands of the Bermuda archipelago. "Sir George Somers, who coasted in his boat about them all," Strachey said, "took great care to express the same exactly and full and made his draft perfect for all good occasions and the benefit of such who either in distress might be brought upon them or make sail this way." In giving the reason for the creation of a map—to aid English mariners—Strachey made it clear that Somers expected to leave Bermuda in the near future. The castaways would continue to work toward that goal.

Knowing that an abundance of fowl awaited the cooks each day allowed the voyagers to turn their thoughts from subsistence to the patterns of a more secure existence. One of those whose attention wandered to new pursuits was George Somers's cook, Welshman Thomas Powell. During the fall Powell grew close to one of the few single women on the island, Elizabeth Persons, the servant who had come aboard the *Sea Venture* in the service of Mistress Horton. Powell's cooking chores kept him close to camp most of the time, and since Horton never strayed far from her cabin, Persons was always nearby. The two developed a friendship through the summer and by fall it turned to something more. If they followed English custom, Thomas and Elizabeth would have bundled together—slept clothed in a single bed—in a thatched cottage during their courtship. Whether they bundled or not, on November 26, four months after the *Sea Venture* brought the castaways to the island, Richard Buck officiated at the wedding of the cook and the servant. The ceremony took place on a Sunday, the day of the week favored by Jacobean wedding couples.

Out of necessity the event was a simple affair. The bride would have worn a traditional wreath of flowers in her hair and carried a coin in her shoe for good luck. A square "care cloth," or wedding canopy, would have sheltered the couple during the ceremony. The wedding feast surely included the recently plentiful cahows roasted over the fire. Powell himself likely prepared the banquet, which may also have featured grilled fish complemented by roasted hearts of palm and fresh picked palmetto berries. A recent vintage of fermented bibby likely completed the convivial table. Though the customary plums and almond paste were lacking, a suitable island version of a wedding cake was undoubtedly created. For good luck the wedding couple would have kissed over the bride cake before serving it to their guests. At the end of the evening when the couple was escorted to their cabin, Persons may have thrown a stocking to her friends as a final gesture. The only record of the event that communicates the festive spirit of the day is John Smith's secondhand report: "amongst all those sorrows they had a merry English marriage."

The easy availability of food also allowed the castaways time to search for treasure. The valuables sought were pearls from the Bermuda lagoons and ambergris washed up on the beach. Ambergris is a waxy substance from the intestines of sperm whales that was highly valued as an ingredient of perfume. Mariners were always on the lookout for the stuff, since even a small lump would bring a fine return in London. According to Jourdain, the *Sea Venture* survivors found what they were seeking: "There is great store of pearl and some of them very fair, round, and Oriental, and you shall find at least one hundred seed of pearl in one oyster. There hath been likewise found some good quantity of ambergris, and that of the best sort." Strachey also reported the discovery of pearls during the voyagers' stay on the island, judging the gems as good as those of the West Indies.

Divers looking for pearl oysters had an opportunity to view the underwater wonders of Bermuda. "In the bottom of the sea," John Smith wrote, "there is growing upon the rocks a large kind of plant in the form of a vine leaf but far more spread with veins in color of a pale red, very strangely interlaced and woven one into another, which we call the feather." The anonymous colonist of a few years later reported another underwater marvel in the bays. "There is one very strange fish, and beautiful to behold. We call it an angelfish (as well as it may be), for as you see the picture of an angel made, so is this, and it shows of many colors both in the water swimming and out of the water and as a dainty a fish of meat as a salmon, or rather better."

Pearls, ambergris, and exotic sea life notwithstanding, the camp of the castaways was not without a continuing undercurrent of tension. The rift caused by the mutiny remained, widening the traditional gulf between mariners and landsmen. The split took the form of segregated campfires within the common clearing, separately planned survival strategies, and an absence of cross-camp chatter. The men at the head of the factions, Admiral George Somers and Governor Thomas Gates, were knights restrained by the genteel traditions of the day, and that restraint veiled the depth of the division. The career seamen formed the core of one group, while the elite landsmen were at the center of the other. Laborers and artisans split between the two factions to some extent, though most remained with the landsmen. The splinter group was that of Somers and his mariners. Seamen traditionally lived a world apart from others of all classes, and so it was on Bermuda. Despite the great disparities of wealth and class among the landsmen, the elite and the poor of the city were familiar with each other and stayed together, albeit as a layered group.

Despite the fires on Strachey's Watch, by late in the fall of 1609 neither Ravens nor rescuers from Virginia had appeared. "Two moons were wasted upon the promontory before mentioned," Strachey said, "and gave many a long and wished look round about the horizon from the northeast to the southwest, but in vain, discovering nothing all the while, which way soever we turned our eye, but air and sea." Everyone knew that the pinnace under construction in Building Bay was not large enough to take everyone to Virginia. The fact that half the castaways would remain behind had been the subject of campfire discussion since late summer, and—despite the desire of some in the company to stay on the island and build a colony there—rumors of such a parting exacerbated the splintering of the company. The assumption by the laborers was that the elite voyagers would take the skilled workmen and the best mariners and sail to safety, leaving them behind. That assessment was undoubtedly accurate and sowed resentment in those who thought they would be abandoned for months or years, perhaps even for the rest of their lives.

In late autumn Somers proposed a new approach to the goal of getting away. "The seven and twentieth of November," Strachey reported, "when then well perceiving that we were not likely to hear from Virginia and conceiving how the pinnace which Richard Frobisher was a-building would not be of burden sufficient to transport all our men from thence into Virginia (especially considering the season of the year wherein we were likely to put off), he consulted with our governor that if he might have two carpenters (for we had four, such as they were) and twenty men over with him into the main island, he would quickly frame up another little bark to second ours for the better fitting and conveyance of our people."

Strachey's description of the governor's reaction to the new plan is overstated, hinting that the writer declined to describe an air of unease in the relationship between Gates and Somers. "Our governor with many thanks (as the cause required), cherishing this so careful and religious consideration in him (and whose experience likewise was somewhat in these affairs), granted him all things suitable to his desire and to the furthering of the work." Somers was assigned "twenty of the ablest and stoutest of the company" for his construction crew, probably composed of the two carpenters and his most trusted mariners. The new strategy was attractive to all, not the least because it separated the seamen from the landsmen and put an end to the daily irritations associated with the rift in the company. Neither leader apparently worried that isolation might increase the alienation of the mariners and embolden their opposition to the governor. Somers's construction crew packed their personal belongings and disassembled their palmetto-leaf huts, packed them into the boats, and rowed to a site on the main island and there created a new camp. Thereafter couriers rowed between the two bases and carried written messages between Gates and Somers.

In the absence of grumbling mariners at the main camp a lighter mood prevailed. On Christmas Eve Richard Buck celebrated Communion. The next day Strachey came across a sign of yuletide renewal on frost-free Bermuda. "At Christmas," he said, "I saw young birds." As December turned to January, though, the weather was more foul than fair. "These islands are often afflicted and rent with tempests, great strokes of thunder, lightning, and rain in the extremity of violence," Strachey said. "The three winter months, December, January, and February, the winds kept in those cold corners and indeed then it was heavy and melancholy being there." Early in January a winter storm nearly destroyed the vessel under construction in Building Bay. Only by wading in the surf and reinforcing the cradle did the carpenters save the pinnace. The near-disaster prompted Gates to order the heaviest work of the Bermuda sojourn, the dragging of rocks into the bay to build a breakwater around the construction site.

Despite the division into two camps, in the early months of 1610 mutinous currents still flowed through the ranks of the castaways. Now that a second vessel was under construction and everyone on the island would be able to leave together, the rebels' old concerns about abandonment were replaced by an unbridled wish to colonize the island. Among the reluctant workers in Gates's camp was Stephen Hopkins, the shopkeeper who was serving as Reverend Richard Buck's assistant. Around the campfire and on work details Hopkins tried to convince his fellows that they were no longer under an obligation to the Virginia Company. The London overseers had promised them safe passage to Jamestown, Hopkins argued, and that promise had been broken when the *Sea Venture* wrecked. The company had defaulted on the contract and left the people on the ship free to do as they saw fit. Not only were the castaways no longer obliged to the Virginia Company, Hopkins said, but in light of the discovery of the potentially lucrative resources of Bermuda, they had a new obligation to claim Bermuda for the company. Similarly, they owed it to their families to seize the opportunity for enrichment they had discovered by chance and at great risk to their lives.

Those who heard Hopkins's whispered urgings around the fire were put in a difficult position. After all, Gates had already made it clear that no talk of altering the course of the expedition would be tolerated. Just by listening to Hopkins they became complicit in his scheme. The traditional punishment for plotting against a commander was death, and while Gates had so far shown restraint, no one knew how long his patience would last. A fear of the consequence of discovery drove Samuel Sharpe and Humphrey Reede to report Hopkins's activities to Gates, and on January 24 the agitator was put on trial in a hearing called by the tolling of the ship's bell.

After testimony against him, Strachey said, Hopkins was "full of sorrow and tears, pleading simplicity and denial." The accused man had left his wife Mary and children Elizabeth, Constance, and Giles back in the village of Hursley in the Hampshire countryside. The misery his execution would cause them was now the subject on which Hopkins focused his impressive rhetorical skills. Strachey was one of those who was moved enough to appeal to Gates for leniency. "So penitent he was and made so much moan alleging the ruin of his wife and children in this his trespass, as it wrought in the hearts of all the better sort of the company who therefore with humble entreaties and earnest supplications went unto our governor whom they besought (as likewise did Captain Newport and myself) and never left him until we had got his pardon." Gates was indeed proving to be a pliant leader, now tolerating a murder and two mutinies without imposing harsh punishment.

After the turmoil of the second mutiny trial, the attention of the castaways was turned in a new direction with the impending birth of the first native Bermudian. The wife of voyager John Rolfe was nine months pregnant and expected to deliver a child soon. A palmetto tent was prepared for Goodwife Rolfe by the other married women of the camp, including Mistress Horton, the just-married Elizabeth Persons Powell, and the wife of Edward Eason, who was herself seven months pregnant. A mattress was laid on a Bermuda-built bed for Goody Rolfe's benefit. At the base of the bed a stool was set for the woman who would act as midwife. Just outside the entrance a fire was kept burning.

At the first pangs of labor, Goody Rolfe sent for her attendants. As a seventeenth-century childbirth manual advised, "the time of delivery being at hand, they must prepare themselves as followeth, which is forthwith to send for their midwife and keeper, being far better to have them too soon than too late." As early labor progressed, Rolfe was encouraged to walk slowly around the clearing to hasten the process. The traditional labor-time nourishments of separate cups of broth and egg yolk (in this case perhaps from one of the first cahow eggs of the season) were offered to her.

As labor progressed and Rolfe was put to bed, one of the attendants may have followed the traditional method of assisting the birth: "Sometimes the midwife, etc., may gently press the upper parts of the belly, and by degrees stroke the child downward, the which pressing down with discretion will hasten and facilitate the delivery." In the wilds of Bermuda not all the traditional remedies of a well-stocked midwife's cabinet were available. The women attending Rolfe likely had no oils of lilies, violets, or roses to use as balms. Surely they did not have ingredients for one traditional mix often prescribed to hasten labor: white wine, mistletoe, and mummy (the dried flesh of mummies—purported to be Egyptian but often domestic and of a more recent vintage—ground fine and sold as medicine).

At the height of labor, one of the attendants surely held Rolfe's hand as others encouraged her to push. The midwife was advised "to give her women good encouragement, desiring them to hold in their breath by stopping their mouths, and to strain downward." When the child finally arrived she was found to be a girl. The cord was cut—close, rather than long for a boy, according to tradition—and a cloth compress was tied around the infant's stomach to protect the cord stump while it was still attached. Rather than the traditional scenting of the compress with oil of roses, Rolfe's attendants may have initiated a tradition that would persist on Bermuda, the use of a potpourri compress of cedar sawdust on the navel of the newborn. "The child being thus anointed, shifted, and well dried and wrapped up, there must be given to it some small quality of wine mixed with sugar," the contemporary childbirth manual says. On Bermuda a spoonful of palmetto bibby may have been the first thing the baby tasted.

The infant girl was baptized soon after birth. Mistress Horton served as a witness at the ceremony. "The eleventh of February we had the child of one John Rolfe christened, a daughter," William Strachey said, "to which Captain Newport and myself were witnesses, and the aforesaid Mistress Horton, and we named it Bermuda." Bermuda Rolfe's legal status as an Englishwoman was arguably in question. The Virginia Company charter stated that any child born in the colony would be treated for "all intents and purposes as if they had been abiding and born within this our kingdom of England." The charter said nothing, however, regarding children born in other foreign places.

Englishwoman or Bermudian, on the warmest February days Bermuda Rolfe was brought outside in a bundle and laid on a dappled spray of palmetto leaves to take in the breezes of the island. After all, as a later anonymous colonist said, the air of her namesake island was clean and

sweet and good for all ages. "Young children do thrive and grow up exceeding well," the colonist wrote, "the climate is so temperate and agree-
able to our English constitutions."

The bounty of Bermuda continued to feed the *Sea Venture* castaways
through the winter. Early in 1610 the cahows the castaways had hunted
since October now began to nest, and the collectors who went to the Bird
Islands returned with a new delicacy for the cooks. Cahow eggs had
white shells and were nearly indistinguishable from hens' eggs, Strachey
said. Scrambled or fried over the fire, they were a welcome reminder of
home.

Green turtles that had been taken occasionally in the summertime
returned in greater numbers in the winter and they too laid eggs. The
Sea Venture, in fact, had come to rest in one of the most active sea-turtle
nurseries of the Atlantic. Hundreds of the huge animals came ashore in
February, each of which provided a meal for as many as seventy people.
The timing of the arrival of the turtles was fortuitous, because the palmetto berries had gone out of season and the hogs that subsisted on them
were growing thin.

The sea turtles were hunted nocturnally as well, according to a later
colonist named Richard Norwood: "We take them for the most part at
night, making a great light in a boat to which they will sometimes swim
and seldom shun, so that a man standing ready with a staff in his hand
which hath at one end a socket wherein is an iron less than a man's finger
four-square and sharp with a line fastened to it, he striking this iron into
the upper shell of the turtle it sticks so fast that after she hath a little tired
herself by swimming to and fro, she is taken by it."

The average sea turtle weighed three hundred pounds. After they
were towed to shore four men were needed to drag each one onto the
sand, where they were flipped over and left alive until eaten. In a macabre addendum, Norwood described the death throes of the sea giants:
"They will live, the head being cut off, four and twenty hours, so that if

you cut the flesh with a knife or touch it, it will tremble and shrink away. There is no meat will keep longer, either fresh or salt." Sea turtles also yielded oil, which provided a medium for cooking, but the prize was the meat in the shell. "The flesh that cleaveth to the inside of this, being roasted against the fire, is excellent meat, almost like the marrow of beef, but the shell itself harder than horn. She hath also a shell on her belly, not so hard, but being boiled it becomes soft like the sinews or gristle of beef."

In February and March cool weather continued, Strachey wrote: "The mornings are there (as in May in England) fresh and sharp." New kinds of animals were found with regularity. The birds were the most remarkable. "Fowl there is great store: small birds, sparrows fat and plump like a bunting, bigger than ours; robins of diverse colors, green and yellow, ordinary and familiar in our cabins, and other of less sort. White and gray herons, bitterns, teal, snipe, crows, and hawks, of which in March we found diverse aeries, goshawks and tiercels, oxen-birds, cormorants, bald-coots, moorhens, owls, and bats in great store." Once in March Gates and another gunner shot two swans over an island pond.

The castaways had been on Bermuda for eight months. Despite the turmoil of the mutinies, they had managed to create an island community that by wilderness standards was remarkably prosperous. Castaway society was a version of English culture with its hard work and class conflict. The unusual elements of island existence, though, were almost all good—swan spit roasted over a fire, bibby shared around a camp table, birds on the nest at Christmastime, and an existence remarkably free of disease. They had found a wonderful place, and many still did not want to leave.

CHAPTER NINE

Rebellion

I do begin to have bloody thoughts.

—Stephano, *The Tempest*

A midst the plentiful flocks the old discontents continued to roil the most recalcitrant castaways. In late winter once again nervous plotters betrayed a rebellious plot to the governor. The mutineers planned an armed attack on the storehouse that held the company's food and equipment, according to Strachey. Even as unnamed informants approached Gates in the main camp, mutineers among the governor's company fled to Somers's construction site and warned cohorts among the mariners. Together they took to the woods, leaving only a few workers with the admiral at the camp on the main island. With accused mutineers at large, Gates ordered the storehouse protected by armed guards and told everyone in the camp to wear weapons. In the days following the revelation of the latest scheme, suspicion pervaded the camp, each person wondering whether mutineers remained among them.

Strachey was among the most wary, alleging the latest plot was "deadly and bloody" and that "the life of our governor with many others were threatened." In a revealing statement, Strachey said the conspirators believed Gates did not have the will to "pass the act of justice upon anyone." The tension broke on March 13. The man charged with treason that day was said to have been stealing tools for the mutineers, but the allegation was likely exaggerated to justify Gates's severe treatment of a quarrelsome man whose temper emerged at the worst possible time. Gentleman voyager Henry Paine refused to stand his assigned night watch, Strachey said, telling the commander there was no need to guard the storehouse from an attack that would never come. Paine addressed the officer with "evil language," and when the commander threatened to report the incident to Gates, "Paine replied with a settled and bitter violence and in such irreverent terms as I should offend the modest ear too much to express it in his own phrase, but the contents were how that the governor had no authority of that quality to justify upon anyone (how mean soever in the colony) an action of that nature, and therefore let the governor (said he) kiss, etc."

The commander made a report to Gates the next morning, complete "with the omitted additions" of words Strachey was too gentile to record. Either Gates's patience finally ran out or he saw that he no longer had any choice if he was to maintain order. Paine was sentenced to die, and this time there would be no reprieve. "Our governor who had now the eyes of the whole colony fixed upon him," Strachey wrote, "condemned him to be instantly hanged, and the ladder being ready after he had made many confessions he earnestly desired being a gentleman that he might be shot to death, and towards the evening he had his desire, the sun and his life setting together."

A resigned and manacled Henry Paine was led into the woods and placed against a tree. Soldiers stood a few paces from and in the twilight shot the condemned man. When death was confirmed, Paine's body was carried to a freshly dug grave next to that of the murdered Edward Samuel. Paine's execution had an immediate effect on the company's perception of their leader. When pushed to the extreme, Gates had finally acted. Mutinous voyagers who had become brazen in their talk now feared that Paine's execution was the first of many. The response was a new wave of desertions. By Sunday morning, March 18, another band had fled to Somers's camp. The latest contingent was composed of conspirators with marginal connections to the plot who feared that their foreknowledge would be discovered and prosecuted. Upon their arrival at Somers's camp they and the remainder of Somers's work crew fled to the woods together, leaving the admiral alone as the only man ostensibly loyal to Gates. Somers's role was a complicated one. The admiral was torn between the mutineers' plan to colonize Bermuda and the sense of honor that bound him to Gates and the Virginia enterprise. True he was now on his own, but he was also in regular contact both with the mutineers in the woods and the governor in the main camp. When the mutineers wanted to send a petition to Gates they brought it to Somers for relaying to the governor. The petition prompted negotiations in the form of letters between the camps over the coming days.

"Whether mere rage and greediness after some little pearl (as it was thought) wherewith they conceived they should forever enrich themselves and saw how to obtain the same easily in this place," Strachey said, "or whether the desire forever to inhabit here, or what other secret else moved them thereunto, true it is, they sent an audacious and formal petition to our governor." In the appeal the men laid out their arguments as to why they should be allowed to remain on Bermuda. They asked only what was fairly theirs, they said, namely that they be provided two sets of clothing each from the warehouse and a year's worth of food.

While the rebels' petition may have struck Strachey as improper, to George Somers the arguments they put forth were not entirely unreasonable. As Hopkins had argued earlier, the mutineers said the failure of the Virginia Company to provide safe transport to Jamestown had released them from any obligation to the organization. Through their own extraordinary efforts during the hurricane, the petitioners said, they had by the grace of God been presented a new opportunity. Surely the people who suffered the failure could not be faulted for embracing the opportunity. Therefore, they said, Gates should provide them the allocations of food and clothing assigned to them for the Jamestown enterprise, allow them to stay and become Bermuda's founding settlers, and ensure that the Virginia Company supported the venture by sending fresh supplies to the island.

Gates did not attempt to refute the arguments of the rebels, but maintained his position that everyone on Bermuda was bound by honor and duty to get to Jamestown. No one on the expedition could presume to rewrite the instructions of the Virginia Company without consulting the members, he argued, and in the absence of new instructions they had no choice but to go on to their intended destination if they were able to do so. Jamestown was the place that company leaders, in their wisdom, had decided to focus their resources. Certainly Gates would report to London about the advantages of Bermuda and the company might well choose to establish a colony there. That was a decision for the Virginia Company to make from a settled perspective, Gates said, and not something for their charges to decide in the wilds of an unintended land. On this point the governor would not waver. His company would go to Virginia.

In his response to Somers and by extension the mutineers, Gates addressed what he assumed was a lingering resentment about who would have been left behind on the island. First, Gates said, he would have left the forsaken part of the company enough supplies to sustain them for a year. Then he would have done everything in his power to send relief to Bermuda as soon as possible, either by appealing to the Virginia Company or by drawing upon his personal resources or those of his friends. Gates then spoke directly to the admiral. If the mutineers were allowed to pursue their plan, he wrote, it would be the ruin of both their reputations. Referring to himself and Somers in the third person, Gates said the Virginia Company would place the blame on the governor and the admiral of the expedition, "so weak and unworthy in their command," rather than on the unruly colonists.

When he reported on the exchange, Strachey maintained the fiction that Somers had no ties to the mutineers, but at the same time made it clear that the friendship between the two leaders was in jeopardy. Gates, Strachey said, appealed to Somers on the basis "of that ancient love and friendship which had these many years been settled between them." In his usual forgiving style, Gates said anyone who disavowed the mutiny would be granted immunity and all who did not would be treated as criminals. When Somers relayed Gates's response to the rebel camp, the mutineers faced the choice of either remaining on the island as outlaws or returning to the fold with their criminal liability erased. Apparently at the urging of Somers, all but two chose the offer of amnesty.

"Sir George Somers did so nobly work and heartily labor," Strachey reported, "as he brought most of them in, and indeed all but Christopher Carter and Robert Waters who (by no means) would any more come amongst Sir George's men, hearing that Sir George had commanded his men indeed (since they would not be entreated by fair means) to surprise them (if they could) by any device or force." Waters was the same man who months before had killed a fellow sailor, and so he was now both a murderer and an inveterate mutineer. If any in the company managed to catch him and bring him into the main camp, he certainly would not survive another trial before Gates. Likewise, Christopher Carter had been a member of the first band of mutineers who had been briefly banished to the small island in September. Both their lives would now depend upon avoiding capture, a consequence that drove them into the remotest woods of Bermuda. From their enclave over the coming weeks they would watch the waters around the island for sight of the departure of the newly built vessels.

For all but the two men hiding in the woods, the execution of Henry Paine and the resolution of the mutiny marked an end to thoughts of remaining on Bermuda. Dreams of a life in an ideal island commonwealth rather than an imperfect Jamestown ended when the mutineers returned to their camp tasks. The man who underwent perhaps the greatest transformation in the turmoil was George Somers. While Somers had always voiced a united front with Gates, the circumstances suggest that he gave his mariners and the other mutineers subtle hints that they were justified in proceeding. The execution of Paine and Gates's decision to stake their friendship and reputations on bringing the whole company to Jamestown apparently convinced him to shift his stance. His thinking remained the same, but no longer would he hint that rebellion was warranted.

The tumultuous events of the execution and final mutiny coincided with the appearance of towering black clouds over Bermuda. A halo around the moon "of a mighty compass and breadth" foretold a violent thunderstorm on March 23. Strachey sat in a palmetto-leaf hut and watched "the mightiest blast of lightning and most terrible rap of thunder that ever astonished mortal men." At times Bermuda lived up to its reputation as an isle of roaring fire, or, as one English chronicler later put it, "a place heretofore—when the devil had a larger power in those territories—so extremely subject to furious rains, lightning, and thunder that it was called the Island of Devils." The storm passed out to sea and left a rain-washed Bermuda to the castaways. Mutiny, too, was gone. All efforts now would be toward leaving the island for Virginia.

The rhythm of the seasons continued as life went on in the camps. A second child was born just as Gates negotiated the end of the mutiny. The baby boy began life just before the Annunciation Day thunderstorm and received the rites of the church just after it. "The five and twentieth of March," Strachey said, "the wife of one Edward Eason, being delivered the week before of a boy had him then christened, to which Captain Newport and myself and Master James Swift were godfathers, and we named it Bermudas."

The godfathers' choice of name was a tribute to the first child born on the island who had lived only a few weeks. Bermuda Rolfe had not survived an infancy marooned on a mid-Atlantic isle. The squalling cries of another child were both a comfort and a burden to the grieving parents. Strachey was a godfather to both children and joined in comforting John Rolfe while the women of the camp ministered to his wife in the seclusion of a palmetto hut. The birth of the second child required the attention of the women, but Goody Rolfe was not left alone. Reverend Richard Buck offered what consolation he could. The child was laid to rest in a small grave in the growing island cemetery.

One among the company who was eager to put to sea for Virginia as soon as possible was William Pierce. For eight months he had not known whether his wife and daughter had survived the hurricane on the *Blessing*. Given the ordeal on the *Sea Venture*, he suspected they were long dead, but he simply did not know. If they did make it through, they would have given up hope that he was still alive. He longed to go to Virginia to learn the truth, and, if his wife and daughter had made it, to resume life with them.

In preparation for departure the castaways laid away food for the crossing. This meant that gathering efforts were increased beyond subsistence hunting and fishing. Everyone not working on the construction of the ships was put to the task. Five hundred fish were salted and packed in barrels. Among the seafood that would be taken were salted grouper and snapper and live conch in their shells immersed in seawater. The castaways also butchered and salted hogs and plucked cahows for salting. Nearer the launch date the voyagers would catch turtles to be carried live on their backs on the decks.

April and early May brought yet another source of food. Huge flocks of "egg birds," probably common terns, arrived on Bermuda to nest. The fowl were as tame as the cahows and even more fruitful producers of eggs. On the Bird Islands they nested in immense numbers, Silvester Jourdain said, and the eggs were easily collected. A thousand eggs could be taken in a morning, he said, and another thousand from the same place later in the afternoon. "They come and lay them daily, although men sit down amongst them." The egg birds were also good roasted, about the size of a pigeon and "very fat and sweet."

Jourdain and Strachey were among the crews who took the boats to the Bird Islands to collect egg birds and cahows. Sometimes as the hunters rowed, migrating humpback whales were visible off the coast. Strachey alleged that he saw whales hunted by teams of swordfish and thresher sharks—a common maritime myth of the day. More probably, if he really observed an offshore attack, he witnessed killer whales attacking humpbacks and expanded on what he saw using a description in one of the books he carried, Gonzalo Fernández de Oviedo's *History of the West Indies.*

During the trips to the Bird Islands other avian beauties could be observed. One was the graceful tropic bird, which performed acrobatic courtship displays and hunted flying fish and squid by diving on them from as high as fifty feet. When dusk fell the distinctive call of another could be heard. The castaways named the bird the pimlico (now known as the Audubon's shearwater). Londoners among the voyagers developed a special fondness for the bird because it sounded as if it were calling the name of a crossroads three miles north of the city that was renowned for the nut-brown ale served in its pubs. Hearing the name of a favorite haunt near home was a reminder that palmetto bibby was a barely adequate substitute for English ale. Many realized, too, that they were becoming eager to leave Bermuda.

Construction of the two vessels that would carry the voyagers to sea proceeded during the spring. The hull of the vessel under construction in Building Bay was now fully built, and carpenters were caulking the seams between each board. Rope from the wreck was shredded and the fibers were pounded between the boards and covered with sealant. A single barrel of pitch and another of tar that had been rescued from the *Sea Venture* were mixed and used to make the seams watertight. An improvised recipe of water, crushed limestone, ground shells, and tortoise oil augmented the traditional material. The carpenters recalled the loss of oakum in the distressed *Sea Venture* and paid special attention to the caulking process in the construction of the successor vessel.

Sealing was complete by the end of March, though much work remained to be done before the vessel was ready to go to sea. The pinnace would be floated and moved to a sheltered bay before masts, rigging, sails, and guns were installed and limestone ballast put in the hold. While the vessel was still light enough to be moved it was launched from Building Bay. A high spring tide at the end of March was chosen for the event. George Somers and his carpenters came from the building site on the main island to assist. Everyone from the main camp walked down what had become a well-worn path to Building Bay to see the pinnace put to sea. All who watched would soon stake their lives on the seaworthiness of the new vessels, so seeing the first of them ride in the water was of great interest to all.

In the cool air of a March morning the vessel was freed from the stocks by teams of men pushing from shore and pulling on ropes while wading in the shallows of the bay. Still others pulled from boats connected to the craft. With each call by master carpenter Richard Frobisher the vessel inched closer to the surf. Once the hull was partially supported by water, less effort was required. Presently the pinnace slid from the bottom of the shallows and floated free. The observers—especially the mariners among them—were pleased to see it prove stable and apparently seaworthy. Following tradition the vessel was named at its launch. "When she began to swim (upon her launching)," Strachey said, "our governor called her the *Deliverance*." Gates chose a name that had been on his mind from the first days after the wreck and through the turmoil of the mutinies: *Deliverance*—deliverance from rebellion, deliverance from oblivion, deliverance from the Devil's Isle. Applause rippled through the crowd after Gates made his announcement.

"The thirtieth of March being Friday we towed her out in the morning spring tide from the wharf where she was built, buoying her with four casks in her run only, which opened into the northwest," Strachey said. "We launched her unrigged to carry her to a little round island lying west-northwest and close aboard to the backside of our island, both nearer the ponds and wells of some freshwater as also from thence to make our way to the sea the better, the channel being there sufficient and deep enough to lead her forth when her masts, sails, and all her trim should be about her."

The *Deliverance* would remain anchored until the second vessel was ready to depart in convoy to Virginia. With a keel of forty feet and a beam of nineteen the *Deliverance* was a little under half the length of the *Sea Venture*. The new vessel was between seventy and eighty tons burden, which meant it could accommodate just over a quarter of the cargo of the larger vessel. The passenger space tween-decks was only four and a half feet high, though it rose to five at the forecastle. The great cabin at the stern had a relatively commodious six-foot ceiling and was appointed with two windows and a tiny gallery balcony aft. "The most part of her timber was cedar," Strachey said. "Her beams were all oak of our ruined ship and some planks in her bow of oak."

Work on the second vessel continued in the coming weeks. The casks of pitch and tar had been spent on sealing *Deliverance,* so Somers's crew had to improvise even more creatively to caulk their pinnace. The castaways' luck held still longer when a beachcomber found a large chunk of wax washed up on the sand. Jourdain guessed that the wax had been bound for manufacture when a ship carrying it wrecked, perhaps near Bermuda but maybe somewhere much farther away. In any case, it was heaven sent, for without it the sealing of the second ship with the homemade limestone mix alone would have been questionable at best. "God in the supplying of all our wants beyond all measure showed himself still merciful unto us," Jourdain said.

At the end of April the second pinnace was pulled from its stocks and floated unrigged. Fewer were on hand at the main-island site to see the second vessel put to sea. Once again a name was chosen that encapsulated the Bermuda experience of the man doing the christening. Somers named the new vessel *Patience,* alluding to the personal resource he had drawn upon most in his days on the *Sea Venture* poop deck and during his mediation between the governor and the mutineers. The *Patience* was towed to the sheltered spot where the *Deliverance* was now almost rigged with sails scavenged from the *Sea Venture.* The second pinnace would be outfitted in the coming days and both would be filled with stores for the weeklong sail together to Jamestown. The *Patience* was even smaller than the *Discovery,* with a keel of twenty-nine feet and a beam of just over fifteen. The entire vessel was made of native wood and, save a single bolt, held together with wooden pegs. Somers had done much of the construction with his own hands.

The castaways, through their hard work over many months, now had before them new vessels to carry them across the Atlantic. Over the next three weeks while the *Patience* was fitted with sails and guns, the castaways packed the camp and transported loads of food and stores to the pinnaces. They would soon leave their sanctuary of nine months. Many had never left England before boarding the *Sea Venture.* Now they were veterans of sea travel—stormy travel at that—and had many months of wilderness life to their credit. Greater challenges lay ahead. At James-town they would be in another wilderness, but in this one they would be under constant challenge from a well-adapted native people. To Ma-chumps, the one Powhatan who would climb aboard one of the two tiny vessels, the trepidation he felt about going to sea again was tempered by the knowledge that after a short time more on the water he would be home.

William Strachey would carry his journal of the storm aboard the *Sea Venture*. At his first opportunity he planned to use it to write a long letter to his prospective patron, the "Excellent Lady"—probably the Countess of Bedford, John Donne's generous patron whom he hoped to make his own sponsor. Strachey's writing abilities had not gone unno-ticed on Bermuda. He was now well known to Thomas Gates, having made a special effort to serve the governor. He would ride to Jamestown on the *Deliverance* with Gates and continue his Virginia project.

In mid-May Gates ordered a memorial set up near the camp to re-cord the presence of the castaways and leave evidence of an English claim to the island. A cedar was selected near the place George Somers had planted his garden. The top of the tree was lopped off to make it less vulnerable to toppling in the wind. A wooden cross was pegged to the tree. At the center a twelve-penny coin with a portrait of King James was attached, and near that a copper plate with an engraved message in Latin and English:

> In memory of our great deliverance, both from a mighty storm and leak, we have set up this to the honor of God. It is the spoil of an English ship (of three hundred ton) called the *Sea Venture*, bound with seven ships more (from which the storm divided us) to Virginia, or Nova Britannia, in America. In it were two knights, Sir Thomas Gates, knight, governor of the English forces and col-ony there, and Sir George Somers, knight, admiral of the seas. Her captain was Christopher Newport. Passengers and mariners she

had besides (which came all safe to land) one hundred and fifty. We were forced to run her ashore (by reason of her leak) under a point that bore southeast from the northern point of the island, which we discovered first the eight and twentieth of July 1609.

Another voyager would leave a personal message behind. Shipwright Richard Frobisher carved a message deep into the trunk of a palmetto tree. The words were in Latin, translating to, "There was built in this place a ship of seventy tons burden by Richard Frobisher, which is destined for Virginia, in order that we all might be transported from this place. In the year 1610, May 4th."

"From this time," Strachey said, "we only awaited a favorable westerly wind to carry us forth." In the second week of May the winds turned and the castaways prepared to depart their refuge. At first light on May 10, Somers and some of his men went out in the rowboats and canoes to lay buoys in the narrow channel that led from the little round island to open water. Everyone climbed aboard the two pinnaces, and the sailors went to work. "About ten of the clock, that day being Thursday," Strachey said, "we set sail."

CHAPTER TEN

Away to Virginia

O brave new world.

—Miranda, *The Tempest*

Bringing the pinnaces through Somers Creek to open ocean was a slow process. Men in small craft called out directions to Christopher Newport on the *Deliverance* and George Somers on the *Patience*. To the horror of everyone, the *Deliverance* struck bottom once with an appalling *thump*. The vessel backed off the obstruction easily, however, and upon inspection the coxswain in the skiff reported no visible damage and said that the obstacle was a reef that gave way on impact. "Had it not been a soft rock, by which means she bore it before her and crushed it to pieces," Strachey said, "God knows we might have been like enough to have returned anew and dwelt there, after ten months of carefulness and great labor, a longer time, but God was more merciful unto us."

The slow wending through the reefs lasted through the night and into May 11, at which point the vessels made deep water at last. Having left Bermuda in a southeasterly direction, the pinnaces would now round the island to the south and head to Virginia. Left behind was a cemetery of graves. "We buried five of our company, Jeffery Briars, Richard Lewis, William Hitchman, and my goddaughter Bermuda Rolfe, and one untimely Edward Samuel," Strachey said. Two others who were lost were not included in his list. Henry Paine who had been executed for treason was apparently no longer considered one of "our company." Strachey also left unexplained the disappearance of Namontack. The Powhatan man was simply gone, and his companion Machumps was leaving Bermuda under suspicion but unprosecuted. Two living men were left behind as well. Robert Waters and his confederate Christopher Carter watched the vessels slowly depart through the reefs. Strachey saw an ironic justice in Waters's staying behind, as if he had been left to tend the grave of the man he had killed—"the body of the murdered and murderer so dwelling, as prescribed now, together."

Once out of the shallows the crossing from Bermuda to Virginia was an unexpectedly easy one. The swifter *Deliverance* carrying Gates and Strachey had to trim sail to allow the *Patience* to keep pace. Twice Newport lost sight of Somers and then found him again. On May 17, only a week after leaving Bermuda, the sailors began to see floating leaves and knew that land was close. The vessels were making a respectable sixty-three nautical miles a day. The deep-sea (or dipsey) line measured thirty-seven fathoms on May 18, then nineteen the next day. Strachey reported that two days later the scent of a verdant jungle reached the pinnaces. "The twentieth about midnight we had a marvelous sweet smell from the shore (as from the coast of Spain short of the straits), strong and pleasant, which did not a little glad us." Perhaps, too, on the midnight approach the foam at the bow of the vessels reflected the glow of the moon. "A well-bowed ship so swiftly presses the water," John Smith said of such midnight runs, "as that it foams and in the dark night sparkles like fire."

"In the morning by daybreak (so soon as one might well see from the foretop) one of the sailors cried land," Strachey said. The well-navigated pinnaces reached the coast as intended at the mouth of Chesapeake Bay. Arriving at low tide, the vessels could not fight the current of the rivers flowing out of the bay and so anchored on the morning of May 21 to await the reversal of tide. "About seven of the clock we cast forth an anchor because the tide (by reason of the freshet that set into the bay) made a strong ebb there and the wind was but easy so as not able to stem the tide we proposed to lie at an anchor until the next flood, but the wind coming southwest a loom gale about eleven we set sail again and having got over the bar bore in for the cape."

As the *Deliverance* and *Patience* came up to Jamestown's coastal Algernon Fort at Point Comfort, a peninsula thirty-five miles downstream from the colony, the expedition had its first contact with other humans in almost a year. "The one and twentieth being Monday in the morning," Strachey said, "we came up within two miles of Point Comfort, when the captain of the fort discharged a warning piece at us, whereupon we came to an anchor and sent off our longboat [or rather skiff] to the fort to certify who we were." As the skiff pulled away from the pinnaces, the passengers and mariners at the rails prepared themselves for reentry into a version of the world they had left behind almost a year earlier on the Plymouth quay. The *Sea Venture* survivors were about to resume their lives in English society—a wilderness form of that world, to be sure, but one that was in contact with the home country. Bermuda was past and some version of a more familiar life lay before them.

Riding before the aromatic Virginia shore, the men and women on the pinnaces had their first look at America. A front of black clouds moved across the bay. Unlike the hurricane that wrecked the *Sea Venture*, this squall could be watched from a sheltered spot on deck in perfect safety. The thunderstorm was a reminder that hazards awaited them in Jamestown. There was time to think about their future in Virginia as rain lashed the vessels. "Being Monday about noon," Strachey said, "where riding before an Indian town called Kecoughtan, a mighty storm of thunder, lightning, and rain gave us a shrewd and fearful welcome."

The *Sea Venture* castaways had no knowledge that a fort stood at Point Comfort. The advance party from the Bermuda pinnaces approached cautiously to be sure the colony had not fallen to an enemy. George Percy, the acting governor of the English settlement, happened to be at the garrison at the time. The unrecognized sails had been spotted the evening before as they came up the bay. Just as Gates was wary that he might be approaching a colony held by a hostile force, Percy, too, worried that an enemy might be preparing an assault. Jamestown had no reason to expect a visit from two small sailing vessels of unknown origin.

"We espied two pinnaces coming into the bay," Percy said, "not knowing as yet what they were, but keeping a court of guard and watch all that night. The next morning we espied a boat coming off from one of the pinnaces, so standing upon our guard we hailed them, and understood that Sir Thomas Gates and Sir George Somers were come in these pinnaces which by their great industry they had builded in the Bermudas with the remainder of their wrecked ship and other wood they found in the country. Upon which news we received no small joy, requesting them in the boat to come ashore, the which they refused and returned abroad again for Sir Thomas Gates."

As the skiff rowed away the men of the fort absorbed the astounding news of the redemption of the *Sea Venture* voyagers. The colonists of Jamestown had long ago concluded that the flagship had broken up or capsized in the hurricane the previous July and that the hundred and fifty-three people aboard were lost. Now, nearly a year later, they reappeared as if by magic. What's more, among the returning lost souls was the governor of Virginia. This not only produced amazement in the colonists of the fort; it also prompted the soldiers to glance at Percy and wonder who would now be in charge of Jamestown. Those coming from Bermuda had dramatic intelligence to take in, as well. The first bit of welcome news was that all but one of the vessels of their original fleet survived the hurricane. Only the ketch the *Sea Venture* towed at its stern had not made it through the storm. The news of the survival of the rest of the fleet reached the *Deliverance* and the *Patience* with the oarsmen of the returning advance boat, and Gates and his entourage were rowed to the fort in a buoyant mood—a fine humor that would be short-lived.

"The good news of our ships' and men's arrival the last year did not a little gladden our governor who went soon ashore and as soon (contrary to all our fair hopes) had new unexpected, uncomfortable, and heavy news of a worse condition of our people above at Jamestown," Strachey said. After Gates waded up the bank and entered the fort, Percy told him that Powhatans had besieged the settlement the previous October and famine had killed many during a winter that became known as the Starving Time. Algernon Fort had sufficient food, but Jamestown up the river was in desperate shape. Gates ordered his pinnaces to the settlement to feed the starving colonists with their Bermuda pork, birds, and turtles, though a lack of breeze made it a slow journey. "From hence in two days (only by the help of tides, no wind stirring) we plied it sadly up the river," Strachey said, "and the three-and-twentieth of May we cast anchor before Jamestown."

The colony was located on a peninsula connected to the mainland by a narrow neck, a strip of land so thin that the Jamestown site was often referred to as an island. The water of the James River scoured the bank as it curved past the peninsula, providing the settlers a natural anchorage close to shore. The deep water along the point was a key reason the site was selected. Marshy shallows separated the peninsula from the mainland, a downside that was viewed as offset by the advantages of the accessible yet easily defended location.

The triangular Jamestown fort was a hundred and forty yards on the river side and a hundred yards on each of the other two. A palisade fence with posts sunk four feet in the ground surrounded houses, a storehouse, a guard station, and a chapel. A lane ran along each perimeter, forming a village square in the center. Guns were mounted on platforms at the three corners to guard the settlement. A main gate opened to the river, and smaller doors provided access at each corner.

Only about ninety of two hundred forty five settlers had survived the winter of starvation—sixty at Jamestown and thirty at the fort. As many as twenty women were among those who began the ordeal at the fort, and some of them were among the survivors. Gates and the Bermuda castaways were at a loss to understand why Jamestown was in such distress. The colonial experiment was expected to be difficult—even the charter of the Virginia Company talked of "great pain and peril" in the New World. Desperate famine, however, was not anticipated.

Laziness was the cause of the troubles, Strachey believed, and he listed the sins of the settlers as "sloth, riot, and vanity." The delay in the arrival of Gates was the other source of difficulty, he wrote, because it deprived the dissolute colonists of their leader. If the governor had made it to Virginia as planned he would have used the powers granted to him by the second charter to rein in the "factionaries" and stifle "their ignoble and irreligious practices." The written orders mandating the new form of government went with Gates to Bermuda, however, and the remainder of the fleet that landed at Jamestown continued to be governed by a ruling council. Steered only by a squabbling assembly, Strachey said, the colony fell to ruin. "No story can remember unto us more woes and anguishes than these people, thus governed, have both suffered and pulled upon their own heads."

The Virginia Company would adopt Strachey's analysis of the sufferings of Jamestown when it learned of the survival of the *Sea Venture* voyagers. In a later publication the company would use a telling metaphor to describe the situation, calling the infighting of the colonial council a "tempest of dissension" that was as damaging as the hurricane that scattered the fleet. While the Virginia Company was blaming the settlers of Jamestown, the colonists were just as adamantly condemning the Virginia Company. To many who lived through the ordeal, the root of the problem was stinginess among the officers of the Virginia Company, especially treasurer Thomas Smith who they contended had not released sufficient money for supplies. The starving colonists were known to berate Smith in absentia as they consumed their meager fare. "The happiest day that ever some of them hoped to see was when the Indians had killed a mare," one account of the Starving Time said, "they wishing while she was boiling that Sir Thomas Smith was upon her back in the kettle."

While laziness and a lack of funding were perhaps factors in the distress of Jamestown, much of the blame must be laid to an insidious force that was working against the success of the colony. In 1607, the very year the first settlers arrived, Virginia began its driest seven-year span in seven hundred and seventy years. The stresses of the drought would induce a period of intense warfare between the settlers and the Powhatans. English observers were not immediately aware of the drought, since the Virginia forest appeared relatively green and full to foreigners unfamiliar with normal levels of moisture. The lack of rain nevertheless had a devastating effect on the food and water resources of people of both nations living in the area. Thus did an invading population that could not grow food as expected meet a resident population whose crops were failing them. The clash of cultures might have been less bloody had it come at a time of plenty. Coming at the time it did, it was exacerbated by a major environmental crisis.

Drought did more than just reduce the amount of crops produced. The Jamestown well drawing water a short distance from the river had a higher than normal salt content during the period of lower runoff from the surrounding hills. To make matters worse, settlers trying to make up for a lack of rain showered their crops with brackish water from the river and further diminished yields. An increase in salinity also reduced fish populations where the waters of the Chesapeake Bay met those of the James River. Strachey reported that the river had provided a great store of fish in the past, but in the spring of 1610 it "had not now a fish to be seen in it, and albeit we labored and held our net twenty times a day and night yet we took not so much as would content half the fishermen."

The English sensed that poor water quality at Jamestown was a problem. "True it is," Strachey said, "I may not excuse this our fort, or Jamestown, as yet seated in somewhat an unwholesome and sickly air, by reason it is in a marish ground, low, flat to the river, and hath no freshwater springs serving the town but what we drew from a well six or seven fathoms deep fed by the brackish river oozing into it, from whence I verily believe the chief causes have proceeded of many diseases and sicknesses which have happened to our people, who are indeed strangely afflicted with fluxes and agues."

In the dry conditions the colonists were at greater risk of disease than they would be in a time of normal rainfall. Lower river levels increased the extent of the marsh zone behind the peninsula and provided disease-carrying mosquitoes a larger breeding area. Settlers stressed by salt poisoning and malnutrition were at increased risk of dysentery, malaria, and typhoid. Malnutrition itself brought on vitamin-deficiency diseases such as scurvy, beriberi, and pellagra. Depression was another danger—what Strachey called laziness might have had a physical basis. A lack of motivation is a symptom of both salt poisoning and malnutri-tion. What's more, since the English were unable to produce sufficient food for themselves, their main sustenance was the unfamiliar food of the Powhatans, a diet likely to upset their constitutions and their moods. Beyond that, depression similar to the sense of hopelessness documented in modern prisoners of war afflicted the besieged settlers in the winter of 1609 to 1610. All of those factors contributed to the celebrated lassitude of the Virginia colonists.

When William Strachey and the other castaways came ashore at James-town on May 23, 1610, they had their first look at the settlement they had been told was a miniature England in the Virginia woodland. What they found instead was a band of skeletal people who had faced starvation while the castaways lived in ease and plenty on the Devil's Isle. When the people of Jamestown told their story to the survivors of the *Sea Venture* wreck, they related a horrible tale indeed. Things had been difficult since the six surviving craft of the hurricane-battered Gates fleet had come into Jamestown in the summer of 1609. The vessels had been pounded as much as the *Sea Venture*, and the people who rode in them were in poor condition.

Gabriel Archer on the *Blessing* reported that his ship had drifted in a stunned state before reuniting with the *Lion*, *Falcon*, and *Unity*. Ignoring Gates's order to rendezvous at Barbuda, the ships limped into Jamestown in mid-August. "The *Unity* was sore distressed when she came up with us," Archer said, "for of seventy landsmen she had not ten sound and all her seamen were down but only the master and his boy with one poor sailor, but we relieved them and we four consorting fell into the king's river happily the eleventh of August." The *Diamond* arrived a few days later, Archer said, "having cut her main-mast overboard and had many of her men very sick and weak, but she could tell no news of our governor, and some three or four days after her came in the *Swallow* with her main-mast overboard also and had a shrewd leak, neither did she see our admiral."

A colonist named William Box also rode on one of the vessels: "In the tail of a hurricano we were separated from the admiral, which—although it was but the remainder of that storm—there is seldom any such in England or those northern parts of Europe. Some lost their masts, some their sails blown from their yards; the seas so overraking our ships much of our provision was spoiled, our fleet separated, and our men sick and many died, and in this miserable state we arrived in Virginia."

The tattered vessels of the Gates convoy had brought only broken and ruined containers of food with the exhausted voyagers. The settlers already in Virginia under the governorship of John Smith had watched in dismay as the newcomers who were supposed to relieve them consumed their stores at an unprecedented rate. One resident recalled that when the hundreds of new settlers came ashore there had been "houses few or none to entertain them, so that being quartered in the open field they fell upon the small quantity of corn—not being above seven acres—which we with great penury and sufferance had formerly planted, and in three days at the most wholly devoured it."

Captain Samuel Argall had arrived at Jamestown in a single vessel just ahead of the hurricane. As the damaged vessels of the Gates fleet began to come in, Argall had left for England carrying news of the great storm. The returning captain would report that the *Sea Venture* had not yet appeared in Virginia a month after the hurricane, not knowing that the people who rode on the ship were stranded on a mid-Atlantic island that he may have seen on the horizon as he sailed back to England.

In September 1609 the Jamestown colonists had lost the services of nominal president John Smith, who, despite being a trigger to factionalism, was the most effective agent for extracting food from the Powhatans. Smith had suffered a grievous wound from a gunpowder explosion and left Jamestown for England when five of the vessels that had survived the hurricane returned home. A day before the convoy left, another English vessel had come up the James River and anchored before the colony. The pinnace *Virginia* had been a part of the original Gates fleet a year earlier but had turned around a week after leaving home. Put in shape for an

Atlantic crossing, the vessel had voyaged to Virginia on its own. The vessels carrying Smith back to England left soon after the arrival of the *Virginia*, taking letters home. A letter from colonist John Ratcliffe reported that hope was almost gone for the hundred and fifty-three aboard the *Sea Venture* and the thirty or so on the ketch towed at its stern. "Sir Thomas Gates and Sir George Somers, Captain Newport, and one hundred and eighty persons or there about are not yet arrived," Ratcliffe wrote, "and we much fear they are lost."

Conditions worsened dramatically during the winter. When Jamestown's two remaining vessels were sent to barter with the Powhatans for food, one crew was massacred and the other betrayed the colony and sailed for England. As the winter deepened the colonists were besieged by Powhatans and suffered starvation. "Famine beginning to look ghastly and pale in every face," George Percy said, and the colonists were forced "to do those things which seem incredible"—eat rats and snakes, resort to cannibalism, and dig up the dead for food. Those emaciated survivors of the Starving Time were the people who greeted the men and women on the *Patience* and the *Deliverance* when they arrived to begin life in the New World.

CHAPTER ELEVEN

Relief from Home

Our royal, good and gallant ship.

—The Boatswain, *The Tempest*

A woman and a girl who survived the Starving Time were happy beyond all expectation when the rude vessels from Bermuda unexpectedly tied up to the trees along the Jamestown shore. After enduring the hurricane on the *Blessing*, Joan Pierce and her daughter of the same name had arrived in Jamestown and waited as the other ships of the convoy came up the river. The *Sea Venture*, with Joan's husband, William, aboard had not come, and after several weeks the survivors gave up hope that the people on the flagship were still alive. The bereaved wife and daughter had finally come to think of William as gone as they struggled through the dreadful winter of 1609 to 1610. Then on a sunny day in May, William Pierce—incredibly, wonderfully, astonishingly—came back from the dead. Truly it was a miracle!

Though no document describes the reunion of William and Joan and their daughter, they surely stood close to one another as Reverend Richard Buck preached a service of thanksgiving. The gathering presumably took place after Gates had offered the famished colonists food. "Our much-grieved governor first visiting the church caused the bell to be rung," Strachey said, "at which all such as were able to come forth of their houses repaired to church, where our minister Master Buck made a zealous and sorrowful prayer, finding all things so contrary to our expectations, so full of misery and misgovernment." The Jamestown church was, according to John Smith, "a homely thing like a barn, set upon crotchets, covered with rafters, sedge, and earth." Some stood outside at the windows as Buck condemned the fallen state of Jamestown and called them to a new beginning.

After the service the leadership of the colony was formally transferred from Percy to Gates. Then the new arrivals walked about the town. "Viewing the fort," Strachey said, "we found the palisades torn down, the ports open, the gates from off the hinges, and empty houses (which owners' death had taken from them) rent up and burnt rather than the dwellers would step into the woods a stone's cast off from them to fetch other firewood."

During the coming days the Bermuda survivors ministered to the sick and fed the hungry. "Our governor Sir Thomas Gates did allow them, as we had, with some pork," Somers said, "and recovered all saving three that did die and were past recovery before our coming. We consulted together what course was best to be taken, for our means would not continue above fourteen days." The starving people of Jamestown rapidly depleted the food brought from Bermuda, now the only food reserves for two hundred and fifty settlers. The famished colonists ate with great relish the salted cahows, pork loins, dried fish, and fresh-killed sea turtles brought from the holds and decks of the *Patience* and the *Deliverance*. The vessels carried only enough food for an ocean crossing to what was expected to be a colony stocked with grains and livestock and run by vital settlers, and it would soon be gone.

After the deliberations with other officers of the colony, Gates decided that everyone in the settlement would starve if they did not leave immediately for England. On June 7 he announced that Jamestown would be abandoned and all would go home. "There was a general acclamation and shout of joy on both sides," Strachey said, "for even our own men began to be disheartened and faint when they saw this misery amongst the others and no less threatened unto themselves." Rather than attempt an ocean crossing in four overloaded craft, the vessels would follow the Virginia coast north. English fishermen working the banks off Newfoundland would be able to take some colonists aboard and augment the food supplies of the rest who would return home on the four pinnaces.

The decision to abandon Jamestown was welcome news indeed to those who had made it through the Starving Time. One who was there recalled the effect of the announcement on the emaciated survivors. "Every man glad of this resolution labored his utmost to further it, so that in three weeks we had fitted those barks and pinnaces (the best we could)."

The most important work to be done before leaving was to properly seal the Bermuda boats by smearing their seams with pitch and tar to augment the island-made sealants. "Most of our men were set to work," George Percy said, "some to make pitch and tar for trimming of our ships, others to bake bread, and few or none not employed in one occasion or another. So that in a small space of time four pinnaces were fitted and made ready, all preparing to go abroad." To expose the underwater portions of the vessels for caulking, they were careened, or tipped on their sides while at anchor by adjusting the ballast and tightening block and tackle connected to a vessel alongside.

As preparations for the voyage were made, Gates had Strachey write out twenty-one new colonial laws to nail to a post in the church. The new rules were rooted in English common law but in their severity were closer to the martial discipline of the battlefield. Allegiance to commander, company, colony, country, and God was demanded upon pain of death. Anyone absent from daily prayers was on first offense to lose food for a day, on second to be whipped, and on third to be imprisoned for six months. A person caught blaspheming would "have a bodkin thrust through his tongue." Anyone found to have used "disgraceful words" would be "tied head and feet together upon the guard every night for the space of one month." Severe sanctions were listed for treason, murder, and theft. A law against rape explicitly protected both English and Powhatan victims—"No man shall ravish or force any woman, maid, or Indian, or other, upon pain of death." The colonists viewed the new laws with sober indifference. Since they were about to leave the colony, they would be subject to them for only a short time. If the colony were to continue they would have looked on them with more concern, but as it was, the laws were not likely to affect their lives.

By early June, preparations for departure were complete. The *Virginia* was sent ahead to tell the soldiers at Algernon Fort that the ships would soon leave. Since they needed to get away soon to ensure that the food did not run out, the vessels were loaded immediately and the colonists assembled on June 7. Some wanted to burn the town, but to ensure order Gates kept a careful watch during the final minutes. "He commanded every man at the beating of the drum to repair aboard," Strachey said. "His own company he caused to be last ashore and was himself the last of them when about noon, giving a farewell with a peal of small shot, we set sail." As the vessels rode the river and the trees finally hid the settlement from view, a colonist said, they "quitted Jamestown, leaving the poor buildings in it to the spoil of the Indians, hoping never to return to repossess them."

That day and evening the voyagers sailed with the current to an isle called Hog Island, and the next morning they went further downriver to another called Mulberry Island, where they paused to await a favorable current. The slow sail down the river allowed the *Sea Venture* survivors to reflect on their New World adventure. Remarkably, it had been exactly one year since they left England. On June 8, 1609, the *Sea Venture* set sail from Plymouth, and on June 8, 1610, its survivors were anchored in the James River awaiting an ebb tide to go home again. Both dates would be turning points in the history of Jamestown.

The longboat approaching the pinnaces as they rode before Mulberry Island first appeared as a smudge on the horizon. A lookout sighted the approaching boat with its rowers taking advantage of the flood tide to counter the flow of the James. Thomas Gates knew there was no longboat at Algernon Fort, so he put the vessels on guard. One way or another, the approaching craft signaled the presence of strangers in Chesapeake Bay.

"About an hour it came up," Strachey said of the longboat, "by which, to our no little joy, we had intelligence of the honorable my Lord La Warr, his arrival before Algernon Fort." To Gates the news was not wholly unexpected. Thomas West, Lord Delaware, was the man who had been

ABOVE: Admiral George Somers remained on the open deck of the storm-swept *Sea Venture* "three days and three nights together, without meal's meat and little or no sleep." This portrait depicts a younger Somers and may have been painted after his death.
(Bermuda Historical Society/ Brimstone Media)

LEFT: Thomas Gates was already a "very remarkable soldier" of the Dutch battlefield when he was appointed to lead the Third Supply to Jamestown. Gates's leadership skills were tested by murder and mutiny during an unexpected sojourn on Bermuda.
(Courtesy of The Library of Virginia)

Bartmann bottles made by Germanic artisans in Europe were among the containers used to hold stores on the *Sea Venture*. This bottle and hundreds of other artifacts were brought to the surface after the wreck was rediscovered off Bermuda in 1958.

(Bermuda Maritime Museum / Brimstone Media)

Divers to the *Sea Venture* wreck found a candlestick wedged between two boards of the hull, perhaps placed there by a sailor as he searched for leaks during the desperate hours of the hurricane. Archaeologists discovered the nub of a burned candle in the bowl.

(Bermuda Maritime Museum / Brimstone Media)

The flagship *Sea Venture*, depicted here in a Bermuda Maritime Museum model, was the largest ship in the Gates fleet at 100 feet and 300 tons. The vessel proved to be a leaky but stalwart transport for the 153 souls onboard. *(Bermuda Maritime Museum/Brimstone Media)*

The *Sea Venture* castaways called the Bermuda petrel the "cahow" for its haunting nighttime call. To Shakespeare, perhaps, it was a "seamel" or "scamel," whose vocalizations helped to inspire the eerie sounds of Prospero's island. A few hundred cahows remain alive on isolated islets. *(Andrew Dobson)*

Green sea turtles came ashore to lay eggs on Bermuda in February 1609 and provided the voyagers a new food source when others were becoming scarce. At three hundred pounds each, two turtles provided enough meat to feed the entire party of castaways.

(Caribbean Conservation Corporation, www.cccturtle.org)

During George Somers's time on the Bermuda archipelago he "coasted in his boat about them all" and drew a map. The Somers Map at the Bermuda Archives is thought to be one of two copies that exist, both of which include later artwork and commentary. *(Bermuda Archives 08:1798)*

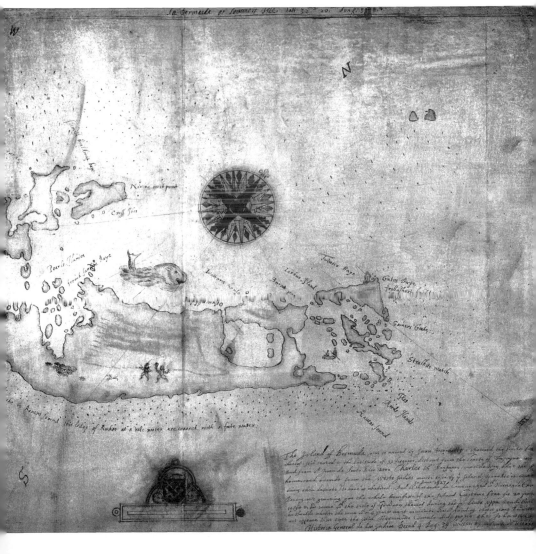

William Strachey sent George Somers's map with a letter to an unnamed "Excellent Lady" in England. A coat of arms later drawn on the map suggests that the lady was Lucy, Countess of Bedford, thought to be the richly attired woman depicted in this portrait.

(National Portrait Gallery, London)

George Percy was the reluctant acting governor of Jamestown when the *Sea Venture* survivors arrived in May 1610. Percy later wrote a narrative to answer critics who saw him as a weak leader, a chronicle that is notable for its frank account of the brutal conditions of Jamestown.

(Virginia Historical Society, Richmond, Virginia)

ABOVE: Thomas West, Lord Delaware, landed in Jamestown weeks after the castaways arrived from Bermuda. Illness eventually drove him from Virginia to the Azores, where he was restored by rest and a diet of island produce, "especially of oranges and lemons."
(Courtesy of The Library of Virginia)

LEFT: Thomas Dale was appointed the colony's military marshal, but upon his arrival the unexpected absence of the ailing Thomas West thrust him into the role of governor. Dale would prove to be a callous leader who used torture and executions to motivate his workers and soldiers.
(Virginia Museum of Fine Arts, Richmond. The Adolph D. and Wilkins C. Williams Fund. Photo: Ron Jennings. © Virginia Museum of Fine Arts)

William Shakespeare probably had this portrait painted by John Taylor about 1610, the year the *Sea Venture* tale was brought back to England. In the autumn of 1611 *The Tempest* appeared on the London stage with unmistakable echoes of the story of shipwreck on a charmed isle.

(National Portrait Gallery, London)

The 1623 First Folio placed *The Tempest* at the front of the book, undoubtedly because it was a recent triumph and one of Shakespeare's most popular works. A legacy of the First Folio was the coining of the word "scamel," apparently a typesetter's misreading of the word "seamel."

(By Permission of the Folger Shakespeare Library)

appointed governor before the *Sea Venture* fleet departed England. During his entire service to the Virginia Company, Gates had technically served as Delaware's deputy, and now the rightful governor was finally arriving. The new fleet was expected to carry a thousand settlers in nine vessels, but news of the loss of the *Sea Venture* had dampened enthusiasm for the venture. Only about a hundred and fifty had signed on, and the convoy numbered only three ships—the *Delaware*, the *Hercules*, and the *Blessing* (the same *Blessing* that had sailed in the Gates fleet and returned to England with John Smith). Still, the small convoy carried ample supplies, and its arrival meant the departing vessels could return to Jamestown without fear of starvation.

To Somers, the timely meeting of the Delaware fleet was good news that "made our hearts very glad." Silvester Jourdain was of the same mind, saying the news "revived all the company and gave them great content." Gladness and contentment, however, were not the emotions of Starving Time veterans who had hailed the news that they would return to England. One colonist said that the announcement from Gates that the vessels would return to Jamestown caused "the great grief of all his company." When they met at Algernon Fort, Delaware told Gates of hearing from the soldiers of the remarkable return of the *Sea Venture* castaways, followed by the terrible news of famine. "It was seasoned with a following discourse, compound of so many miseries and calamities, and those in such horrid changes and diverse forms, as no story I believe ever presented the wrath and curse of the Eternal Offended Majesty in a greater measure."

Delaware and his fellows in turn told the colonists what had transpired in England over the previous year. Samuel Argall had returned in November 1609 with news that the *Sea Venture* had been lost. Later in November more disaster had befallen the Virginia Company. Two of the ships in the convoy carrying the injured John Smith had encountered a storm off France and "were dashed to pieces on the rocks off the coast of Brittany with all hands on board, one man being saved." Spanish ambassador Pedro de Zúñiga reported that the four others had arrived home between November 30 and December 21, 1609: "They tell me that the sailors do not come very happy, because [they] are suffering great hunger there and they bring nothing of any consequence in the ships."

Returning sailors and landsmen alike had spread stories of misery and death. In response the Virginia Company had launched a fresh publicity drive to protect their considerable investment in the enterprise. First an announcement was rushed into print that attacked the character of the returning voyagers and anyone who believed their reports. Those arriving home were "unruly youths" disseminating "vile and scandalous reports" to "color their own misbehavior and the cause of their return with some pretense." Likewise, those who took up and spread the reports were cowards content to remain in England and "cheer themselves with the prevention of happy success in any action of public good." The devil was ultimately responsible for the vicious reports: "These devices infused into the tongues and heads of such devisors (by the Father of Untruths) do serve for nothing else but as a cloak to cover the wretched and lewd pranks of the one sort and the stupidity and backwardness of the other." The company invited right-thinking adventurers to join in a new expedition under Delaware. This time it pledged to accept no "lascivious sons, masters of bad servants, and wives of ill husbands."

In the winter of 1610, as colonists in Jamestown starved to death, the Virginia Company crystallized its latest defense in a less hysterical form in the pages of *A True and Sincere Declaration of the Purpose and Ends of the Plantation Begun in Virginia*. That twenty-six-page pamphlet would stand as the company's most complete response to the scandal that had seized the attention of everyone in London. In *True Purpose* the company conceded that the venture was facing unmitigated criticism on street corners and around tavern tables, attributing the negative talk to "ignorant rumor, virulent envy, or impious subtlety." All was not well in Jamestown, the company acknowledged. "We will call before us all the objections and confess ingenuously all the errors and discouragements which seem to lie so heavy as almost to press to death this brave and hopeful action." The problems, however, were the fault of lazy colonists and incompetent commanders rather than the company. Now the Virginia venture faced new adversity caused by a storm that no one could have anticipated. Should it abandon the project at the most difficult hour, the company asked, or should its members carry on like proper Englishmen? "Is he fit to undertake any great action whose courage is shaken and dissolved with one storm?" No, the company concluded, the colony would go on, and what began as "so small a root" would continue to flower with a "blessed and unexpected growth" into a successful enterprise.

Five months after the loss of the *Sea Venture* and five months before it was known that the people aboard it had survived on Bermuda, *True Purpose* audaciously suggested that those on the ship might still be alive. Gates, the Virginia Company said, was "perhaps bound in with wind, perhaps enforced to stay the masting or mending of some what in his ship torn or lost in this tempest, we doubt not but by the mercy of God he is safe with the pinnace which attended him and shall both, or are by this time, arrived at our colony." The company admitted of Gates that "the loss of him is in suspense," but supposed that there was reason to hope for his survival—"against some doubt." The pamphlet apparently had the desired effect, for soon after its publication at least one Englishman reported that, "some say that the admiral is now safely come to Virginia."

In the winter of 1610 the officials of the Virginia Company used every forum they had at their disposal, including the pulpits of London churches, to bolster sagging confidence in the Jamestown venture. On February 21, Reverend William Crashaw delivered a sermon before Lord Delaware as he prepared to sail, echoing the themes of *True Purpose* but using more colorful language. The "loose, lewd, licentious, riotous, and disordered men" of the earlier expeditions were "the very excrements of a full and swelling state." Yet, Crashaw said, "such fellows as these that be the scum and scouring of the streets and raked up out of the kennels are like to be the founders of a worthy state." All that was needed was discipline imposed by a robust commander. "Let no wise man object that our last fleet was dispersed and sore shaken by a storm, for he cannot but know that such a sail by sea must as well expect tempests of wind as travelers on the land showers of rain."

The latest effusion of words represented the Virginia Company at its vehement best, but in the post–*Sea Venture* climate yielded only a hundred and fifty recruits, a fraction of the hoped-for thousand. Delaware left London on March 10 and traveled overland to Southampton, from which his ships weighed anchor on April 1. As it turned out, if he had waited even a few days longer, he would have arrived at a vacant settlement.

CHAPTER TWELVE

Forest People

Savages and men of Ind.

—Stephano, *The Tempest*

After two months on the water the convoy of Lord Delaware reached Point Comfort and intercepted Gates's departing vessels at the mouth of the river. The new governor arrived at Jamestown in June, when summer foliage was nearly full. Delaware made an entrance with more pomp than had yet been displayed at Jamestown. Strachey carried Gates's heraldic flag as the outgoing governor welcomed the new one.

"His lordship landing fell upon his knees and before us all made a long and silent prayer to himself," Strachey said, "and after marched up into the town where at the gate I bowed with the colors and let them fall at his lordship's feet, who passed on into the chapel where he heard a sermon by Master Buck." After the service Delaware had his ensign, Anthony Scot, read his commission. To complete the transfer of power, Gates turned over the seal of the Virginia Company to the new governor. Delaware then spoke to the assembled colonists, both veteran and new.

"I delivered some few words unto the company," Delaware said afterward, "laying some blames upon them for many vanities and their idleness, earnestly wishing that I might no more find it so lest I should be compelled to draw the sword in justice to cut off such delinquents which I had much rather draw in their defense to protect from enemies."

After the assembly Delaware inspected the fort. None of the existing houses met his standards as a residence, so he returned to his cabin aboard ship. Two days later he named more than a dozen officers of a new government. The three knights of the colony were given high posts—Gates and Somers retained their positions as lieutenant governor and admiral, while newcomer Sir Ferdinando Weynman (Delaware's first cousin) was appointed master of ordnance.

Delaware also appointed Strachey secretary of the colony, probably on the recommendation of Gates. The former secretary had died before the *Sea Venture* survivors came to Jamestown, and the constantly scribbling Strachey was an obvious choice as a replacement. This was a gratifying turn of events for the aspiring writer. Now he would do in an official capacity what he hoped to do on his own, write about the events and people of the New World. A colonial position was also sure to gain him the notice of potential patrons on both sides of the Atlantic.

The first order to the new secretary was to write a report of the events on Bermuda and Jamestown to be carried back to England with the next ship. Strachey had already written most of a long letter to his potential patron, probably the Countess of Bedford. Drawing from that, he would fashion a similar report to serve as an official communication from Delaware to the Virginia Company. While Strachey sat in his hut writing for the colony—an eminently satisfying role indeed—other colonists set about the more physically taxing labor of restoring Jamestown. "I set the sailors a-work to unlade ships," Delaware said, "and the landsmen, some to cleanse the town, some to make coal for our forges. I sent fishermen out to provide fish for our men to save other provisions." An immediate concern was the colony's lack of livestock. During the Starving Time the colonists had consumed all the hogs, chickens, and horses, leaving not a single domestic animal alive.

Somers proposed a solution—he would go back to Bermuda, fill a vessel with pork, fish, and fowl, and return to Jamestown. The mid-Atlantic isle was a week's sail from Virginia in good weather and offered live animals and easily accessible food of many varieties. Delaware enthusiastically accepted the offer and appointed Samuel Argall to accompany the admiral in a second vessel. "I dispatched Sir George Somers back again to the Bermudas," Delaware wrote in a letter home, "the good old gentleman out of his love and zeal not motioning [wavering] but most cheerfully and resolutely undertaking to perform so dangerous a voyage and, if it please God he does safely return, he will store us with hogs' flesh and fish enough to serve the whole colony this winter." Delaware's praise of Somers's sacrifice in offering to return to Bermuda reflected the persistent view that the shallows around the Devil's Isle were extremely dangerous despite the admiral's earlier success.

After a residency in Virginia of less than a month, Somers set sail again for the island that had been his home for most of the past year. He and Argall left Jamestown in the *Patience* and the *Discovery* on June 19. As they sailed downriver Somers wrote an optimistic letter home, to be left at Algernon Fort as they passed and delivered to England on the next departing ship. "Now we are in a good hope to plant and abide there," Somers wrote, "for here is a good course taken and a greater care than ever there was. I am going to the Bermuda for fish and hog with two small pinnaces and am in a good opinion to be back again before the Indians do gather their harvest." The vessels made the open ocean before dawn on June 23 after seeking shelter from a rainstorm in the lee of a headland.

Back upriver at Jamestown, Delaware ignored the rain and ordered the refurbishing of the colony to continue. After a basic cleanup was finished, the "pretty chapel" received workers' attention. The restored church, Strachey said, "shall have a chancel in it of cedar and a Communion table of the black walnut and all the pews of cedar, with fair broad windows to shut and open as the weather shall occasion of the same wood, a pulpit of the same with a font hewn hollow like a canoe, with two bells at the west end. It is so cast as it be very light within and the lord governor and captain general doth cause it to be kept passing sweet and trimmed up with diverse flowers."

Four preachers who came with Delaware joined Richard Buck on a rotating schedule. The five clerics were able to offer a full slate of services: sermons once on Thursday and twice on Sunday and prayers daily in midmorning and late afternoon. "Every Sunday when the lord governor and captain general goeth to church," Strachey said, "he is accompanied with all the counselors, captains, other officers and all the gentlemen— and with a guard of halberdiers in his lordship's livery, fair red cloaks— to the number of fifty, both on each side and behind him, and being in the church his lordship hath his seat in the choir in a green velvet chair with a cloth with a velvet cushion spread on a table before him on which he kneels."

A few days after the arrival of the Delaware fleet, illness began to attack the colonists fresh from England. New colonists expected a period of seasoning, but the disease that swept the new group of men and women was more severe than usual. Among the colonists who suffered was Delaware himself. "Presently after my arrival in Jamestown," Delaware reported, "I was welcomed by a hot and violent ague." The expedition doctor, Lawrence Bohun, used the common treatment of bloodletting as a curative, but it had little effect on the illnesses that assailed Delaware in regular succession over the next month. In a state of weakness the new governor was afflicted with diarrhea, gout, and scurvy. The entry into Virginia, the new governor believed, brought him near death. "I was upon the point to leave the world," he wrote.

Under attack from disease, the colony also received no quarter from the Powhatans besieging the settlement. Soon after his arrival Delaware sent two emissaries to demand that Wahunsenacawh stop ambushing English colonists and return guns he had acquired. If he refused, Delaware said, the English would attack and burn his villages. The soldiers who were sent did not bring back a positive report. "Powhatan returned no other answer but that either we should depart his country or confine ourselves to Jamestown only without searching farther up into his land or rivers," Strachey said, "or otherwise he would give in command to his people to kill us and do unto us all the mischief which they at their pleasure could and we feared, withal forewarning the said messengers not to return any more unto him unless they brought him a coach and three horses, for he had understood by the Indians which were in England how such was the state of great *werowances* [rulers] and lords in

England to ride and visit other great men." This exchange with the English emissaries may also have been the time that Wahunsenacawh claimed that months earlier his men had intercepted and killed Henry Ravens and his crew after they reached Virginia from Bermuda in their rigged longboat just after the wreck of the *Sea Venture*.

Powhatan attacks continued unabated. Even just beyond the palisade the colonists were in danger. Strawberries grew among the stumps in the cleared area beyond the wooden walls, but picking them put one in range of the bowmen who waited in the woods at all hours. The colonists were continually under observation. On July 6 downriver at Point Comfort, Gates ordered a man named Humphrey Blunt to retrieve a boat that had drifted from Algernon Fort to a nearby shore. "Certain Indians (watching the occasion) seized the poor fellow and led him up into the woods and sacrificed him," Strachey said. Seeing his man slain steeled Gates to a new resolve. "Now being startled by this, he well perceived how little a fair and noble entreaty works upon a barbarous disposition and therefore in some measure purposed to be revenged."

Three days after the killing of Blunt, the newly resolute Gates—perhaps driven, too, by latent frustration over the mutinous behavior of his own flock during the previous year—led a punitive expedition against the nearby town of Kecoughtan. Strachey went along, remaining safely in the rear. Gates sent a lone drummer into the village to draw out the men and women. "Being landed he caused the taborer to play and dance," Percy wrote, "thereby to lure the Indians to come unto him." When the unsuspecting residents emerged from their houses to meet the visitors, the soldiers "fell in upon them, put five to the sword, wounded many others, some of them being after found in the woods with such extraordinary large and mortal wounds that it seemed strange they could fly so far." No English were injured or killed. Afterward the soldiers took grain, tobacco, and clothing from the homes.

Two garrisons were established on the site to make use of unripe corn standing in fields around the village. Some of the Kecoughtan houses were set aside for the use of the soldiers who would reside at the outposts, and the others were burned. A tent and thatched cabins served as additional housing. Walking the site after the fight, Strachey said the location was well chosen and the fields of two to three thousand acres about it were expertly cultivated. In addition the colonists found "many pretty copses or bosks" nearby in which grew gooseberries, mulberries, cherry trees, and a plant he called a "maracock apple," today known as the maypop passionflower.

The most important fruit found flourishing at Kecoughtan was grapes. The Virginia Company hoped wine for the English market would be one of the products of Jamestown. To establish the industry, Delaware carried French vintners who had promised the Virginia Company they would begin sending wine home within two years. To that end, a vintner was placed with the garrison at Kecoughtan. "We proposed to set a Frenchman here a-work to plant vines, which grew naturally in great plenty," Strachey wrote.

When not attending to sick colonists, Delaware's physician, Lawrence Bohun, managed to turn out a passable young wine. "Behold the goodly vines burdening every neighbor bush and climbing the tops of highest trees and those full of clusters of grapes in their kind, however draped and shadowed soever from the sun and though never pruned or manured," Strachey wrote. "I dare say it, that we have eaten there as full and luscious a grape as in the villages between Paris and Amiens, and I have drunk often of the rathe [early] wine which Doctor Bohun and other of our people have made full as good as your French-British wine. Twenty gallons at a time have been sometimes made without any other help than by crushing the grape with the hand, which letting to settle five or six days, hath, in the drawing forth, proved strong and heady."

While the Powhatans would never return to Kecoughtan, they soon retaliated with a raid on Jamestown. Two of the attackers were captured and brought into the palisade. Still smarting from the rejection of his earlier emissaries, Delaware decided to send a bloodier message to Wahunsenacawh. The colonists identified one of the men as a participant in an earlier attack, and he was dragged to a stump where his right hand was hacked off with a sword. The grievously wounded warrior was sent away with a demand to Wahunsenacawh that he cease all hostilities. If those steps were not taken, the man was told, his companion would be executed.

The departure of the mutilated captive coincided with preparations by Gates and Newport to return to England to lobby for more supplies. The *Hercules* and the *Blessing* would also carry two reports written by Strachey. The first was the official communication to the Virginia Company carrying Delaware's signature. A second was the letter from Strachey to the "Excellent Lady," probably the Countess of Bedford. The map of Bermuda that George Somers had drawn during his months on the island was enclosed with the letter. Since the countess was a prominent stockholder of the Virginia Company, Strachey hoped that his letter to her would be circulated among company officials—all the better for establishing himself as a chronicler of Virginia.

In order to send the ships home with something in their holds, the colonists took lumber and iron ore from the forest near a town called Warraskoyack. While lading the ships the English captured the leader of the town, Tackonekintaco, along with his son, Tangoit, and a third man. The three were brought to Algernon Fort, where Delaware was waiting to see the ships off. There Tackonekintaco was induced to agree to exchange five hundred bushels of grain after the fall harvest for copper, beads, and hatchets. With that promise Tackonekintaco and Tangoit were released, while the third man was held to ensure compliance. The colonists planned to send the man to England and then return him to Virginia for redelivery to his people after the tribute was paid. Before the ships left for England, however, the hostage leaped overboard and made it to shore despite being bound. "The Indians of Warraskoyack would oftentimes afterward mock us," Strachey said, "and call to us for him and at length make a great laughter and tell us he was come home; how true or false is no great matter, but indeed the old king after that time refused to perform the former bargain."

~~

After Gates departed for England, an ailing Lord Delaware returned to Jamestown, still residing on his ship rather than on land. Receiving no answer to the message sent to Wahunsenacawh with the handless combatant, he ordered George Percy to take seventy men and attack the nearby town of Paspahegh. Strachey accompanied this raiding party as well, again remaining in the rear guard of the action. On August 9 the soldiers left by water and landed three miles from the town. A captive named Kemps was forced to guide their march through the forest. He attempted to lead the troops astray, Percy said, but upon threat of death finally led them to the outskirts of the town. The troops attacked upon the firing of a pistol, taking the villagers by surprise. "We fell in upon them, put some fifteen or sixteen to the sword, and almost all the rest to flight."

In the aftermath of the attack a soldier delivered to Percy a Powhatan man, woman, and children who had been taken prisoner. Percy scolded the solider for sparing the prisoners, and the Powhatan man was immediately executed. The woman and children were marched back to the boats. "My soldiers did begin to murmur because the queen and her children were spared," Percy said. "So upon the same, a council being called it was agreed upon to put the children to death, the which was effected by throwing them overboard and shooting out their brains in the water. Yet for all this cruelty the soldiers were not well pleased and I had much to do to save the queen's life for that time."

Percy then sent Captain James Davis and a column of soldiers ashore again to pursue the fleeing Paspaheghs. Davis and his men, "marching about fourteen miles into the country, cut down their corn, burned their houses, temples, and idols, and amongst the rest a spacious temple, clean and neatly kept, a thing strange and seldom seen amongst the Indians in those parts. So having performed all the spoil he could, returned aboard to me again and then we sailed down the river."

At Jamestown, Davis rowed to Delaware's ship to report on the raid (inexplicably, Percy remained behind in the pinnace). When Davis returned he told Percy that Delaware had ordered the prisoner executed by burning. The prospect was too horrible for Percy. "I replied that having seen so much bloodshed that day, now in my cold blood I desired to see no more, and for to burn her, I did not hold it fitting, but either by shot or sword to give her a quicker dispatch. So turning myself from Captain Davis, he did take the queen with two soldiers ashore and in the woods put her to the sword." Upon reflection—perhaps even at the time—Percy suspected that Delaware had made no such order, though he kept his doubts to himself. "Although Captain Davis told me it was my lord's direction," Percy wrote later, "yet I am persuaded to the contrary."

CHAPTER THIRTEEN

Blood in the Snow

To see a dead Indian.

—Trinculo, *The Tempest*

On the last day of August 1610 the ship that had been dispatched to fetch food from Bermuda with George Somers—Samuel Argall in the *Discovery*—returned to Jamestown without having reached the mid-Atlantic isle. Argall and Somers had encountered contrary winds that kept them from heading into the Atlantic. Rather than remain in waters barren of fish, they had sailed first for Cape Cod and then Sagadahoc. They had then become separated in fog off the coast. Argall had fished with some success, paused on August 27 to name Delaware Bay after his commander, and made his way back to Jamestown after ten weeks at sea. The fate of Somers and the *Patience* was unknown.

Delaware sent the newly returned Argall to Warraskoyack with two companies of soldiers to continue his campaign of violence against Wahunsenacawh and to avenge the perceived treachery of Tackonekintaco. Having heard of the devastation at Kecoughtan, the people of Warraskoyack fled from the approaching soldiers and Argall met no opposition. Strachey remained at Jamestown this time, writing that the soldiers "fell upon two towns of his and burnt them to the ground with all their goodly furniture of mats, dishes, wooden pots, and platters."

Soon after Argall's raid, a single vessel from England arrived in Jamestown. The *Dainty* brought a dozen men and one woman and at least two horses. The arriving colonists reported that just before they left England a ship arrived from Jamestown with news of the Starving Time. Eight months earlier the *Swallow* had abandoned a trading expe-

dition and sailed for home instead of bringing food back to the strug-
gling colony. Those on board deflected accusations that they had stolen
the ship by saying they had no choice but to leave a desperate situation.
To bolster their claim, they had described to all who would listen the
events of the Starving Time in graphic detail.

"The Indians hold the English surrounded in the strong place which
they had erected there, having killed the larger part of them," a new
Spanish ambassador, Alonso de Velasco, wrote to his king after having
heard reports by the *Swallow*, "and the others were left so entirely without provisions that they thought it impossible to escape, because the
survivors eat the dead, and when one of the natives died fighting they
dug him up again two days afterwards to be eaten. The swine which
they carried there and which commenced to multiply, the Indians killed,
and almost all who came in this vessel died from having eaten dogs, cat
skins, and other vile stuff."

In response to the renewal of the public relations disaster they had
worked to overcome, Virginia Company officials employed their usual
tactic of disparaging the reputations of the returning voyagers. "These are
that scum of men," the company said, "that failing in their piracy, that
being pinched with famine and penury, after their wild roving upon the
sea, when all their lawless hopes failed, some remained with other pi-
rates they met upon the sea, the others resolved to return for England
[and] bound themselves by mutual oath to agree all in one report to dis-
credit the land, to deplore the famine, and to protest that this their coming away proceeded from desperate necessity." With the new charges
against the colony the Virginia Company's ability to raise money and
recruits was further compromised. "Thus it looks," Velasco wrote, "as if
the zeal for this enterprise was cooling off."

As autumn 1610 came to full leaf in Jamestown, William Strachey witnessed a second execution for mutiny. The Virginia Company had outfitted a crew of miners and sent them to the colony with Delaware. Some
of the miners allegedly conspired to take a ship and return to England

(perhaps planning to look for precious metals on their own before sailing). The plan was betrayed to Delaware, who ordered an immediate hanging.

"My lord for an example adjudged one of them by marshal law to be executed," Percy reported. "The party being thrown off the ladder, what with the swing and weight of his body the rope did break and he fell upon the ground, and in regard of the accident my lord pardoned him, although it nothing availed him, having received his death with the gird of the rope and extremity of the fall so that within two days after he died."

This was another gruesome scene, the kind Strachey witnessed but declined to describe in his writings. The journals he kept in Jamestown included their share of violent episodes, but the worst things he saw were written in veiled language or left out altogether. Readers of narratives would not want to hear about botched hangings of colonists or murders of women and children. There was no need to write about that for his own use, and the Virginia Company certainly would not want such material included in official dispatches from secretary of the colony. Thus Strachey remained mute about some of the worst aspects of colonial life.

Soon after the hanging, and perhaps even prompted by it, Delaware ordered a company of men up the James River to march into the interior in search of a lode of shiny metal that had been found on an earlier expedition. Too sick to join the initial venture, the governor appointed George Yardley and Edward Brewster to lead the company. The men living at Kecoughtan had finished harvesting the corn there and so were ordered to abandon the post and prepare to join the expedition. They would travel by boat as far as possible and then hike into the interior. A palisade would be constructed at the mine site and they would spend the winter there digging for silver. Strachey remained behind in Jamestown when the boats departed.

On the voyage upriver a longboat of fourteen miners searching for fresh water went ashore at the village of Appomattox. The residents asked the visitors to leave their weapons in the boat, which turned out to be a fatal decision. During a meal the Englishmen were set upon and killed. Only Dowse the drummer (the same man who had drawn out the

Powhatans at Kecoughtan) survived by running to the longboat and making his way out into the river. Learning of the massacre from the escaped drummer, the rest of the force immediately attacked, burning the town and killing and scattering its residents. The depleted company continued as far as they could with the boats, but did not go farther than the riverside.

Late in the fall Delaware left Jamestown to winter with the miners at the northern campsite, and before going he sent Samuel Argall north to the Potomac River to trade for food. Being outside the Powhatan confederacy and not directly affected by English settlement, the Patawomecks proved willing to barter. Argall acquired four hundred bushels of grain and stacks of furs in exchange for scrap copper and lead, ninety-six hatchets, sixty knives, some bells, and twelve pairs of scissors.

On the expedition Argall also recovered an English boy named Henry Spelman who had lived among the Powhatans and Patawomecks for a year. The fifteen-year-old had come to Jamestown in the Gates fleet aboard the *Unity*. Only a few weeks after arrival he had been left with Wahunsenacawh to learn the Powhatan language, but after a while he ran off and walked through the forest many miles to Patawomeck country. "With this King Patawomeck I lived a year and more," Spelman said, "at a town of his called Passapatanzy, until such time as a worthy gentleman named Captain Argall arrived."

Argall and Spelman returned to Jamestown in early winter 1611. When Strachey heard the story of the expedition and learned Spelman's history, he was pleased to have a new source of information on the people of Virginia. Spelman had learned the language of the Powhatans and the Patawomecks, which would be a great help to the colonists in general and the secretary in particular. Strachey interviewed the teenager and made notes about the circumstances of his release. Spelman told him that just before his release his overseer, Iopassus, came aboard Argall's ship "about Christmas" and had a long conversation "sitting (the weather being very cold) by the fire upon a hearth in the hold with the captain." During the visit Iopassus asked to see a Bible a sailor was reading. After examining the illustrations in the book, he offered to tell of the beliefs of the Patawomecks.

"We have five gods in all," Iopassus said. "Our chief god appears often unto us in the likeness of a mighty great hare; the other four have no visible shape but are indeed the four winds which keep the four corners of the earth. Our god who takes upon him this shape of a hare conceived with himself how to people this great world and with what kind of creatures." The deity in the shape of a hare created a great deer to live upon the earth, Iopassus said, but the gods from the four corners of the earth were envious and slew the deer. The god in the shape of a hare then made each hair of the deer into another deer and placed people upon the earth—"a man and a woman in one country and a man and a woman in another country, and so the world took his first beginning of mankind."

Argall then asked what happened to the Patawomecks after death, and Strachey described Iopassus's answer, as translated by Spelman. "After they are dead here they go up to a top of a high tree and there they spy a fair plain broad pathway, on both sides whereof doth grow all manner of pleasant fruits as mulberries, strawberries, plums, etc. In this pleasant path they run toward the rising of the sun, where the godly hare's house is and in the midway they come to a house where a woman goddess doth dwell who hath always her doors open for hospitality." There, Iopassus said, they have a feast of boiled corn, walnut milk, and fruit before continuing on to their destination. "They find their forefathers living in great pleasure in a goodly field, where they do nothing but dance and sing and feed on delicious fruits with the great hare, who is their great god, and when they have lived there until they be stark old men they say they die there likewise by turns and come into the world again."

Soon after Argall and Spelman came back to Jamestown, blood fell again on the snow of Tsenacomoco. The blockhouse that guarded the neck leading from the colony to the mainland was attacked on February 9 by

Wowinchopunck, the leader of Paspahegh, the town the English had overrun in August. The soldiers in the blockhouse went outside and attempted to seize Wowinchopunck, but seeing that he could not be taken alive the captain of the guard stabbed him twice and fled back to the building. The attackers picked up the fallen man and carried him into the woods. One of the blockhouse guard pursued the carriers and catching one, "overthrew him and with his dagger sent him to accompany his master in the other world."

Late in the winter, the still-ailing Delaware and the remainder of his company abandoned the upriver palisade and returned to the colony. Disease was rife in Jamestown that winter, and among those who died was Kemps, the Powhatan captive who was forced to lead Percy against the Paspaheghs. Percy also reported the demise of Sir Ferdinando Weynman, whose "death was much lamented, being both an honest and a valiant gentleman."

By March, Delaware's health was so fragile that he decided to sail to the West Indies, where he might bathe in the geothermal hot springs of Nevis. Leaving the colony he was charged to govern was sure to anger officials and investors of the Virginia Company, but Delaware felt his life depended upon it. At his sailing the governor reported that he left two hundred in the colony supplied with enough food for ten months. In the estimation of those left behind, however, the food stores were meager and the expectations low. "At his going he left Captain George Percy deputy governor, the people (remaining under his command) provided for three months at a short allowance of victuals," a colonist reported.

After Delaware's ship was out of view, the warriors from Paspahegh assaulted Jamestown in one of the most successful attacks against the colony. George Percy had doubled the guard at the blockhouse and ordered his men not to be drawn from the tower, but the soldiers stationed there disobeyed his orders, with fatal results. The guards, Percy said, "showing more valor than wit, more fury than judgment," pursued a small band of Powhatans who appeared near the blockhouse. The interlopers withdrew into the forest and the soldiers followed, only to fall into an ambush, "where being five or six hundred of savages let fly their arrows as thick as hail amongst our handful of men and defeated and cut them all off in a moment, the arrows which they had shot being so many in number that the ground thereabouts was almost covered with them." The attackers' cries of "Paspahegh, Paspahegh" brought fifty reinforcements from the palisade, but when they arrived all that remained to do was recover the bodies of the soldiers. A spooked Percy dispatched a boat in an unsuccessful attempt to catch Delaware. To the colonists, the move revealed the deputy governor's reluctance to lead. For the first time, William Strachey was in the wilderness of the New World without the guidance of a governor he trusted. From his first days under the leadership of Percy, Strachey began to mull the possibility of returning home to London.

Just over a week after the blockhouse ambush, to the relief of the colonists, one of the two ships that had carried Gates back to England came up the James River. The *Hercules* under Captain Robert Adams carried only thirty people, but in addition to replacing the twenty killed at the blockhouse the arrival did a bit to revive the morale of the dispirited colony. The vessel carried important news for the survivors of the *Sea Venture* wreck—for the first time they knew that their families and friends were aware they had survived on Bermuda.

One man aboard the *Hercules* was a new recruit named Robert Evelyn, a Londoner deep in debt who hoped to return from the New World with riches for his wife and children. "I am much grieved at my heart for it that my estate is so mean," Evelyn had written to his mother as he prepared to leave. "I am going to the sea, a long and dangerous vo[yage with] other men to make me to be [able] to pay my debts and to restore my decayed estate again; which I beseech God of His mercy to grant it may be [made] prosperous unto me to His honor and my comfort in this world and in the world to come; and I beseech you if I do die that you would be good unto my poor wife and children, which, God knows, I shall leave very poor."

Adams, Evelyn, and the others on the *Hercules* reported that Thomas

Gates had stunned London and all of England by coming back from the grave. When his ships arrived at the Thames quay in September, the story of the survival of the *Sea Venture* voyagers had spread rapidly through the city. To satisfy the demand for information on the wreck, two who had lived through it immediately published accounts. Silvester Jourdain was first into print with his *Discovery of the Barmodas*, a short pamphlet telling the story in spare prose. Another *Sea Venture* passenger, Richard Rich, calling himself a "soldier blunt and plain," offered the tale in verse under the title *Newes from Virginia: The Lost Flocke Triumphant*.

Neither Jourdain nor Rich mentioned the fate of Namontack, the Powhatan emissary who had twice been to London before departing on the *Sea Venture* with Machumps. Gates retold the Bermuda story many times, however, and a Dutch writer living in London heard one of those tellings. Emanuel van Meteren reported that Gates included among his list of the Bermuda dead "a *casicke* or son of a king in Virginia who had been in England and who had been killed by an Indian, his own servant." Gates's suspicion that Machumps had killed Namontack was reported as a certainty, and the former castaway apparently did not mention that the suspected murderer continued to circulate among the colonists in Jamestown without sanction for the alleged crime.

As in earlier times, the most anticipated publication in the weeks after Gates's return was the one issued by the Virginia Company itself. Now instead of having to explain the death of one of its most promising leaders, the company could hail his survival as proof that God intended the English to prevail in Virginia. As the basis of *A True Declaration of the Estate of the Colonie in Virginia*, the company drew upon Strachey's letter to the "Excellent Lady" and the derivative report that the secretary had drafted for Delaware's signature. The company highlighted the successes of Bermuda and Virginia and downplayed or omitted the episodes of mutiny, murder, and bloody battles with the Powhatans. Highlighted was the miraculous—some might even say magical—survival of Thomas Gates and his company on an enchanted island.

This series of fortuitous events proved the intervention of the divine, according to the Virginia Company. Could these coincidences, the company asked, mean anything but that God intended Jamestown to succeed? If Gates had not come from Bermuda, the Virginia settlers would have starved; if Gates had not saved the colony from burning, the palisade could not have been reoccupied; if Jamestown had been abandoned much longer, the Powhatans would have destroyed it; if Gates had left sooner, his fleet would not have met Delaware; if Delaware had not brought ample supplies, his arrival would not have made a decisive difference. This was the hand of God at work, the Virginia Company said, and the preservation of the castaways on Bermuda was final proof that God wanted the English to succeed in the New World.

In crafting their publicity campaign, the Virginia Company made use of the positive elements of Strachey's unexpected report. His vivid prose was a great help in crafting their publication, and the company wanted more. The organization's secretary and friend of Strachey's, Richard Martin, was enlisted to write him and ask for additional writings. The *Hercules* carried a letter from Martin to Strachey, complimenting his literary efforts and requesting a new report. Strachey may have sent back an additional description of the country when the *Hercules* returned to England in a few weeks' time, but more likely he sent nothing immediately and the request by Martin spurred him to begin work on his comprehensive history of Virginia. Strachey was now convinced that he would realize his opportunity for literary success. At long last he had wealthy and well-placed patrons asking him to write something that would have a lasting impact on the literature of the age. He did not intend to let the chance slip by.

The most important news arriving with the *Hercules* was that it was part of a new supply fleet. The ship had separated from two companion vessels on the way over, but others were expected soon in the Chesapeake. The convoy was under the leadership of Sir Thomas Dale, a career soldier with twenty-three years' military service. Dale had distinguished himself against Celtic forces in Ireland and the Spanish in the Netherlands, rising from common soldier to knight. While serving in the field with Gates in both conflicts, Dale had used strict discipline, in sharp contrast to Gates's preference for compromise. The Virginia Company had given Dale the rank of marshal and placed him in charge of the colony's military activities. He had departed with three ships carrying cattle, armor, and three hundred settlers, including sixty women. While Dale was assigned to oversee military activities only, in the unexpected absence of Delaware he would become the highest-ranking official in the colony and take over as acting governor. The marshal would prove to be a strict leader.

CHAPTER FOURTEEN

Poison

I fear a madness held me.

—Alonso, *The Tempest*

The sails of the remaining two ships of Thomas Dale's fleet appeared on the horizon off Point Comfort in May 1611. The Virginia Company's primary order to Dale was to expand the settlement beyond Jamestown and Point Comfort. The two abandoned forts at Kecoughtan, now named Fort Henry and Fort Charles, were to be reoccupied and planted with corn. The settlement at Jamestown was to become a fully functioning village. Once those goals were accomplished, Dale was to reoccupy and develop the upriver site where Delaware had spent the winter. The new leader's efforts were to be spent strengthening the colony rather than seeking silver.

"The twelfth of May we seized our bay," Dale reported, "and the same night with a favorable southeast gale (all praise be to God for it) we came to an anchor before Algernon Fort at Point Comfort, where to our no small comfort again we discovered the *Hercules* even then preparing to take the advantage of the present tide to set sail for England." The *Hercules* had exchanged its cargo of settlers for one of fish and was set to return home. Percy was at the fort to see the ship off, and the veteran colonist greeted Dale with the news that Delaware had left Virginia a month earlier and Dale would consequently be in charge of the entire colony rather than just its military activities.

Given the rapid advance of the growing season, the marshal immediately took his ships to Kecoughtan instead of going upriver to Jamestown. There he found that the English encampment remained vacant. Housing and corn were his priorities, so he wasted no time in establishing both at Kecoughtan. Dale ordered carpenters to restore the cabins at the site, and put the rest of the colonists in his ships to work planting the fields around the destroyed Powhatan village. After a week, he left a contingent of settlers at Kecoughtan to tend the fields and moved on to Jamestown.

Arriving at the Jamestown palisade on Sunday, May 19, Dale found the residents living an undisciplined existence. As colonist Ralph Hamor sarcastically put it, the people were found to be going about "their daily and usual works—bowling in the streets." The lack of crops in the ground and the perceived lack of effort angered Dale, who vented his frustration on Christopher Newport. The former captain of the *Sea Venture* had returned to Virginia with him, apparently after supporting the contention of Virginia Company treasurer Thomas Smith that the colony was adequately provisioned. "Sir Thomas Dale, at his arrival finding himself deluded by the aforesaid protestations," a witness said, "pulled Captain Newport by the beard, and threatening to hang him, for that he affirmed Sir Thomas Smith's relation to be true, demanding of him whether it were meant that the people here in Virginia should feed upon trees."

Dale immediately set the colonists to work restoring the settlement. William Strachey was always quick to show loyalty to a strong leader, and he was careful to avoid being among those who were subjected to Dale's wrath. The new acting governor would retain Strachey as secretary of the colony, and one of their first joint projects was an expansion of the laws first imposed by Gates. Strachey spent hours with Dale as the marshal dictated dozens of new civil and military regulations. By the time they were posted on June 22, the original list of twenty-one civil laws had been expanded to thirty-seven, and fifty-one military commandments had been laid out as well. Few colonists were happy with the new rules. "Sir Thomas Dale immediately upon his arrival," one resident said, "to add to that extremity of misery under which the colony from her infancy groaned, made and published most cruel and tyrannous laws, exceeding the strictest rules of marshal discipline."

Dale's civil laws were much like those imposed by Gates. Anyone killing a domestic animal without permission would be punished by the branding of a hand and the loss of both ears. Despite the threat of attack, settlers were told to go at least a quarter of a mile from the fort "to do the necessities of nature, since by these unmanly, slothful, and loathsome immodesties, the whole fort may be choked and poisoned with ill airs." Colonists were to keep their houses clean, with the beds at least three feet off the ground to escape contagious vapors. Some of the laws were directed at women—any laundress who stole clothes or surreptitiously replaced new articles with worn ones, for example, was to "be whipped for the same and lie in prison till she make restitution of such linen." Beyond the civil laws, a new section of military decrees applied only to the male colonists when they were acting as soldiers. If they transgressed while on duty they might be whipped, held in irons, forced to ask forgiveness on their knees, run a gauntlet of pikes, lose a hand, or be executed by their own weapons. Soldiers were subjected to a strict code of honor and were not to "outrage or injure anyone without a cause, in deed or in words, privately behind his back like a sly coward or openly to his face like an arrogant ruffian."

A bond formed between Strachey and Dale as they drafted the expanded laws. The new leader of the colony found a loyal lieutenant in the secretary, and would trust him thereafter with personal projects. After living for a short period under the unsure leadership of George Percy, Strachey admired Dale's imposition of fierce discipline on what the secretary had always seen as an unbridled rabble. Strachey would stay close to the acting governor's side for the remainder of his time in Jamestown.

Dale and his council of advisers developed a list of construction projects to restore Jamestown. They made plans to repair the church and storehouse and to construct a stable, barn, armory, powder house, fish-drying shack, wharf, forge, second well, and additional blockhouse. First on the agenda were the church, stable, and wharf. As work commenced on those, it became clear to colonist Ralph Hamor that Dale would be "severe and strict" in his rule and expect each of his orders "with all severity and extremity to be executed."

In addition to reinvigorating Jamestown, Dale wanted to expand the colony to a new site. To that end, in early summer he undertook a scouting expedition with a hundred colonists, including Strachey. First Dale planned to explore the Nansemond River, a tributary of the James that branched off downriver from Jamestown. He would then return past the colony and go upriver to inspect the rude fort Delaware had built there. Machumps would serve as a guide. The Powhatan traveler had returned to Virginia with the *Sea Venture* castaways, apparently telling Wahunsenacawh that Namontack had stayed behind in England. The colonists continued to suspect him of foul play in Namontack's disappearance in Bermuda but continued to use him as a guide and interpreter. Machumps, Strachey said, "comes to and fro amongst us as he dares and as Powhatan gives him leave." When in Jamestown he would occasionally dine with the leaders of the colony. "Before their dinners and suppers the better sort will do a kind of sacrifice, taking the first bit and casting it in the fire and to it repeat certain words," Strachey wrote. "I have heard Machumps at Sir Thomas Dale's table once or twice (upon our request) repeat the said grace, as it were, howbeit I forgot to take it from him in writing."

On one of his extended visits to Jamestown, Machumps told a story that the colonists wanted to believe. At an inland village, he said, "the people have houses built with stone walls and one story above another, so taught them by those English who escaped the slaughter at Roanoke." The fate of the 1587 colony located down the coast at Roanoke had been of intense interest to the English since a supply ship found the site deserted in 1590. Machumps claimed that the colony was overrun and the attackers "preserved seven of the English alive—four men, two boys, and one young maid (who escaped and fled up the river of Chanoke)." Though the colonists would search as best they could and inquire at parlays, no further evidence of the seven captives has ever been discovered.

Machumps was aboard when the expedition departed for Nansemond. As the vessels of the colony made their way up the tributary river, the English and Powhatans encountered each other and clashed. The soldiers wore armor brought over by Dale, which deflected most arrows. Nevertheless, Captain Francis West was impaled in the thigh and Captain John Martin in the arm, and an arrow pierced the brim of Dale's helmet, just missing his head.

"In these conflicts many Indians being also slain and wounded and, not being acquainted nor accustomed to encounter with men in armor, much wondered thereat," Percy said, "especially that they did not see any of our men fall as they had done in other conflicts. Whereupon they did fall into their exorcisms, conjurations, and charms, throwing fire up into the sky, running up and down with rattles and making many diabolical gestures with many necromantic spells and incantations, imagining thereby to cause rain to fall from the clouds to extinguish and put out our men's matches and to wet and spoil their powder. But neither the devil whom they adore nor all their sorceries did anything avail them, for our men cut down their corn, burned their houses, and besides those which they had slain brought some of them prisoners to our fort."

Reverend Alexander Whitaker, who had arrived in Virginia with the Dale fleet, was a witness to the battle. The Nansemonds' call for rain was successful, according to Whitaker, though it failed to dampen the English powder. "As our men passed by one of their towns there issued out of the shore a mad crew, dancing like antics [as] our Morris dancers before whom there went a *quiockosite*, or their priest, [who] tossed smoke and flame out of a thing like a censer. An Indian by name Machumps amongst our men seeing this dance told us that there would be very much rain presently, and indeed there was forthwith exceeding thunder and lightning and much rain within five miles and so farther off, but not so much there as made their powder dank."

Dale and his men returned to Jamestown, and while there they received a Powhatan delegation that delivered a warning from Wahun-senacawh. The English were not to venture upriver, the Powhatan leader said, and were immediately to return the prisoners they had taken at Nansemond. "Otherwise he threatened to destroy us after strange manner," Whitaker reported. "First, he said he would make us drunk, and then kill us, and for a more solemnity he gave us six or seven days' respite. Sir Thomas was very merry at this message and returned them with the like answer."

Days later Dale and his men proceeded up the James as planned, and during the venture Wahunsenacawh attempted to make good on his threat. "One night our men being at prayers in the court of guard," Whitaker said, "a strange noise was heard coming out of the corn towards the trenches of our men like an Indian *hup hup!* with an *oho oho!* Some say that they saw one like an Indian leap over the fire and run into the corn with the same noise, at the which all our men were confusedly amazed. They could speak nothing but *oho oho* and all generally taking the wrong end of their arms."

"Thanks be to God this alarm lasted not above half a quarter of an hour and no harm was done, excepting two or three which were knocked down without any further harm," Whitaker said. "For suddenly as men awakened out of a dream they began to search for their supposed enemies but finding none remained ever after very quiet."

The Powhatans had tried to use poison against the English once before, and may now have managed to slip a hallucinogenic herb into the water of the company, perhaps a tea made from the seeds of jimsonweed. "A fantasy possessed them," Percy said of Dale's men, "that they imagined the savages were set upon them, each man taking one another for an Indian and so did fall pell-mell, one upon another, beating one another down and breaking one of another's heads, that much mischief might have been done but that it pleased God the fantasy was taken away whereby they had been deluded and every man understood his error."

After the disturbing but harmless episode, the expedition continued up the river, stopping at the deserted village of Appomattox that Delaware's men had attacked the previous fall after the killing of the miners. The men walked through partially burned houses looking for artifacts, and in one of them Strachey found a pair of severed cat paws hanging on a wall. The claws probably belonged to a bobcat taken by a Powhatan hunter, though the colonists envisioned something larger. "I found in an Indian house certain claws tied up in a string," Strachey wrote. "They are assured unto me to be lion's claws." After going on and inspecting the upriver fort, Dale decided to build his satellite settlement at that location. After a few days the company returned to Jamestown, with plans to return with a construction team as a prelude to the permanent occupation of the site.

Plans to develop an upriver settlement were delayed by an event that occurred soon after the expedition returned to Jamestown. The colonists had long feared they would encounter the Spanish in the New World, and now for the first time it came to pass. The sight of the sail of a Spanish caravel off Point Comfort caused the soldiers of the fort to immediately prepare for war. On board the approaching ship, most of the sailors were just as tense. All but three of them were confused as to why their commander was directing their vessel to approach an English fort. Only Captain Diego de Molina, Ensign Marco Antonio Perez, and pilot Francisco Lembri knew that the true purpose of their voyage up the coast from the Caribbean was to spy on the English colony. The rest had been told their mission was to search for a lost munitions ship.

The Spanish claimed the New World wholly for themselves and were still on uneasy terms with their former enemy. They saw the establishment of an English settlement on the Virginia coast as a dangerous precedent. Three years earlier Spain almost launched an attack on Jamestown. A fleet was outfitted in 1608, but the ships were diverted to the war in the Netherlands and the plan went no further. Now in the spring of 1611 the Spanish had decided they were content to allow England to pour capital into an enterprise that was yielding little return. The Spanish Council of War was still interested in knowing the strength of the colony, however, and on its orders the caravel *Nuestra Señora del Rosario* had headed north from Havana to scout Jamestown.

The misinformed Spanish sailors were mystified by their captain's insistence that they sail toward the fort, and equally baffled by his suggestion that the English ship they saw anchored there might be the lost Spanish vessel. The soldiers at Point Comfort fired a warning shot as the Spaniards approached, and the caravel anchored and responded with a shot of its own. Molina, Perez, Lembri—an Englishman formerly named Limbrecke who had been living in Spain for many years—ordered ten armed men to join them in a longboat and row to shore. As they neared the beach, the oarsmen saw sixty or seventy men near the fort and asked Molina to turn around. The captain responded sharply, according to an official report by one of the sailors: "Don Diego said no one should say a word or he would break his head." The longboat continued on until it was just off the beach. There the Spaniards saw footprints of boots they identified as English or Flemish. The sailors refused to leave the longboat, and only Molina, Perez, and Lembri splashed into the surf. As the longboat pushed off, fifty Englishmen emerged from hiding, surrounding the three Spaniards on the beach, disarming them and leading them to the fort.

Inside the Point Comfort palisade, the Spaniards told Commander James Davis that they wanted to search the James River for the lost vessel. Somewhat surprisingly, Davis agreed to send an English pilot aboard the caravel to help it navigate the James, apparently judging it an opportunity to get the vessel to Jamestown, where Dale and his three English vessels could take it at will. English pilot John Clark was thus sent to the caravel. Signals from Molina on the beach brought the Spanish longboat back in. To ensure that Clark would not get his clothes wet, the sailor's report said, the Spaniards carried him to the longboat—"one of the mariners put him into the boat, carrying him on his shoulders."

The master of the caravel was not inclined to sail up the James. His only desire was to extract himself from his present situation, retrieving if he could the three colleagues who had in his view embarked on a reckless

venture. Instead of being allowed to take the ship up the river, Clark was
held prisoner. The next morning the master of the caravel came near
shore himself and, in shouted negotiations with Davis on the beach, proposed that the three Spaniards be traded for Clark, an offer Davis refused. At that the longboat returned to the caravel and the vessel set sail
for Havana. The standoff thus ended with the three Spaniards in the
hands of the English and pilot John Clark bound for Cuba.

The captive Spaniards were brought up the river to Jamestown. After
a report from Davis, Dale ordered the three men questioned by Percy
and Newport, with Strachey taking notes. After an extensive interrogation in a mixture of Spanish and English, Percy reported to Dale that
"their intent was as evil as we imagined." The men would be held prisoner at Jamestown for the time being. The Spanish incursion worried
Dale, and in a report to the Virginia Company he said he feared it was a
precursor to an invasion. The colonists, Dale said, "are here so few, so
weak and unfortified" that they would have little chance against even a
small Spanish force.

A few weeks later it appeared Dale's fears would be realized. On August
2, Davis sent a longboat from Point Comfort to Jamestown with word
of nine sails off the coast. Dale immediately began preparations to meet
the enemy. Since the palisade at Jamestown would provide little defense
against the guns of Spanish ships, Dale ordered everyone in the colony
onto the three vessels then on hand—the *Starre*, the *Prosperous*, and the
Deliverance. Meanwhile he sent a boat with thirty armed men back down
the river to return as soon as possible with more intelligence. When the
scouts came back in three hours' time, they brought good news. "It was
an English fleet, Sir Thomas Gates general thereof," Ralph Hamor reported. Instead of a bloody battle with the Spanish, the colonists would
welcome a large company of fresh settlers. This new flotilla under Gates
was the largest since the 1609 convoy led by the *Sea Venture*. Nine vessels
had departed England in May with three hundred people and a hundred
domestic animals. On board were "the choicest persons we can get," the

Virginia Company said, because "it is not intended anymore to burden the action with vagrant and unnecessary persons."

In the English Channel Gates had encountered the incoming ship of Lord Delaware, who had abandoned the plan to go to Nevis and sailed for home. The two leaders paused at the Isle of Wight to confer on the state of the colony. At harbor in the island town of Cowes, Delaware told Gates that contrary winds had forced his ship to abandon its course for Nevis in favor of making for the Azores. A few weeks spent on those islands had proved beneficial to the governor, whose ailments apparently included scurvy: "I found help for my health, and my sickness assuaged by means of fresh diet, and especially of oranges and lemons, an undoubted remedy and medicine for that disease."

Gates had left Delaware at the Isle of Wight and sailed for Virginia. The voyage had been uneventful, except for a deep personal loss for Gates himself. Among those who traveled with him were his wife (whose name is now lost) and three daughters. Only Gates and daughters Mary, Elizabeth, and Margaret reached Jamestown, however, as "his lady died by the way in some part of the West Indies." Thus it was a grieving Thomas Gates who brought his fleet into Jamestown in August 1611.

William Strachey and the other *Sea Venture* survivors who had remained in Jamestown had not seen their former leader for a year. Those who had stayed behind when Gates returned to London in the summer of 1610 had now spent more time in Jamestown than they had on Bermuda. Gates was a year removed from the wilderness, his recollections of the Bermuda stay and a brief stop in Jamestown overlaid with the routine memories of a year at home. Now an officer of the colony, Strachey resumed his friendship with Gates. As his former commander told stories of life in London—about the theaters, the houses, the food, the social life—the flood of reminiscences was enough to convince Strachey that he had spent sufficient time in the wilderness.

Gates immediately took over the leadership of the colony and Dale returned to his intended role as marshal. Gates's arrival removed any impediment to Dale's immediate deployment upriver to build the new fort. A month after the new settlers arrived, Dale and a large force of 350 headed up the James to the site of the new palisade, while Gates remained at Jamestown with the aim of revitalizing the main settlement. Others headed in the opposite direction—downriver toward the open ocean. To some the arrival of Gates meant their own departure from the New World and return to England. Among those who were homeward bound was William Strachey.

When Strachey boarded the *Prosperous* in the late summer of 1611, he carried his journals, a packet of letters from the colonists to officials and family members in England, and a copy of the laws set down by Gates and Dale. At their request he would publish the laws in England and send them back in book form. Strachey also carried two hooded and tethered New World birds of prey as gifts for patrons of the enterprise. "I brought home from thence this year myself a falcon and a tiercel," Strachey later wrote, "the one sent by Sir Thomas Dale to his highness the prince and the other was presented to the Earl of Salisbury—fair ones." He also carried the cat claws he had found on his last expedition. As the ship cast off from the Jamestown shore and the river gave way to open ocean, William Strachey prepared to resume life in England.

CHAPTER FIFTEEN

Bound for England

Carry this island home in his pocket.
—Sebastian, *The Tempest*

The *Prosperous* reached London in late October or early November 1611. The vessel returned to the city with no advance warning, and so only workers and passersby were on the quay when William Strachey exchanged the woodland paths of Virginia for the muddy lanes of London after more than two years in the wilds.

Strachey's return to his wife, Frances, and sons William Jr., now fifteen, and Edmund, now seven, is undocumented. Surely the appearance of his carriage at the front walk of their house in Crowhurst, Surrey, was a shock to his family. Their initial excitement would have been mixed with surprise at the rough appearance of their husband and father. When the frenzy of the greeting was over, the boys probably stroked the smooth backs of the tethered hawks and examined the dried cat claws their father had carried home. The earthy scent of the Virginia mementos would have brought forth many questions. Strachey certainly recounted his travels in greater detail than the official reports that had reached the family. Frances and the boys probably started the conversation by telling Strachey they had thought him dead for a year—until learning of his survival on Bermuda after a titanic struggle with an Atlantic tempest.

The returning voyager did not linger long in Crowhurst. Strachey was eager to exploit the interest in his writings that had been shown by the letter from Martin. First he would deliver the hawks Thomas Dale had sent by him to Prince Henry and the Earl of Salisbury. Then to put himself in close proximity to members of the Virginia Company, he would again leave his family behind and take a room in the Blackfriars district of London. Once settled, Strachey intended to fulfill his pledge to Dale to publish the Jamestown laws.

On December 13, Strachey formally registered the laws for publication with the Stationers' Company of London under the title *For the Colony in Virginea Britannia, Lawes Divine, Morall and Martiall*. To exploit the exposure the book would provide him, he included an introductory letter of his own addressed to the Virginia Company. Since he suspected the readers might not make it through the letter, he summarized his message in the first sentence: "During the time of my unprofitable service" in Virginia, Strachey said, he had taken it upon himself to serve as a "remembrancer of all accidents, occurrences, and undertakings thereunto." The message was clear—Strachey's time in Virginia had left him poor, but if he were now properly financed he would produce a comprehensive chronicle of Jamestown.

Upon his return to England Strachey found himself once again in need of money for daily subsistence, a disconcerting change after having his food and shelter provided for him in Virginia. The truth was that he had come back from Jamestown without a coin in his pocket. Old friends were generous in the excitement of his return and lent him money, but the attention and funds soon faded. To make matters worse, as soon as moneylender Jasper Tien learned of Strachey's return home he filed suit to recover thirty pounds the Virginia voyager had borrowed years earlier.

What Strachey needed was a patron. He had high hopes that the recipient of his letter from Virginia, Lucy, Countess of Bedford, would be that patron. If he could convince the countess to fund his work just as she did the writings of John Donne, things would be fine. Strachey realized soon after returning home, however, that such an arrangement was an unlikely prospect. Donne had acquired a new patron, Sir Robert Drury, and an angry countess had cut off contact with him (and undoubtedly anyone associated with him as well). In any case, just weeks before Strachey returned, the countess had lost a one-day-old baby and was in seclusion. Thus, all the preparation Strachey had made in sending his letter to the countess and cultivating her favor would be for naught. What's more, Donne would shortly leave on an extended trip to Italy with the family of his new patron, so there would be no opportunity to exploit new connections through him, either.

On the positive side, as a courier for the leaders of Jamestown, Strachey had opportunities to come in contact with wealthy people in the days following his return. He had delivered the hawks Dale sent to Prince Henry and the Earl of Salisbury. In both cases, however, he had been treated as little more than a deliveryman. The lack of attention was perhaps understandable, since just as Strachey returned to London the court of King James was in the midst of hosting a visit by Frederick V of the Palatine, the leading suitor for the hand of James's daughter, Princess Elizabeth. Festivities surrounding the visit were a subject of conversation throughout the city. To Strachey the most notable events associated with the visit were theater productions that had been presented to the royal guest. The highlight of the slate of dramas was a new play by William Shakespeare called *The Tempest*. The production took place at the royal Masquing House on the grounds of Whitehall Palace. The date was November 1, 1611—All Hallows' Day—within a day or two of Strachey's return to London.

The Masquing House was England's most sumptuous theater. In 1606, James had ordered a 1518 banquet hall rebuilt as a theater. The new building was a hundred and seventy feet long and sixty feet wide. A forty-by-forty-foot stage stood at one end, raised three feet off the floor. Tiers of backless wooden benches separated into columned bays accommodated noble members of the audience, while the king and his family sat on a raised platform directly in the center of the audience section. A canopy covered the king's throne, which was even with the height of the stage. Special guests sat on stools at the edge of the royal platform. Candle-filled chandeliers hung from the ceiling.

Thirteen men and four boys presented *The Tempest* (men still played all women's roles onstage). King James and Queen Anna were attired much as they would be a few days later when the Venetian ambassador described them at another event: "The imagination could hardly grasp the gorgeousness of the spectacle. The king's own cloak, breeches, and jacket were all sewn with diamonds, a rope and jewel of diamonds also in his hat of inestimable value." Queen Anna, the ambassador said, "had in her hair a very great number of pear-shaped pearls, the largest and most beautiful in the world; and there were diamonds all over her person, so that she was ablaze."

A contemporary description of a Masquing House drama involving ships at sea—one that may well be an account of this very performance—provides a glimpse of the opening scene of Shakespeare's new play. A Londoner named James Shirley described "waves capering about tall ships" and "a tempest so artificial and sudden in the clouds with a general darkness and thunder so seeming made to threaten, that you would cry out with the mariners in the works, 'You cannot escape drowning.'" On the night of the *Tempest* debut, the applause was as loud as the thunder that had rolled through its opening scene. Backstage, Shakespeare and the King's Men knew that the royal approval would translate into big crowds when they opened the play at the Blackfriars and the Globe.

What Strachey heard about the play intrigued him because it featured a storm and a shipwreck on an enchanted island, much like the one he had just experienced himself. To some in the Masquing House audience the play seemed to be Shakespeare's commentary on England's colonial ambitions. If that was the case, Strachey was eager to see the new drama himself. Fresh from the successful performance at the Masquing House, Shakespeare's King's Men probably opened the play at the Blackfriars Theater soon afterward. One may imagine Strachey attended a show as soon as possible. After all, he was no stranger to the theater—in the old days he had been a part owner of the Blackfriars and visited as often as three times a week—and this was no ordinary play.

Two years earlier when William Shakespeare began contemplating *The Tempest* in 1609 at the age of forty-five, he was the leading playwright of the day—not a giant of literature but an author of popular works of wit and insight. In the months after the *Sea Venture* departed he was contemplating retirement despite being in the midst of his most creative decade. The closing of the theaters during the plague cost him dearly, however, and leisure would have to wait. While he anticipated the end of the plague in the relative safety of Stratford-upon-Avon, he looked for a subject for a new play. As usual, his method of looking for the framework of a new drama was to read widely and to gauge the current interests of his audience.

A book that may have met Shakespeare's gaze as he searched for a theme was William Thomas's 1549 *Historye of Italye*. Thomas tells the story of Prospero Adorno, a duke of Genoa who was deposed in 1461. The book also tells of King Alphonso of Naples, who married a daughter of the Duke of Milan and abdicated in favor of his son Ferdinand. Shakespeare often built his history plays on outlines he drew from accounts of real people of the past. Perhaps these Italian stories offered possibilities. He was partial to the Old World as a setting for his plays, and England's flourishing trade to ports on the Mediterranean Sea made the classical world of current interest to Londoners. Perhaps he could find a way to bring in elements of both the New and Old Worlds, to knit a classical setting onto a colonial theme.

Shakespeare also used ancient texts as a reliable source of ideas. He enjoyed making classical literary allusions in his plays even though many patrons of London's theaters were unable to read. The allusions were included for the benefit of literate theatergoers who considered it a point of pride to identify his sources. Virgil's *Aeneid*, with its story of the founding of an empire, had much to offer. In addition, the playwright surely had Arthur Golding's 1567 translation of Ovid's *Metamorphoses* on his table. Ovid's evocation of a Golden Age intrigued him, especially in light of another work—John Florio's recent translation of Renaissance philosopher Michel de Montaigne's essay "Of the Cannibals." Montaigne moved Ovid's theme of a Golden Age ahead in time, suggesting that the people of the New World were living a Golden Age of coexistence with each other and the natural world.

Reading Montaigne reminded Shakespeare of current events. Here was an intersection of classical and contemporary themes, just the kind of interconnection the playwright could use to craft a play that spoke to the latest concerns of Londoners. The presses of the city were dominated by publications about the New World. At that very time, in fact, the Virginia Company was shifting from its attempt to motivate potential colonists with talk of treasure to a more philosophical approach that imagined the founding of an ideal commonwealth in Virginia. Competing visions of a Golden Age and a savage world were at the ambivalent root of the contemporary debate about New World exploration, and, as Shakespeare knew, conflict is a fine thing to have at the heart of a play.

The obvious books to read for ideas about the New World were collections of explorers' chronicles such as Richard Willes's *History of Travayle in the West and East Indies* (a copy of which William Strachey had taken aboard the *Sea Venture*). Shakespeare had used travel narratives in crafting earlier plays, and perhaps this new one would be no exception. Willes's 1577 collection of writings by explorers included an abridged version of *The History of the West Indies* by Gonzalo Fernández de Oviedo (spelled "Gonzalus Ferdinandus Oviedus" by Willes). Always on the lookout for engaging language sounds, Shakespeare may have paused when he came across the name of that author. Gonzalus Ferdinandus: perhaps that name might adorn a character or two in a play about the New World if he ever put one to paper.

As he read Willes's book, the playwright came across the story from the Magellan voyage about the captured Patagonian native appealing to the deity Setebos. As he read the description of the events that had happened nearly a century earlier at the bottom of the world, Shakespeare mulled the idea that a character in his play might recapitulate the Patagonian's call to Setebos. Such a character might call out to this god as he struggled to understand forced servitude imposed by Europeans who invaded his land. If Shakespeare also picked up Richard Hakluyt's *Principal Navigations, Voyages, Traffiques and Discoveries of the English Nation*, he may have read Job Hartop's story of the Bermuda sea monster—

the part human, part fish monster who resembled a New World man. Maybe the playwright would create a man-monster of his own.

An example of a wild man character was fresh in Shakespeare's mind. The King's Men were at that moment preparing to launch a revival production of the popular anonymous play *Mucedorus*. One of the characters of the play is Bremo—a classic wild man of the forest who displays a mixture of brutishness and refinement. Bremo is a recluse who attacks everyone he encounters, everyone, that is, except a young woman who captures his imagination. A knight kills Bremo, an outcome that always prompts a mixed reaction in the audience. Shakespeare was intrigued by the possibilities of creating a new wild man for the stage, one who might also have an incongruous mix of coarse and sophisticated attributes. If he were to create such a character, a New World play would be a natural setting.

Encounters Shakespeare surely had with indigenous people of Virginia reinforced the playwright's preoccupation with experimenting with Old World perceptions of New World people. During the playwright's lifetime more than thirty-five people were brought across the Atlantic to England, most as curiosities to be displayed to the paying public of London (envoys Namontack and Machumps were conspicuous exceptions). Though many of the kidnapped men and women died soon after arrival, their value as attractions did not cease with their passing. Preserved corpses, decorated with paint and faux costumes, were sometimes made available to the viewing public.

Namontack's presence in London in the summer of 1608 and the winter of 1609 is especially significant, for Shakespeare likely encountered the visitor who his rival Ben Jonson immortalized with a brief mention in a new play, *Epicoene*. Here was a New World man of a "shrewd, subtle capacity" who was encountering the wonders and deceits of the Old World. The technologies of England were marvels to the Powhatan from Tsenacomoco, while the subterfuge of his handlers was not immediately apparent to him (as demonstrated by his positive report to Wahunsenacawh between his two London trips). Just as Jonson saw theatrical possibilities in Namontack, so, too, might Shakespeare. Perhaps he would create a stage version of the Powhatan visitor that was more complex than Jonson's mere mention, a character that might arise from Shakespeare's perception of Namontack as a wild man learning western ways in the service of a European master.

Since the first Jamestown fleet departed England in 1607, exploration of the New World had been the talk of London. The value of that public interest was not lost on William Shakespeare. The playwright possessed a keen ability to discern popular taste and the inclinations of patrons. He surely heard the latest news from Virginia from such well-placed sources as his patron Henry Wriothesley, the Earl of Southampton, who was the most prominent official of the Virginia Company. The ultimate patron of the arts was King James, in whose court any play would have to appear to be deemed a success. Though somewhat skeptical of the value of the Jamestown expeditions and willing to allow the private Virginia Company to do the work, James was closely monitoring the New World enterprise and would want to see any new play that treated it.

Shakespeare's King's Men were well named. The troupe performed at court thirty-seven times in 1610 and 1611. The players even provided private performances for the king during the plague epidemic. Part of their appeal was their cooperation with royal directives. Shakespeare offered little resistance to attempts to shape his plays to the tastes of kings and queens. The approval of the royal Office of the Revels was required before any play was permitted to appear at court. As one observer put it, the royal censors made sure the plays were "rehearsed, perfected, and corrected before they come to the public view of the prince and the nobility." Giving up some creative control could prove lucrative to playwrights and their companies, of course, since shows that did well at court usually played to large audiences when they appeared before the public.

Whatever Shakespeare gave up in fashioning his work to royal and public taste, he could nevertheless be counted on to recapitulate ongoing social debates with keen insight. If the Golden Age dreams of the Virginia Company were being shattered in Jamestown, Shakespeare's audience could be sure that a vision of the New World from his quill would reflect that reality. If critics of the Virginia enterprise were charging that colonists were invading, exploiting, and brutalizing the people of the New World, a Shakespeare play with a colonial theme would certainly incorporate that criticism. Those deeper themes were the most important elements the playwright would draw from the Jamestown chronicles. The turns of phrase he would purloin would be clues leading to that treasure.

The influence of playwrights as social commentators was stronger than ever during the period in which *The Tempest* was written. The Virginia Company was exquisitely sensitive to its depiction on the stages of the city. In his February 1610 sermon to the departing Lord Delaware, William Crashaw made a special point of disparaging the influence of "the players" on the Virginia enterprise. "Nothing that is good, excellent, or holy can escape them," Crashaw said. "How then can this action? But this may suffice, that they are *players*. They abuse Virginia, but they are but *players*. They disgrace it, true, but they are but *players*. And they have played with better things."

A Shakespeare play about the New World would, of course, be deeper than a simple lampooning of the Jamestown enterprise. The Virginia Company could be counted on to oppose even the most innocuous depiction, but that didn't bother Shakespeare. His aim was to create art that would both resonate with a general audience and subtly fulfill the wishes of the most important member of the audience, King James. In fact, a current development in the royal family provided a sure way to curry royal favor. All London was aware that King James's daughter, Princess Elizabeth, would soon choose a royal suitor from the continent, and that the likeliest choice was Frederick V of the Palatine. A play in which a fictional father with transcendent powers saw a daughter happily betrothed would certainly interest the royal family and might even be an appropriate entertainment for a royal engagement celebration.

All those strands of thought were well and good, but Shakespeare still needed a dramatic center around which to build a play. The inherent interest of the theatergoing public was there, as were the pithy themes that naturally arose from the clash of Old and New World cultures. But something more was needed, something vivid, dramatic, and heart pounding that would set the audience on edge from the first line. He would read the printed announcements and pamphlets along with his classical texts, talk to as many people as possible, and wait for something to inspire him.

When Thomas Gates returned from the dead to London in September 1610, Shakespeare had his story. One of the most dramatic sea tales to reach London in years would provide the framework of his new drama. First he read Silvester Jourdain's *Discovery of the Barmodas* and Richard Rich's *Newes from Virginia*. Then the Virginia Company's *True Declaration of the Estate of the Colonie in Virginia* appeared in London bookstores. Ironically, in the pages of its triumphant account of the survival of its colonial governor, the company called the loss and return of the *Sea Venture* survivors a "tragical comedy." In the hands of England's preeminent playwright, it would become just that.

Shakespeare's most important source, William Strachey's letter to his "Excellent Lady," came into the playwright's hands sometime in the weeks after it reached London in September 1610. He may have been given a copy by an acquaintance associated with the Virginia Company, but perhaps the most likely place he saw it was at a printer's shop in St. Paul's churchyard, a few doors from the Blackfriars Theater. William Welby was the publisher of most of the Virginia chronicles. In an introduction he wrote to a 1613 reprint of Jourdain's 1610 *Sea Venture* account, Welby said that he had in his possession an unpublished account of the Bermuda shipwreck that was a "more full and exact description of the country and narration of the nature, site, and commodities, together with a true history of the great deliverance of Sir Thomas Gates and his company upon them." This was almost surely Strachey's letter, and given the animosity officials of the Virginia Company felt toward the players of London, it is more likely that Shakespeare borrowed the narrative from Welby than from a company official.

The Blackfriars Theater was a wood-framed stone structure with dormer windows that held five hundred paying customers. Some of the most popular seats were stools lining the sides of the stage (a tradition that annoyed the actors but was too lucrative to give up). Theater was the primary mode of entertainment for men and women of all classes, and fifteen thousand Londoners saw plays each week. Most attended large open-air playhouses like the Globe, which accommodated audiences of up to twenty-five hundred. Theaters were also housed in smaller roofed buildings that provided a more comfortable all-weather experience and appealed to the upper class. As playwright John Marston put it, in the roofed theater "a man shall not be choked with the stench of garlic nor be pasted to the barmy jacket of a beer brewer" as he might be if he watched a play among the groundlings of an open-air house.

The Blackfriars Theater reopened in 1608 as the first enclosed venue for adult actors, having featured child actors in the early years when William Strachey was part owner. The Blackfriars was the first playhouse of any kind within London's city walls. The owners managed to circumvent a prohibition against theaters within the city because the building was a former monastery and a religious exemption to local laws remained in place. The increasing popularity of the more intimate setting of the enclosed theater prompted changes in the plays themselves—more music and dancing were presented; facial expressions became more important than grand gestures; and plays were broken into acts for the first time so that workers could replenish candles for lighting. *The Tempest* had all of those characteristics and was the first play Shakespeare tailored to the demands of the Blackfriars venue.

The Tempest did indeed play to large crowds at the Blackfriars following the Masquing House triumph. If William Strachey saw a performance, he would have entered comfortably in advance of the King's Men's regular 2:00 p.m. start time. The audience entered the Blackfriars by way of a stately staircase that led to the former monastery dining hall. The theater was housed in the very chamber in which Roman Catholic officials had heard arguments about whether they should grant a divorce to Henry VIII and Catherine of Aragon. The interior was lit with light from windows, but candelabra provided much of the illumination and would remain lit during the performance. The stage was plain, and a small balcony provided a second level for the players. Strachey would have selected a seat on a bench and waited for the show to begin.

CHAPTER SIXTEEN

Blackfriars Surprise

Into something rich and strange.
—Ariel, *The Tempest*

As William Strachey awaited the beginning of *The Tempest* in the Blackfriars, he may have mulled the associations evoked by the very title of the play. Those connections may have been truer than he realized, as the title is the most conspicuous of the language Shakespeare may have drawn from the Virginia chronicles. "Tempest" was a common synonym for "storm," but one example of its use in the *Sea Venture* narratives stands out. The anonymous author of a Virginia Company pamphlet gave the word special emphasis even by the standards of the day. In listing the problems caused by the storm that scattered the Gates fleet, the writer capitalized and italicized the word: "First, the *Tempest*: and can any man expect an answer for that?" Perhaps Shakespeare answered the rhetorical question with a storm of his own.

The Tempest opened on the deck of a ship at sea in a storm. "A tempestuous noise of thunder and lightning" filled the theater, according to the play's stage directions. Pebbles rolled in a drum created the rumbling and a hand-cranked canvas fan just offstage provided wind. The Blackfriars was too small for pyrotechnic squibs, so sound and wind effects sufficed to create the *Tempest* storm. As the stage directions also specify, when the *Tempest* actors appeared onstage their hair had been doused with water.

Wind, rain, and thunder—to Strachey the stage action would already have been a reminder of the hurricane of July 1609. Then the parallels began to appear. One of Shakespeare's storm-swept wayfarers—in one of only two times the playwright used the word *glut*—said the ocean did "gape at widest to glut" the boatswain of the *Tempest* ship. Strachey may have recalled that in his narrative he had described the air as filled with a "glut of water." The *Tempest* passengers then expressed their fear that the ship would break up in the violent sea, saying, "Mercy on us!— We split, we split!" That seemed odd to Strachey, since he had written of the *Sea Venture* passengers that "there was not a moment in which sudden splitting or instant oversetting of the ship was not expected." On the stage the boatswain complained that the cries of the passengers were louder than the storm or the calls of the mariners: "A plague upon this howling. They are louder than the weather or our office." Why he, too, had written that the lamentations of the *Sea Venture* passengers were lost in the wind and shouts of the officers. Both ships, too, were taking on water. The pervasive leak that hampered the *Sea Venture* was a relatively rare occurrence, yet one of Shakespeare's characters said the *Tempest* vessel was "as leaky as an unstanched wench." This was a revelation to Strachey—it was almost as if the storm that tossed the *Sea Venture* was swept in its tumultuous whole from the pages of his own narrative to the seas surrounding the *Tempest* ship. Shakespeare had his attention now.

As the opening scene of the play continued, noblemen arrayed in the finery of an Italian court joined the sailors on deck. The characters revealed that the ship was carrying Alonso, the king of Naples, and his son Ferdinand. The king's adviser, Gonzalo—called in the cast list "an honest old councillor"—then began a testy exchange with the boatswain. Gonzalo told the mariner to keep in mind that the king was aboard his vessel, and the annoyed boatswain told the elite passenger to get out of the way and allow him and his sailors to battle the storm. To Strachey the appearance of Gonzalo, the aged adviser to the king in *The Tempest*, may have reminded him of George Somers, the gray-haired counselor of the governor on Bermuda. Both Gonzalo and George established early on that they were as comfortable wrangling with sailors as they were advising leaders. Each straddled the visceral world of the sailors and the intellectual world of the colony's noblemen.

Next the enchanted *Tempest* isle was revealed to Strachey and the other patrons in the Blackfriars audience. The action moved to the island of the magician Prospero, who emerged onstage attired in a long robe. With him was his daughter, Miranda, who was played by a boy dressed as a noblewoman. Miranda asked her father whether he conjured up the storm and, seeing the ship in distress offshore, pleaded with him to calm the waters. The description of the storm by the fair Miranda, to Strachey's ear, sounded remarkably familiar. Strachey remembered that he had written of a "roaring" storm that was "a hell of darkness turned black upon us." Miranda seemed to evoke those images when she asked her father whether he "put the wild waters in this roar" and created a sky as black as "stinking pitch." Furthermore, Strachey knew he had written "the sea swelled above the clouds, and gave battle unto heaven" and "at length did beat all light from heaven." Thus it added to his surprise when Miranda used a similar image, saying "the sea, mounting to th' welkin's cheek"—in other words, to the edge of heaven—"dashes the fire out."

Strachey may have noticed a clever twist in Miranda's description of the storm. The play had been originally written for the Masquing House, and in that well-appointed venue squibs hanging above the stage would have flashed lightning during the storm scene. Smoke from the squibs would have drifted over the audience, and the scent of gunpowder would have permeated the hall as Miranda spoke her lines. The aroma would have given special meaning to her description of the black sky as "sulphurous" and resembling "stinking pitch." Those words best describe stage effects used to create a theatrical storm rather than a real one. The playwright thus subtly reinforced to the audience that Prospero created the *Tempest* storm with magic tricks, just as the stagehands had created the theatrical storm they were watching onstage.

The scene continued with Prospero reassuring his daughter that, while he did use his magic to create the storm, the people on the ship were in no danger. "No more amazement," he told Miranda. "Tell your piteous heart there's no harm done." Prospero's use of the word *amazement* likely pleased Strachey. *Amazement* was a favorite word of his, too—in fact he had used it three times in his description of the reaction of the *Sea Venture* passengers to the storm. By the closing act of *The Tempest*, Strachey would learn that three times, too, Shakespeare's characters would use the word.

Twelve years earlier, Prospero told Miranda, he was the rightful duke of Milan. His brother Antonio, in league with Alonso, the King of Naples, overthrew him and set Prospero and Miranda adrift at sea. His friend Gonzalo managed to smuggle them the magician's treasured books and clothes before they were set to sea in a small boat. Father and young daughter eventually shipwrecked on the island, and there Prospero raised Miranda. Now, by chance, Alonso and Antonio's ship was passing the island, and so the magician raised a storm to bring his enemies to the island.

Using his magic Prospero then induced Miranda to fall asleep and called for the sprite Ariel. Ariel entered dressed in a costume that probably featured a multicolored silk tunic and silver wings. The young man playing the part would have several costume changes as the play progressed, appearing later as a water nymph in a crown of seashells, in a cape depicting invisibility, and as a giant batlike harpy. As Ariel and Prospero talked, it was revealed that a now-dead witch named Sycorax had come to the island before Prospero and imprisoned the sprite in a split pine trunk. The magician had released the nymph and now treated him as an indentured servant whom he promised one day to set free. At the bidding of his master, Ariel had flown to the storm-tossed royal ship to put a fright into those on board. He reported to an eager Prospero that he haunted the vessel as a glowing apparition: "I boarded the King's ship: now on the beak, now in the waist, the deck, in every cabin I flamed amazement. Sometime I'd divide and burn in many places—on the topmast, the yards and bowsprit would I flame distinctly, then meet and join."

The image left William Strachey bemused. The mariners of the *Sea Venture* who saw St. Elmo's fire in the rigging were apparently not the only ones to "make many constructions of this sea fire." Shakespeare's description of the flitting sprite appeared to be a brilliant reworking of his own account of the darting light on the masts and ropes of the Jamestown-bound ship. Strachey had written of "an apparition of a little round light like a faint star, trembling and streaming along with a sparkling blaze half the height upon the mainmast, and shooting sometimes from shroud to shroud, tempting to settle as it were upon any of the four shrouds, and for three or four hours together, or rather more, half the night it kept with us, running sometimes along the main yard to the very end, and then returning." Though the buoyant sprite of *The Tempest* came of age in the imagination of the master playwright, it seemed he was born in the early morning hours of Friday, July 28, 1609, in the rigging of the distressed *Sea Venture*.

Shakespeare enhanced his portrait of Ariel by giving him an attribute of St. Elmo's fire not mentioned in the Virginia chronicles but known to mariners of his day. Through the ages, those who have seen the mesmerizing electrical glow have told of a bizarre side effect: the luminescent force can also make the heads and hands of people glow and cause their hair to stand on end. Ariel described just such an effect in his report to Prospero: "All but mariners plunged in the foaming brine and quit the vessel; then all afire with me, the King's son Ferdinand, with hair up-staring (then like reeds, not hair), was the first man that leapt." The line makes it clear that Strachey and Shakespeare both had St. Elmo's fire in mind as they wrote.

Ariel then noted from the Blackfriars stage that Prospero used his magic to hold the king's ship unharmed in a "nook," a place that sounded suspiciously like the cleft in the rock that held the *Sea Venture* upright in the Bermuda surf. "Safely in harbour is the King's ship," Strachey heard Ariel tell Prospero when the magician asked about the location of the *Tempest* vessel, "in the deep nook where once thou called'st me up at midnight to fetch dew from the still-vexed Bermudas; there she's hid." *Bermudas*—the word came as a shock to William Strachey. Why had Shakespeare chosen to include in a play set on a Mediterranean island a reference to another island thousands of miles away, an allusion that was inexplicable unless *The Tempest* was inspired by the startling news of the survival of the *Sea Venture* castaways on the mid-Atlantic isle. Here in another guise was the gentle wreck of the flagship of the Virginia fleet, a ship that had grounded in a "nook" while its passengers removed in safety to "the still-vexed Bermudas." Strachey needed no more convincing. Now he knew he was watching his letter to the "Excellent Lady" transformed by Shakespeare into his latest stage magic.

To Strachey, Bermuda's enchanted reputation seemed to survive within *The Tempest* as the magical qualities of Prospero's isle. The origin of Bermuda's charmed character lay in the oft-reported stories of generations of sailors who believed Bermuda a stormy place of treacherous shallows and strange howlings. Strachey and his fellow castaways had long before marveled at the contrast between that reputation and the miraculous delivery of the *Sea Venture* voyagers from a foundering ship to an island of bounty. The Devil's Isle that was Bermuda before the wreck seem to provide the darker facets of *The Tempest*—indeed, Strachey probably noticed that characters on the stage would repeat the word *devil* a dozen times in the play. From the bountiful paradise discovered after the wreck seemed to have come the lighter elements. *The Tempest* artfully combined the two faces of Bermuda that Strachey knew so well—the Devil's Isle it once was and the gentle land it became.

Onstage the dialogue between Ariel and Prospero continued. The people who the magician had wanted to come ashore had done so, the sprite told his master, and the others were put to sleep inside the ship. If Strachey had read the pamphlet his fellow *Sea Venture* passenger Silvester Jourdain had published after arriving back in London, he may have noticed that the sleeping mariners of *The Tempest* may have had an origin in the *Sea Venture* chronicles as well. Strachey himself had written that the people on the flagship were in such despair that they nearly resolved to "shut up hatches" and wait for the vessel to sink. Jourdain added the detail that may have caught Shakespeare's eye when he said that the passengers and crew of the *Sea Venture* "were so overwearied" during the final hours at sea that they had "fallen asleep in corners and wheresoever they chanced first to sit or lie." In the combination of the two passages Shakespeare may have found the kernel of the weariness that would afflict his *Tempest* sailors—the place coming from Strachey and the overwhelming drowsiness from Jourdain. "The mariners all under hatches stowed, who," Ariel said, "with a charm joined to their suffered labour, I have left asleep." Toward the end of the play Prospero would order Ariel back to the ship to wake the crew: "To the King's ship, invisible as thou art; there shalt thou find the mariners asleep under the hatches." After they emerged from their slumber, a bleary-eyed boatswain would be mystified as to why they had fallen asleep: "We were dead of sleep and—how we know not—all clapped under hatches."

The image of a broken fleet bereft of its governor was another image that William Shakespeare apparently could not resist. Once again, a detail of the Jamestown story reemerged in the playwright's remaking of the *Sea Venture* chronicles of the New World. Ariel reported to Prospero that after the magical storm scattered the ships of King Alonso's convoy, "the rest o'th' fleet, which I dispersed, they all met again, and are upon the Mediterranean float, bound sadly home for Naples, supposing that they saw the King's ship wrecked and his great person perish." Thus Shakespeare seemingly recapitulated the story of a leader lost on a rain-whipped night and a dispirited fleet reuniting and sailing on without him. The image reminded Strachey of the stories he had heard in Jamestown about the reuniting of the Third Supply after the hurricane and their sadness at apparently losing their leader in the wreck of the flagship. Perhaps the playwright even drew on Strachey's description of the castaways sailing "sadly up the river" when they finally reached Point Comfort and learned of the difficulties Jamestown had experienced after the disappearance of the governor.

The first act of *The Tempest* continued with Prospero's dismissing Ariel and awakening his daughter to tell her they would visit Caliban. The *Tempest* cast list calls Caliban "a savage and deformed slave." He is the son of the witch Sycorax, who arrived pregnant on the island. By the time Prospero and Miranda arrived, Sycorax was dead and Caliban was wandering the island alone. At first the father and daughter treated the wild man kindly, until he attempted to rape Miranda. From that time on he was a slave for life.

Caliban's entrance on the Blackfriars stage was the most dramatic of the afternoon. The servant monster's costume was of the earth and sea, probably consisting of a leather tunic, long hair, and beard. *The Tempest* was peppered with comments about the appearance of the "savage and deformed slave." He was called a "deboshed fish," "half a fish and half a monster," "puppy-headed" (meaning foolish looking rather than literally having the features of a dog), and "mooncalf." To Antonio he was "a plain fish"; to Alonso "a strange thing as e'er I looked on"; and to Prospero a "misshapen knave." Despite all of those word portraits, Caliban's costume was relatively simple, and it was the skill of the actor that animated his character.

As Strachey watched Caliban onstage, he kept coming back to the descriptions of sea turtles he had included in his *Sea Venture* narrative. Caliban had a strange mix of attributes that seemed a hodgepodge of animal allusions from a particular line of Strachey's narrative. Strachey wrote that the sea turtle is "a kind of meat, as a man can neither absolutely call fish nor flesh," and that it spends its days "feeding upon sea grass like a heifer, in the bottom of the coves and bays." In *The Tempest* Prospero called the slow-moving Caliban "tortoise," and another character wondered whether he was "a man or a fish." Caliban appeared to be "half a fish and half a monster" and a kind of sea-turtle man—"legged like a man and his fins like arms." Strachey's suggestion that sea turtles were like grazing cows also seemed to reemerge in Caliban. On five occasions Stephano and Trinculo called the *Tempest* monster a "mooncalf," a term for a deformed child born on a full moon, but one also with bovine overtones that may have reminded Strachey of his own image of a marine heifer.

Bermuda cedars may have made an appearance that day on the Blackfriars stage, too. The idea of seething berries in fresh water seemed to have piqued Shakespeare's interest. In a reference that seemed odd to Strachey unless the source was the *Sea Venture* chronicles, Caliban mentioned that when Prospero first came to the island the magician "wouldst give me water with berries in't." True, in describing their homemade liquor the castaways had spent most of their time talking about bibby, a libation made from the sap of the palmetto tree. Strachey, however, had written of a second drink made from cedar berries. As he watched *The Tempest* he may have even been able to recall the passage. He remembered writing about the cedar tree, "the berries whereof our men seething, straining, and letting stand some three or four days made a kind of pleasant drink." Remarkably, the fermented berry liquor he himself had drunk on Bermuda seemed to be a favorite of the monster he was watching on the Blackfriars stage.

The birthplace of the mother of the *Tempest* monster was also familiar to William Strachey. Shakespeare set the play in the Mediterranean, and a mention of a city on its coast seemed to link the play to Strachey even though the *Sea Venture* was far removed from those waters. Strachey stopped in Algiers on the North African coast in 1606 as he voyaged to Turkey to serve as secretary to the British merchant company there, and in his account of the *Sea Venture* storm he mentioned that he did so. In describing the hurricane, Strachey recalled that he experienced less violent storms "upon the coast of Barbary and Algeere, in the Levant." Shakespeare seemed to have picked up on that allusion, for twice in *The Tempest* it was mentioned that Caliban's mother, the witch Sycorax, was banished from Algiers before she came to Prospero's island.

Caliban and Miranda may have bloodlines in another Jamestown narrative. John Smith's book *True Relation of Such Occurrences and Accidents of Noate* was published—probably without his permission—in 1608 before Strachey departed on the *Sea Venture*. The work was available on the shelves of London booksellers when Shakespeare was writing *The*

Tempest. In it Smith tells of a visit to Jamestown by Wahunsenacawh's daughter Pocahontas: "Powhatan," Smith wrote, "understanding we detained certain savages, sent his daughter, a child of ten years old, which not only for feature, countenance, and proportion much exceeded any of the rest of his people, but for wit and spirit, the only nonpareil of his country." Caliban echoes the most distinctive word of Smith's *True Relation* account, suggesting that the heart of Pocahontas may beat in Shakespeare's Miranda. While Shakespeare used the term *nonpareil* in five of his plays, his use of it in *The Tempest* just after it had appeared in a work of relevance to the theme of the play suggests the playwright may have read Smith. "And that most deeply to consider is the beauty of his daughter," Caliban said from the stage as he described Prospero's view of Miranda, "he himself calls her a nonpareil." Along with his description of Pocahontas, Smith describes a man that Wahunsenacawh sent to accompany Pocahontas on the visit. Smith characterizes the chaperone as the Powhatan leader's "most trusty messenger, called Rawhunt, as much exceeding in deformity of person, but of a subtle wit and crafty understanding." The description is suggestive of Caliban's description in *The Tempest*'s list of actors, in which the wild man is described as "a savage and deformed slave."

Strachey couldn't help but think that Namontack and Machumps, too, may have contributed to the character of Caliban. The *Tempest* monster was probably singing about New World fish traps when he celebrated his impending liberation from Prospero with a song that began, "No more dams I'll make for fish." While all the printed mentions of the two Powhatans on the *Sea Venture* were published after Shakespeare composed his play, their presence on the ship and the disappearance of Namontack on Bermuda were a topic of discussion in London while the playwright composed *The Tempest*. There was good reason to believe it, since characters portrayed on the Blackfriars stage that afternoon explicitly alluded to New World visitors to London when Trinculo suggested that he and Stephano would become rich if they brought Caliban home and exhibited him as a curiosity in exchanges for coins:

"When they will not give a doit to relieve a lame beggar," Trinculo says, "they will lay out ten to see a dead Indian." When Trinculo alluded to a "painted" Caliban he may have been referring to cosmetics sometimes applied previous to the display of a New World inhabitant (whether alive or dead): "Were I in England now (as once I was) and had but this fish painted, not a holiday fool there but would give a piece of silver."

Just as Caliban and Miranda might have roots in Jamestown, so, too, might Ferdinand, the son of the king of Naples and Miranda's love interest. Hearing the name that Shakespeare chose for his leading man, Strachey would have been reminded of Sir Ferdinando Weynman, the man who had arrived at Jamestown with Delaware and later died there. Weynman was the second man Strachey had mentioned in his letter to the "Excellent Lady" who had a variant of the name Ferdinand, the first being *History of the West Indies* author Gonzalo Fernández de Oviedo (known as "Gonzalus Ferdinandus Oviedus" to the author of the book Strachey carried). Perhaps the repetition of the name had been enough to fix it in Shakespeare's mind as he mulled what to call the lover of the fair Miranda.

At the close of the first act, Prospero asked Ariel to draw in Ferdinand, who was wandering the island alone. During the course of the play, Miranda would be smitten with the prince, and the two would fall in love. Ferdinand would choose a peculiar way to prove his love. Miranda would discover him stacking wood on Prospero's orders, and she would beg him to rest. Ferdinand would refuse, saying he carried the wood on her behalf. His "wooden slavery" was a self-imposed condition for her benefit, he would say: "For your sake am I this patient log-man." To Strachey the scene was reminiscent of his description of Thomas Gates on Bermuda patiently cutting wood for the construction on the pinnaces. In Strachey's account, the governor did so to show his workers that he was willing to work himself and thereby convince them by example "to fell, carry, and saw cedar fit for the carpenters' purpose."

Early in the play, however, Ferdinand was preoccupied with grief over the supposed death of his father, Alonso. In Ferdinand's musings, Strachey might have wondered whether Shakespeare imagined the undersea world of the Bermuda pearl divers. Ariel described a tropical lagoon as he sang a lament about the supposedly drowned king. As he did so, he evoked the magic of the *Tempest* isle: "Full fathom five thy father lies, of his bones are coral made; those are pearls that were his eyes, nothing of him that doth fade but doth suffer a sea-change into something rich and strange."

At the end of the second act of *The Tempest*, William Strachey relaxed on his bench and mulled the scenes that had just passed before him. The transformation of his narrative captivated the former Virginia voyager. He was pleased to have a part in Shakespeare's entertainment, and the insight it provided into the playwright's literary method fascinated and inspired him. Strachey would watch the rest of the play with interest and see if he could discern more of his own words in the lines and themes of the magical drama unfolding at the Blackfriars.

CHAPTER SEVENTEEN

Bermuda Ghosts

Such stuff as dreams are made on.

—Prospero, *The Tempest*

As the second act of *The Tempest* opened, William Strachey and the rest of the *Tempest* audience watched Ferdinand and his father, Alonso, wander Prospero's island, both unaware that the other was alive. Both were under the impression that the other had perished, even though—perhaps not surprisingly, given the play's origin in the *Sea Venture* story—no one on the *Tempest* ship had actually suffered harm. As he grieved for his son, Alonso imagined that a grotesquely large fish had eaten his castaway son, lamenting, "What strange fish hath made his meal on thee?" The line is oddly reminiscent of Strachey's aside about the remora—a fish that in legend grows to enormous size and intervenes in human affairs.

The scene suggested another parallel between the *Sea Venture* story and *The Tempest*. Publications put out by the Virginia Company after the loss of the flagship suggested that its voyagers might have survived on some remote shore. In light of the facts then known, the suggestion was excessively optimistic, even if in hindsight it proved to be entirely accurate. William Shakespeare included in *The Tempest* a similar case of misplaced optimism that turned out to be true. In the play, Alonso's servant Francisco tried to comfort him by arguing without rational basis that Ferdinand had survived the wreck, which in fact he had. Sebastian had trouble believing Francisco's overly cheerful assessment, saying that the cities to which the *Tempest* voyagers would return would "have more widows in them of this business' making than we bring men to comfort them." Furthermore, as the king and his handlers wandered after the

wreck, Adrian called the *Tempest* island "uninhabitable and almost inaccessible." The statement is a succinct echo of the *Sea Venture* voyagers'
assessment of Bermuda (or more precisely, their perception of the island
before they landed and found it eminently habitable if accessed by luck).
Few ocean islands in the world were *inaccessible,* and so Shakespeare's
use of the term to describe the *Tempest* isle would have been especially
telling to Bermuda veteran William Strachey.

The action of *The Tempest* then shifted to yet another band of castaways wandering the island unaware that others had survived the storm.
Now began a dual story line of plots against the leaders—one a serious
conspiracy by Prospero's brother Antonio against King Alonso, and the
other a comic scheme against the life of Prospero by the drunken butler
Stephano, the court jester Trinculo, and Caliban. The manner in which
the three comic mutineers met reinforced Caliban's origin as a sea-turtle
man. As the scene opened, Caliban mistook an approaching Trinculo
for a spirit of the isle and lay down to feign death. When a thunderstorm
threatened, the jester climbed on top of the prone Caliban, joining the
wild man underneath his cloak to avoid the rain. Stephano then came
upon the other two, unaware that Trinculo had survived the wreck. All
that was sticking out from under the cloak—turtlelike—was Caliban's
head between Trinculo's feet at one end and Caliban's feet at the other.
Stephano mistakes his find as "some monster of the isle, with four legs,"
until he recognizes Trinculo's voice and pulls him out from under the
cloak.

Trinculo's entrance reinforced the frivolous tone of the scene, his
costume cuing the audience that he was a comedian. During the course
of the play Caliban would insult him as a "pied ninny" and a "scurvy
patch." True to those hints, when the jester appeared onstage he wore the
patchwork apparel of a court comedian, including the classic belled cap
of a motley fool. The costume of his companion Stephano was nothing
unusual, but his name may have struck one member of the audience as
curious. William Strachey may have sensed an echo of the inept mutiny
of Stephen Hopkins of Bermuda in the comic rebellion of Stephano of

The Tempest. In reading Strachey's narrative of the castaways' time on Bermuda, Shakespeare may have seen a clownish stage character in the pathetic supplications of Hopkins. The conspiracy of Stephano, Trinculo, and Caliban would serve as a comic version of the more significant machinations of Antonio and Sebastian against Alonso. In the plot of the Bermuda mutineer named Stephen, Shakespeare may have seen the possibility of a slapstick rebel named Stephano.

Stephano's method of getting to shore from the distressed *Tempest* ship may also have had an origin in Strachey's chronicle. Strachey wrote that when *Sea Venture* voyagers lightened the leaking ship, they threw overboard trunks, chests, and heavy guns, and dumped the contents of "many a butt of beer, hogshead of oil, cider, wine, and vinegar." While casks of wine were dumped over the side of the *Sea Venture*, at least one had been pitched intact from the *Tempest* ship. "I escaped upon a butt of sack," Stephano said, "which the sailors heaved o'erboard." The cask of wine proved a double benefit, serving Stephano both as a float at sea and a source of drink on the island. He gave Caliban his first drink of alcohol, and the servant monster so enjoyed the result that he proclaimed Stephano to be heaven-sent and pledged his loyalty.

In order to impress his new master, Caliban promised to gather them the fine things of the island. To the ear of the Virginia voyager, the bounty the monster pledged to gather was something that sounded suspiciously like the cahows the *Sea Venture* castaways found living in holes in the Bermuda ground. What Strachey probably heard that afternoon from the Blackfriars stage was Caliban say he would gather nuts, capture marmosets, and "get thee young seamels from the rock." The word is presumably pronounced "sea-mell," a variation of the term Strachey used in his narrative to identify the cahow—"sea-mew." Twelve years after the *Tempest* debut, the word would apparently be inadvertently changed to "scamel" when a typesetter misread Shakespeare's now-lost manuscript, mistaking an "e" for a "c" and in the process adding a new word to the English language. The highly influential First Folio version of *The Tempest* would give the word as "scamel," evidently enshrining a casual error as a new word that has been dutifully included in dictionaries ever since.

The cries of sea-mews seemed to be heard in more ways than one on the afternoon Strachey watched *The Tempest*. The nighttime hunting technique of the *Sea Venture* survivors, which Strachey in his narrative called "lowbelling," has a corollary in *The Tempest* as well. From the stage Sebastian proposed that the shipwrecked *Tempest* party go "bat-fowling," or nocturnal hunting with clubs and lights. The haunting calls that the voyagers heard on those hunting trips also seemed to echo in the play. On Prospero's island Sebastian reported hearing a "hollow burst of bellowing, like bulls, or rather lions." Later the theater was filled with music played by the invisible Ariel. "Be not afeard," Caliban told Stephano and Trinculo as the music began. "This isle is full of noises, sounds and sweet airs that give delight and hurt not. Sometimes a thousand twangling instruments will hum about mine ears." Still later, the boatswain described being awakened by "strange and several noises of roaring, shrieking, howling, jingling chains and more diversity of sounds, all horrible." Strachey would surely have heard all of these mysterious wails as the nocturnal cries of Bermuda birds transformed into enchanted airs on the Blackfriars stage.

Just as William Strachey had written about "bloody issues and mischiefs" arising in the Bermuda camp of the castaways, so, too, did Shakespeare put "bloody thoughts" in the heads of his *Tempest* mutineers. Life on Bermuda also featured punishment imposed by a leader who was at once harsh and indulgent, and so did Shakespeare's drama on the stage. Strachey described discontent among the *Sea Venture* castaways as a "desire forever to inhabit here"; in *The Tempest* he may have recognized his phrase transformed into Ferdinand's declaration "Let me live here ever!" and the musings of Gonzalo on what life would be like "had I plantation of this isle." In Ariel and Caliban the Virginia voyager in the audience may have sensed a kinship with the laborers and artisans of the *Sea Venture*, whose indentures to the Virginia Company served as their tickets to Jamestown. In *The Tempest* Ariel acted as the loyal indentured servant to the most powerful man on the island, chafing under onerous contractual terms but nevertheless serving without complaint. Ariel is the descendant of William Strachey and his ilk, including the informants who betrayed mutinies hatched by their compatriots. At the other end of the spectrum, Caliban's plots of murder mirror those of the rebellious voyagers of the Bermuda expedition.

As Strachey mulled the ideas put forth in the speeches of the characters onstage, the stark contrast of Jametown's inexplicably apathetic populace in the midst of an imagined paradise also may have come to mind. The failure of expectations to match reality in the New World was a principal point of contention in an ongoing public debate about the value of exploration, and Strachey would not be surprised to find that it was a theme of *The Tempest*, as well. Sure enough, the issue emerged in explicit form when Gonzalo launched into an extended rumination on what he would do "had I plantation of this isle." Gonzalo pictured a Golden Age on Prospero's island—using the signature phrase of philosopher Michel de Montaigne, who suggested that the people of the New World lived in an uncorrupted Eden. The *Tempest* counselor said that were he to possess the *Tempest* isle he would establish a society in which there was no need for a legal system; poverty would cease to exist, food would be plentiful, and there would be "no occupation, all men idle, all; and women, too, but innocent and pure; no sovereignty." Sebastian and Antonio served as foils in the scene, badgering Gonzalo as he mused. When Gonzalo said the *Tempest* isle offered "everything advantageous to life," Antonio sarcastically responded, "True, save means to live." Gonzalo's proposal that the ideal state would feature "all men idle" in particular drew the derision of the wits. "All idle—whores and knaves," said Antonio.

To a Jamestown veteran such was William Strachey, the musings of Gonzalo would have seemed a virtual recapitulation of the Virginia Company pamphlets that depicted Jamestown as a paradise awaiting the establishment of an ideal commonwealth. Gonzalo's imagined plantation was Shakespeare's distillation of the arguments of the colonialists at their wildly optimistic peak. The playwright, demonstrating why his literature would be so enduring, presented both sides of the question in equally strong terms. The pointed repartee of Sebastian and Antonio perfectly reflected the pessimism of reports that depicted drought-ravaged Jamestown as a barren and spiritless colony of helpless laggards. These were arguments the people of London would recognize, and Shakespeare delivered them as usual with the best and worst aspects of both positions fully explored. Here was an example of his ability to penetrate a debate on current events and lay it gleamingly bare in a way that is eminently entertaining.

To Strachey the coincidences were tumbling from the Blackfriars stage. He would probably have noticed that the characters of the play were preoccupied with water quality. Both Prospero and Caliban threatened to punish others by withholding fresh water and forcing them to drink salt water. Caliban especially seemed to evoke Strachey's fears of the Jamestown well when he wished Prospero to suffer the consequences of poor drinking water: Strachey described "fens, marshes, ditches, muddy pools," while Caliban in *The Tempest* said, "all the infections that the sun sucks up from bogs, fens, flats, on Prosper fall, and make him by inchmeal a disease!" Ariel also commented on the questionable water of the *Tempest* isle, mentioning a "filthy-mantled pool" near Prospero's cave from which Trinculo emerged to complain, "I do smell all horse piss." Like the briny flow of the James River, it seemed, the contaminated water of Prospero's island was a source of illness.

Shakespeare and Strachey were equally fond of classical allusions, and the playwright may have written one into *The Tempest* that he read in the voyager's account. Strachey was drawing on Virgil's *Aeneid* when he said the Jamestown fort was located on "a low level of ground about half an acre (or so much as Queen Dido might buy of King Hyarbas, which she compassed about with the thongs cut out of one bull hide and therein built her castle at Byrza)." Queen Dido makes an appearance in *The Tempest*, as well, when the play's characters debate whether she was from Carthage or Tunis on the Barbary Coast. Though Shakespeare needed no excuse to draw on one of his favorite classical texts, his prominent allusion to Dido suggests that he was reading Strachey's chronicle at the time. Perhaps Strachey's aside even nudged the playwright's attention to the Mediterranean coast of Africa when he was considering places in which to set *The Tempest*.

While Shakespeare resisted the trend toward including audience-participation masque dances in his play, he could not avoid the spectacle associated with the masques if he hoped to maintain the favor of the king and queen. *The Tempest* therefore included the lavish dance and music interludes marked by special effects that the royals had come to expect, even if they were never invited to leave their seats. In the debut of the play at the Masquing House, Shakespeare and the set designers did not disappoint the royal family. Complex scenery and costume were used during the onstage masque in the third act of the play. At the Blackfriars it was a lesser version of the pageantry, but dramatic nevertheless.

At the Masquing House a full consort of musicians had provided the music. Bandoras and citterns with their wire strings and lutes with their gut strings composed the plucked instruments. A musician played the keyboard of a virginal, while others used bows to play viols and violins. Wind instruments included cornets, flutes, recorders, sackbuts, and shawns. Drummers provided percussion on kettledrums, side drums, and tabors. The Blackfriars had no keyboard musicians, but it did feature a small group on string, wind, and percussion instruments.

Prospero watched from the stage balcony as the masque scenes began that afternoon at the Blackfriars. As instructed in the stage directions, to "strange and solemn music" wraiths of "several strange shapes" carried a fully set banquet table onstage and danced around it with "gentle actions of salutations," inviting Alonso and his entourage to feast. After the dancers withdrew and Alonso and the noblemen moved toward the table to eat, they were interrupted by Ariel emerging from the clouds in the shape of a harpy. In a costume resembling a giant bat, Ariel descended from the rafters of the theater with the assistance of a hidden levitation machine. Such devices were new to the English stage, recently copied from Italian designs by the king's stage technicians. At the Masquing House heavy post-and-beam frames covered by scenery supported small movable platforms. Hidden stagehands operated ropes and pulleys to raise and lower the actors. The Blackfriars lacked such expensive equipment, and so Ariel descended on a simple rope and pulley. Truly, it was a bit of an awkward entrance—one theatergoer likened the appearance of a Blackfriars descent to watching the lowering of "a bucket into a well."

Ariel descended from the *Tempest* clouds, landed on the stage, approached the table, and enveloped it with his wings. The cover of the giant wings allowed other actors surreptitiously to turn a revolving panel in the tabletop that made the dishes of food and drink seem to vanish when the wings were withdrawn. Ariel then proceeded to break the tension of the play by telling the king and his noblemen that Prospero still lived and that they had been brought to the island to answer for their crimes against him. Ariel then exited to the sound of thunder, and the dancing wraiths returned and carried the table out. Prospero, hidden from the other characters on his balcony perch, then declared to himself that his spells were working and exited the stage.

Grand spectacle continued in the fourth act of the play. The action opened with Prospero embracing Ferdinand and welcoming him to the family. An engagement celebration then commenced, featuring more dancers. The most elaborate costumes were reserved for the goddesses Iris, Juno, and Ceres, who continued the masque with more levitation, dance, and song. Their appearance on the Masquing House stage likely resembled Ben Jonson's presentation of Juno in a production three years earlier: "Sitting in a throne supported by two beautiful peacocks; her attire rich and like a queen, a white diadem [crown] on her head from whence descended a veil, and that bound with a fascia [chinstrap] of several-colored silks, set with all sorts of jewels and raised in the top with lilies and roses; in her right hand she held a scepter, in the other a timbrel [tambourine]; at her golden feet the hide of a lion was placed."

A less richly attired Juno entered from the heavens and descended slowly to the Blackfriars stage. A succinct stage direction—"Juno descends"—calls for the character to enter from above the stage over the course of several lines. Stagehands behind the scenes worked the pulleys while musicians played to cover the creaks of the apparatus. Nymphs who served the goddesses did the dancing this time, along with "sun-burned sicklemen, of August," costumed as "reapers properly habited." The dance played out for two or three minutes as the main characters watched, until Prospero recalled that Caliban and his accomplices were plotting to kill him and ended the revelry with a clap of his hands. A stage direction suggests that the scene change is barely covered by music, saying of the dancers that "to a strange hollow and confused noise, they heavily vanish."

Caliban, Trinculo, and Stephano appeared next on the stage, and their costumes again contributed to the spectacle. As the trio approached Prospero's cave they were distracted by "glistering apparel" that Ariel had hung on a linden tree. Stephano and Trinculo took down the clothes from the branches and tried them on, and as they did so mirrored span-gles sewn on to the costumes reflected the light of the candelabra. Caliban urged his two cohorts to ignore the clothes and proceed with their plan to murder Prospero, but the butler and jester put on the garments and mar-veled at their good fortune.

Strachey in the Blackfriars audience may again have been taken back to his time on Bermuda. The newfound clothes of the *Tempest* mutineers seemed to recapitulate the unexpected request of the last group of Ber-muda mutineers for "two suits of apparel." Strachey probably found it hard to believe, but his account of the rebels' request seemed bizarrely close to the *Tempest* trio's comic interest in the glittering clothes on the tree. Perhaps Shakespeare paused at the section of the Bermuda narra-tive where Strachey derided the apparel request of the *Sea Venture* muti-neers as "the murmuring and mutiny of such rebellious and turbulent humorists."

There were more tidbits, too, that seemed to mimic the *Sea Venture* experience. The conspiracy of the *Tempest*'s comic trio failed when Prospero confronted them. In an echo of the Bermuda hog hunts, the three were chased from the stage by dancers costumed as baying hounds named Mountain, Silver, Fury, and Tyrant. Musicians behind the screen provided "a noise of hunters" as the dancers in dog masks pursued the mutineers offstage. A reminder of the Bermuda hog hunts had already come to Strachey's mind earlier, when Caliban accused Prospero of holding him prisoner by saying "you sty me."

The play culminated in the fifth and final act when Prospero forgave the enemies who exiled him and announced his plan to return to Milan. After his declaration, the lovers Miranda and Ferdinand were revealed at the back of the stage playing chess. In addition to confirming the play's romantic association, the scene served to reunite the lost father and son when King Alonso and his son Ferdinand each realized that the other was still alive. The drama ended with the lovers safely betrothed, the enemies of the court neutralized, and the rightful king returning to his land. Ariel was released from servitude and Caliban was presumably left to roam the island alone.

Prospero closed the play with a soliloquy delivered from center stage. As Strachey listened to the closing lines of the ruler of the *Tempest* isle, he may have been reminded of Thomas Gates of Bermuda. Each was a well-read governor marooned on a wild island; each threatened severe punishment but was ultimately satisfied with spoken assurances of renewed allegiance by the condemned; and each modeled dutiful behavior when his countrymen suggested that expediency trumped responsibility. In crafting the character of Prospero, Shakespeare may have taken special notice of Strachey's description of the transformation in Gates's personality after the ambush of Humphrey Blunt. Gates was freshly arrived in Virginia when he sent Blunt to retrieve an errant boat on the James River, only to watch from afar as his man was set upon and killed by Powhatans. The experience steeled Gates's resolve and precipitated his attack on the unsuspecting people of Kecoughtan. Throughout his narrative Strachey depicted Gates as a patient patriarch who abhorred violence but who was forced into the role of a wounded overseer resigned to delivering punishment. Shakespeare would lead the character of Prospero through a similar passage in *The Tempest*. In Virginia the killing of Blunt caused the conversion; in *The Tempest* it was brought on by Caliban's attempted rape of Miranda. That difference aside, the transformations of Gates and Prospero are remarkably similar. "Thou most lying slave, whom stripes may move, not kindness," Prospero said of Caliban, "I have used thee (filth as thou art) with humane care and lodged thee in mine own cell, till thou didst seek to violate the honour of my child." In *The Tempest* as in Virginia, the perceived recalcitrance of the indigenous person moves the interloper to use force instead of the moderate persuasion he prefers.

Prospero may also have received a bit of Shakespeare himself in his personality. In the magician's closing speech some critics have sensed that the playwright was announcing his own retirement. Prospero told the audience that he would give up his spells and lead a quiet life in Milan, just as Shakespeare mulled an end to his stage magic and a new life of retirement in Stratford-upon-Avon. Carrying the interpretation further, Ariel may be understood as Shakespeare's creative imagination being released from servitude and Caliban as his darker impulses being left to roam in a private place unseen by the world. There are parallels, after all, between a magician who conjures up storms and manipulates people with magic and a playwright who creates theatrical storms and manipulates characters with stagecraft. Shakespeare might even have been referring to his most famous venue, the Globe theater, when Prospero in his closing speech said, "the solemn temples, the great globe itself, yea, all which it inherit, shall dissolve, and like this insubstantial pageant faded, leave not a rack behind."

Strachey would have been amused as he watched a dreamlike version of his Bermuda and Virginia experiences play out in candlelight. Many moments of recognition would have taken place as he heard variations of his own language in the lines of the actors. The play would have seemed strangely familiar yet incredibly distant in the shadowy theater as his thoughts turned to his days in Bermuda and Jamestown. Even so, to Strachey the drama on the Blackfriars stage would have been little more than an ephemeral diversion. While he would have been flattered to see his words so used, he would also have thought that *The Tempest* was popular entertainment that would soon fade into oblivion as all popular entertainments eventually did. This version of his story would not last; no, it was up to him to create a work of literature that would have the enduring impact that this fleeting stage show would never enjoy.

Perhaps as soon as that evening, in his spare room a few doors from the theater, William Strachey took out his diaries and the memoirs of his Virginia voyage. He may also have reread his introductory letter to the *Lawes Divine, Morall and Martial*. "I have both in the Bermudas and since in Virginia been a sufferer and an eyewitness," he had written, "and the full story of both in due time shall consecrate unto your views." He intended to keep that promise, and so perhaps even that night he put down the book, picked up a quill, and began to write.

CHAPTER EIGHTEEN

After the Storm

Our revels now are ended.

—Prospero, *The Tempest*

While William Shakespeare was destined to be remembered as the greatest writer of his age, William Strachey would enjoy no such fate. Despite his determined efforts to acquire a patron, he was unable to interest a benefactor in financing the publication of his history of the exploration of Virginia. The reality was that while Strachey had been in Jamestown for a reasonably long period, he had only ventured beyond the palisade a few times in the rear guard of major expeditions. The most successful author on the subject, John Smith, had gone into the wilds many times and was himself the source of much of what was known about Virginia. Strachey simply did not have the experience to match Smith's eyewitness accounts of the early years of the colony.

In later years a detention for debt left Strachey begging for money in a note to a friend: "This last dismal arrest hath taken from all my friends something and from me all I had," he wrote, "and today I am to meet with some friends at dinner returned from Virginia, and God is witness with me I have not to pay for my dinner, all my things be at pawn." Strachey's wife, Frances, died sometime after his return from Jamestown and he married a second time. He lived to see his son William wed, but also to endure the death of his granddaughter Helen at four months of age in April 1620.

Late in life Strachey wrote a poem that reflected thoughts of his own mortality: "My hour is come, false world adieu / That I to death untimely go. / Thy pleasures have betrayed me so." He died in June 1621, and four years later Samuel Purchas published his letter to the "Excellent Lady" in a collection of travelers' accounts entitled *Purchas His Pilgrimes*. Strachey's work appeared under the title "A True Reportory of the Wracke, and Redemption of Sir Thomas Gates Knight." The manuscript was subsequently lost, leaving the 1625 book as the only version of the text that would endure. Strachey died without the literary legacy he had longed for, save one to which he paid little heed—his account of a shipwreck on an enchanted isle had inspired a magical drama by a playwright who would someday be considered a literary master.

The Tempest remained a London favorite for years after its debut. King James liked the play so much that he ordered it performed on the royal stage eighteen months later for the celebration of the wedding of his daughter Elizabeth on Valentine's Day, 1613. To give it a fresh feel, two songs were added for the encore performance. "Full Fathom Five" and "Where the Bee Sucks" enlivened the wedding spectacle. The venue for the show was again the Masquing House, and again it was a great success.

The Virginia Company continued a defensive posture against the ridicule its enterprise received in the London theaters. A 1612 company publication lamented that "the malicious and looser sort (being accompanied with the licentious vain of stage poets) have whet their tongues with scornful taunts against the action." Now William Shakespeare was also a target, for in his popular *Tempest* the audience surely recognized the *Sea Venture* story. What probably bothered officers of the Virginia Company more than Shakespeare's dissection of their Golden Age aspirations was King James's obvious appreciation of the play.

Whether or not Shakespeare meant to announce his retirement in Prospero's soliloquy, *The Tempest* was his final solo work. He coauthored three more plays with John Fletcher—*All Is True*, or *Henry VIII*; *The Two Noble Kinsmen*; and the lost *Cardenio*. About the time he finished *The Tempest* he moved from London to Stratford-upon-Avon to live in what a contemporary called a "gentlemanlike" home called New Place, a rambling dwelling fronted by sixty feet of vine-covered walls and appointed with ten fireplaces and a bay window. The playwright continued to spend time in London, however. In March 1613 he purchased an apartment near the Blackfriars Theater as a real estate investment, and perhaps also as a place to stay on visits to London.

Three months after Shakespeare's apartment purchase, on June 29, 1613, the King's Men suffered a catastrophe that could have been an even greater disaster for English literature. During a performance of *All Is True*, sparks from a stage cannon set the roof of the Globe ablaze. "Some of the paper or other stuff wherewith one of them was stopped did light the thatch," a Londoner wrote to a friend soon after, "where being thought at first an idle smoke and their eyes more attentive to the show, it kindled inwardly and ran round like a train, consuming within less than an hour the whole house to the very grounds. This was the fatal period of the virtuous fabric, wherein yet nothing did perish but wood and straw and a few forsaken cloaks; only one man had his breeches set on fire, that would perhaps have broiled him if he had not by the benefit of a provident wit put it out with bottle ale." Luckily the company's playbooks were carried from the house as the fire spread. If they had not been, the only copies of half of Shakespeare's works would have burned with the theater.

Away from London in his retirement, Shakespeare was preoccupied with the marriage of his daughter, just as Prospero was obsessed with Miranda's matrimonial fate in *The Tempest*. Lacking the ability of Prospero to cast spells, the playwright was less able to ensure the happiness of his daughter Judith. She and local vintner Thomas Quiney married without the permission of the church during Lent in early 1616 and were excommunicated for doing so. The apparent reason for their hurried wedding became clear a short time later, when Quiney admitted to a premarital affair with an unmarried woman who had died in childbirth. As a result of the confession, Shakespeare rewrote his will to give Judith's portion of his estate directly to her rather than to her husband. The bulk of his estate went to his other surviving child, daughter Susanna, who had a stable marriage (the playwright's third child, a son named Hamnet, had died young). During the same revision of the will, Shakespeare added his only bequest to his wife Anne, notoriously leaving her only his second-best bed, a brief reference scholars have plumbed ever since for clues to the playwright's enigmatic relationship with his spouse.

Within a month of writing his will, William Shakespeare was dead. On April 25, 1616, the playwright's body was buried in the chancel of Holy Trinity Church in Stratford-upon-Avon. The only known documentation of the cause of death is a note written a half century later by the vicar of Stratford-upon-Avon: "Shakespeare, [poet Michael] Drayton, and Ben Jonson had a merry meeting and it seems drank too hard, for Shakespeare died of a fever there contracted." Shakespeare ended his life as a successful playwright whose popular entertainments had made him relatively wealthy. At his death he had not the remotest idea that posterity would lionize him as the most eloquent voice in the English language.

The Tempest remained in the King's Men manuscript playbook for seven years, until 1623, when the troupe consented to the publication of the First Folio. Since buyers would best remember Shakespeare's most recent triumph, *The Tempest* was placed first in the volume of his collected works. The text from the playbook was published complete with stage directions that were probably written for the Whitehall debut, and consequently *The Tempest* is considered one of the least adulterated of Shakespeare's works (since no manuscripts of any of his plays survive, all of the texts are based on published copies). In the introduction to the First Folio, Ben Jonson indulged in the usual exaggeration of such prefaces, but in this case the hyperbole proved true. Of Shakespeare, Jonson said, "he was not of an age, but for all time!"

The triumph of *The Tempest* prompted other playwrights to write New World dramas. George Chapman's *Memorable Maske of the Two Honorable Houses of Inns of Court* debuted at the 1613 wedding alongside Shakespeare's returning play. Chapman felt no need to transform the raw material of exploration as Shakespeare had done. An island in *Memorable Maske* is populated by "Virginians" rather than magical characters with New World roots. The action follows rather obviously what Chapman apparently believed the king wanted to see—his fictional New World society included princes and knights who acted like aristocrats of the Old World. A delegation of those noble Virginians traveled to England to attend the wedding of the king's daughter. At the height of the drama, flats were rolled back to reveal a Virginia gold mine filled with glittering ore. Chapman's intuition that a more straightforward story line would please the king turned out to be incorrect, as James preferred the subtlety of Shakespeare to the overt wish fulfillment of Chapman.

Much to his annoyance, Ben Jonson also found the durable popularity of *The Tempest* difficult to ignore. In the introduction to the published version of his 1614 play *Bartholomew Fair*, Jonson uses a light touch in trying to fend off criticism that his *Fair* lacks a character like Caliban. "If there be never a servant-monster i' the fair, who can help it?" he asks, adding of himself in the third person, "He is loth to make nature afraid in his plays, like those that beget tales, tempests, and such like drolleries." After Shakespeare's death, Jonson relented and attempted a *Tempest*-like play of his own with *News from the New World Discovered in the Moon*. The 1620 work featured a Golden Age society on the moon that sent emissaries to earth. In an allusion to *The Tempest*, Jonson has a character use one of Caliban's nicknames: "O, I, moon-calves! What monster is that, I pray you?" Another character then answers, "Monster? None at all; a very familiar thing like our fool here on earth."

A third playwright also imitated Shakespeare's New World masterwork. John Fletcher eventually took his predecessor's place as the primary dramatist of the King's Men. As the troupe continued to stage *The Tempest*, Fletcher tried to exploit its popularity by writing *The Sea Voyage*. The new drama was indebted to both *The Tempest* and the *Sea Venture* accounts, featuring "Happy Islands" that were simultaneously a paradise and a frightful place.

Bermuda also emerged in the work of John Taylor the Water Poet, a master of nonsense verse whose pamphlets parodying contemporary authors enjoyed a large popular market in the years following the *Sea Venture* wreck. Taylor mocked the travel accounts of writer Thomas Coryate with his "Epitaph in the Barmooda tongue, which must be pronounced with the accent of the grunting of a hog." The poem consisted of unintelligible doggerel lines modeled on New World languages that each ended in a grunted *"ogh."* Taylor lampooned Bermuda's new image as a heavenly place by attributing a "translation" of an accompanying "Epitaph in the Utopian tongue" to a fictional "Caleb Quishquash, an Utopian born, and principal secretary to the great Adelontado of Barmoodoes."

The other voyagers who rode the *Sea Venture* through the hurricane lived out their lives on both sides of the Atlantic. George Somers would be celebrated as the founder of Bermuda. The last anyone in England or Jamestown had heard from the admiral was just before he lost touch with Samuel Argall in the fog off the coast of Sagadahoc in the summer of 1610. Somers had volunteered to go to Bermuda to restock Jamestown with food, and did in fact go on to the mid-Atlantic isle after losing contact with Argall. The admiral had reached Bermuda late in the summer of 1610, perhaps after stopping briefly on the Connecticut shore. The two mutineers who had hidden in the woods and stayed behind had greeted Somers's pinnace and rejoined his company. Somers and his crew had spent six weeks hunting hogs, turtles, and birds to bring back to the Virginia colony.

The hunt had suddenly halted in early autumn when Somers was taken ill after a meal of fire-roasted pork. The admiral probably suffered from a lethal variety of food poisoning now known as necrotizing enteritis, or "pig-bel." Vulnerability to clostridial bacteria in undercooked pork is especially acute when feasting follows a period of protein deficiency. Somers would have suffered through bloody diarrhea, abdominal pain, and vomiting before dying on November 9 of what his fellows described as "a surfeit in eating of a pig."

Somers's nephew Matthew had assumed command, ordering his uncle's body embalmed instead of buried, with the intention of bringing it home to England. In accord with a knightly tradition that dated back to the Crusades, the embalmers removed Sir George Somers's heart for a separate interment. The body itself was preserved in a wooden box under a heavy layer of salt from the Bermuda salt house. Removing the internal organs was a normal part of the embalming process, but in this case it served a ceremonial as well as a practical purpose. Somers would leave his heart on the island that had provided him salvation in the midst of a terrible tempest. "His heart and bowels were there buried," a contemporary wrote a decade later, "a great cross of wood being pitched over his grave."

During the months that followed Somers's death, a debate ensued in the Bermuda camp. Having seen the desperate straits of the Virginia colony firsthand, none of the men on the island wanted to return there. The problem was one of honor, since the admiral pledged to return with food that all the colonists on Bermuda knew was essential for the survival of Jamestown during the upcoming winter. Arguments over the campfire resulted in a stalemate that lasted through the winter. Finally in late spring the men of the Bermuda expedition seem to have justified to themselves that no matter how terrible the winter had been, Jamestown's need for food was lessened with the coming of the spring. Thus the decision was made to sail for England. The returning colonists hoped that their report of the attractiveness of Bermuda as a settlement site would overshadow any condemnation they received for failing to supply the colony the previous fall. In the spring the *Patience* departed for England, this time leaving behind three volunteers to hold a claim to the island.

Matthew Somers headed for his uncle's homeport of Lyme Regis in Dorset, far from London and thus insulated from the criticism of the Virginia Company. The timing of the arrival of the *Patience* served the returning colonists well. Word of their return reached London at about the time that the convoy under Thomas Gates departed for Jamestown in the late spring of 1611, and so the perception was that Jamestown would soon be well supplied. They had been correct, too, that most of the discussion surrounding their return would be about the possibility of settling Bermuda rather than about their decision not to return to Virginia.

The body of George Somers was interred in the village of Whitchurch Canonicorum on June 4. John Smith later described the service. "His body by his friends was honorably buried, with many volleys of shot and the rights of a soldier," Smith said. "And upon his tomb was bestowed this epitaph:

> Alas Virginia Somer so soon past
> Autumn succeeds and stormy winter's blast,
> Yet England's joyful spring with April showers,
> O Florida, shall bring thy sweetest flowers."

The next month the admiral's estate was divided among his heirs. After bequests to the poor of Lyme Regis and to servant George Bird, the property of the childless knight was divided between his widow, Joan, and his nephews and nieces. Soon after his funeral, the Reverend William Crashaw published an appreciation of the departed mariner, recalling "Sir George Somers, that famous seaman, our worthy admiral, that true and constant friend to Virginia, who in his old age left a pleasant seat in Dorsetshire, a good living, and an easy life to live and die for the good of Virginia."

In 1612, Bermuda was renamed the "Somers Islands" in honor of the deceased admiral. The name persisted for a while, often spelled as Summer Isles to emphasize the mild climate, but it never supplanted the name Bermuda. In 1619, Governor Nathaniel Butler ordered a memorial stone installed over the island burial place of Somers's heart. In the inscription he took the liberty of adding a year to the death date, apparently for rhyming purposes:

> In the year 1611,
> Noble Sir George Somers went hence to heaven;
> Whose well tried worth that held him still employed,
> Gave him the knowledge of the world so wide.
> Hence it was by heaven's decree, that to this place
> He brought new guests, and name to mutual grace.
> At last his soul and body being to part,
> He here bequeathed his entrails and his heart.

Back in England Matthew Somers engaged his aunt in a long legal battle over his uncle's estate, which ended only with Joan Somers's death in 1618. Matthew continued his litigious ways in later years—a counterclaim in a future lawsuit alleged that he pursued a "riotous and disorderly course of living."

Soon after returning to Jamestown, Thomas Gates sent his now-motherless daughters home with Christopher Newport on the *Starre*. "He hath sent his daughters back again," a London official wrote to a colleague in December 1611, "which I doubt not is a piece of prognostication that himself means not to tarry long after." That assumption proved incorrect, however, and Gates remained in Jamestown for three more years. While Thomas Dale ruthlessly drove his men to build Henrico and Bermuda Hundred, Gates used a lighter hand to develop the original settlement of Jamestown. Among his accomplishments was the construction of a governor's house with a hearth made of Bermuda limestone from the ballast of the *Deliverance* or the *Patience*. Gates finally returned to England in April 1614. When war between Spain and the Netherlands resumed in 1621 he returned to his command in the Low Countries, dying of fever at Schenck in September 1622.

Joan Pierce, who saw her husband William come back from the dead when the *Sea Venture* survivors arrived in Jamestown, prospered in Virginia. Her husband became a wealthy planter, and together they enjoyed the success all Virginia-bound colonists had hoped to achieve. John Smith reported in 1629 that on a visit to London, Joan Pierce told of her prosperity in the wilderness. "Mistress Pierce, an honest industrious woman, hath been there near twenty years and now returned saith she hath a garden at Jamestown containing three or four acres where in one year she hath gathered near a hundred bushels of excellent figs and that of her own provision she can keep a better house in Virginia than here in London for three or four hundred pounds a year, yet went thither with little or nothing." The Pierces' daughter, Joan, married John Rolfe after the death of his second wife, Wahonsonacock's famous daughter, Pocahontas.

The brief Spanish incursion at Point Comfort in 1611 was a monumental event in the life of English pilot John Clark, who was taken away on the Spanish ship. Clark was kept prisoner in Cuba and Spain until he was exchanged for his counterpart, Diego de Molina, in 1616. Four years after gaining his freedom he sailed to the New World on the *Mayflower*. Also on board the Pilgrims' ship was Stephen Hopkins, the Bermuda rebel who returned to England soon after reaching Jamestown. Since Clark was a mariner, he returned to England with the *Mayflower*, whereas Hopkins and his family remained in Plymouth to live and die and eventually be revered as Pilgrim founders.

Epilogue

While the seventeenth century passed and the people associated with the *Sea Venture* died off, *The Tempest* of William Shakespeare endured. Characters of the play were given permanent places in the literary universe when in 1851 an astronomer named a newly discovered moon of Uranus after the sprite Ariel. In 1948 a sister moon of the same planet became Miranda. Then when improved telescopes yielded a spate of new discoveries between 1997 and 2001, Uranus was given moons named Caliban, Sycorax, Prospero, Setebos, Stephano, Trinculo, Francisco, and Ferdinand. For all time a celestial blue giant will be circled with the characters of Shakespeare's otherworldly play.

As *The Tempest* underwent a transformation from popular entertainment to literary masterpiece, scholars began to interpret the work as the playwright's commentary on the colonial experience. In 1797 an observer first suggested that Shakespeare drew on Virginia travel narratives in writing the *Tempest*. In 1808, Silvester Jourdain was identified as a source, then much later, in 1892, William Strachey's letter home was proposed to be one as well. In the twentieth century *The Tempest* became firmly established as Shakespeare's New World play.

Ironically, a direct descendant of William Strachey attempted unsuccessfully to ensure that the play was not placed among the transcendent works of the English language. Literary critic Lytton Strachey's 1906 article "Shakespeare's Final Period" declared *The Tempest* a mediocre work. Fourteen years earlier the work of the critic's ancestor was suggested as a progenitor of the play, though whether Lytton Strachey knew of William Strachey's apparent influence on the work he was assessing is unknown.

The reading of Shakespeare's last play as a commentary on Britain's colonial aspirations reached a peak in the 1960s and 1970s when the attention of critics focused on Caliban as the indigenous person and Prospero as the European oppressor. Leo Marx in his 1964 book *The Machine in the Garden* crystallized the concept of the *Tempest* as "a prologue to American literature." During the final twenty years of the century a new line of inquiry reemphasized the play's classical roots. Critics began to argue that the colonial interpretation imposes a modern viewpoint on to a historical text, rendering Prospero's island "a kaleidoscope" or "a complex Rorschach blot that exposes its observers' habitual presuppositions." Yet in the twenty-first century the colonial reading remains firmly embedded in *Tempest* scholarship and in the costumes and manners of *Tempest* characters onstage.

Also in the twentieth century a controversy about Shakespeare's identity found new life. The lack of copious documentation of the playwright's life long ago led to the suggestion that someone other than William Shakespeare authored the plays attributed to him. The leading candidate as an alternate author is Edward de Vere, the seventeenth Earl of Oxford. Proponents of that theory, however, must overcome the obstacle that de Vere died in 1604, five years before the *Sea Venture* wrecked on Bermuda. Consequently, advocates of de Vere are in the position of either denying that *The Tempest* was inspired by the Bermuda chronicles or denying that the play was written by "Shakespeare" (both approaches have been attempted). Despite the arguments of de Vere supporters, mainstream Shakespeare scholars remain convinced that the best interpretation of the documentary record is that William Shakespeare of Stratford-upon-Avon, the King's Men actor, was the author of the plays.

The work of William Strachey attracted new attention in the nineteenth and twentieth centuries, as well. The comprehensive history of

Virginia that Strachey wrote (and to a large extent copied from John Smith) after returning to England was finally published after more than two centuries in 1849 as *The Historie of Travaile into Virginia Britannia*. Fifty years after that his *True Reportory* was reprinted in a 1907 edition of *Purchas His Pilgrimes*, and scholars began to recognize Strachey's importance as an observer of colonial life. While *Historie of Travaile* owes much to John Smith, *True Reportory* is largely original and has earned its author a reputation as an unflinching observer (despite his bias in favor of colonial leaders). One modern scholar calls *True Reportory* "magnificent—it has some sentences which for imagination and pathetic beauty, for vivid implications of appalling danger and disaster, can hardly be surpassed in the whole range of English prose." Another designates it "one of the finest pieces—clear, specific, descriptive, critical—in the literature of the whole period of seventeenth-century American enterprise." Strachey is said to be "notably good as an interpreter of Indian life, being both shrewd and sympathetic in his comments." His original dictionary of the Powhatan language included in *Historie of Travaile* has particular importance: "The large Strachey vocabulary of Powhatan Indian words—with six times as many as are to be found in Smith's writings—is invaluable for modern students of Algonkian languages."

The stories that Strachey and his fellow *Sea Venture* chroniclers told inspired writers and artists of the nineteenth and twentieth centuries, just as they did those of the seventeenth. In 1840 Washington Irving wrote two essays on the wreck, noting that his interest was especially drawn to the founding of the Bermuda islands because he "could trace, in their early history, and in the superstitious notions connected with them, some of the elements of Shakespeare's wild and beautiful drama of *The Tempest*." Irving unfortunately slipped once and identified the wrecked ship as the "*Sea Vulture*" and made the exaggerated claim that a "bitter feud" on the island resulted in "a complete schism" between Gates and Somers. The Irving essays are best known for their depiction of the men Matthew Somers left behind as "the three kings of Bermuda."

Rudyard Kipling learned of Shakespeare's connection to Bermuda when he took a cruise to the island in 1894. In 1896 he wrote a letter to the editor of the *Spectator* suggesting that the playwright might have overheard the *Sea Venture* story from a sailor in a London tavern. Kipling believed that the wind in the Bermuda coral caused the strange sounds of Prospero's island and a particular cave on the shore near Hamilton was a likely model for the magician's cell. Kipling went on to imagine that a castaway taking refuge under the ribcage of a whale skeleton inspired the scene of Trinculo hiding under Caliban's cloak. Thirty-four years later Kipling incorporated his ideas into a poem entitled "The Coiner." In it he pictured Shakespeare meeting *Sea Venture* sailors at a tavern in 1611 and hearing about the Bermuda shipwreck. Shakespeare buys them drinks to keep them talking about their "seven months among mermaids and devils and sprites, and voices that howl in the cedars o' nights." The sailors eventually fall asleep and awake the next morning to find that coins had been left in their pockets. They congratulate themselves on their luck, without realizing that Shakespeare—the "coiner" of the title—got the better of the deal by acquiring a story he would turn to gold on the London stage.

The *Sea Venture* and *The Tempest* bewitched another twentieth-century literary great as well. In 1924 James Joyce mentioned both in his monumental novel *Ulysses*. Episode Nine of the stream-of-consciousness work is thick with allusions to Shakespeare and includes the following line: "The *Sea Venture* comes home from Bermudas and the play Renan admired is written with Patsy Caliban, our American cousin." Joyce was referring to Ernest Renan, who wrote *Tempest* criticism. *Our American Cousin* was a nineteenth-century work of the American theater, but the play lacks a character named Patsy and Joyce's reason for joining it to the name of Shakespeare's servant monster remains obscure.

Novelist Cothburn O'Neal also discovered the story of William Strachey and *The Tempest* and in 1954 turned it into his novel *The Dark Lady*. In a riff on the authorship question, the story features the fictional Rosaline, an illegitimate daughter of Edward de Vere, who is pretending to be a man playing women on the Jacobean stage. Rosaline is also the true author of London's most popular plays, which she publishes with the cooperation of a King's Men actor named William Shakespeare. Rosaline, who has a daughter named Miranda, is the "Excellent Lady" who receives Strachey's letter from Jamestown. When King James discovers that she is the secret author of Shakespeare's work he forbids her to write any more plays. The novel ends when the inexplicably blond-haired Strachey, conveniently widowed after the death of his wife, Frances, offers to take her away to Bermuda.

Later in the twentieth century other artists drew upon *The Tempest* as a play about the colonial world. Martinique playwright Aimé Césaire in 1969 debuted a rewritten *Tempest* he called *Une Tempête*. The new version transformed Caliban into an African slave and Ariel into a person of mixed race. Césaire succeeded in "unmasking the brutality which underlies colonization," according to one commentator. "In *Une Tempête*, Caliban effectively demonstrates that Prospero's 'humanism' is decidedly inhuman (and inhumane) precisely because it does not accord Caliban the status of a human being."

In the 1990s Cherokee artist Jimmie Durham embraced the colonial theme of the play as well, creating a series of masks and fictional diary entries depicting the pre-*Tempest* Caliban as a student of Prospero. Durham imagines the young Caliban as obsessed with finding a reflection of his face on a mirrorless island, a metaphor for his search for identity. Just as *The Tempest* has an undercurrent of cruelty in the relationship between the magician and the monster, so, too, does Durham's work. "One time Prospero was going to spank me because I was playing with mud," a fictional diary entry reads. "When I resisted I caused him to accidentally hit me in the nose."

The radical transformation of the Bermuda landscape that began with the introduction of hogs by the Spanish has continued to the present time. The feral hogs were gone within a few years of settlement. By 1623 the colonial government introduced laws to protect cahows, cedar trees, and tortoises, all of which were threatened with extinction only fourteen years after settlement. Prickly pears and palmettos faced the same threat. Bananas, oranges, lemons, pomegranates, and domesticated mulberries were soon introduced to the island, further stressing native species. Since the colonists arrived, more than a thousand foreign plants have been brought from all over the world. Today Bermuda is home to seventeen species of flora unique to the island, a hundred and sixty species native both to Bermuda and other locations, and thirteen hundred introduced plants. One of the unique species, the Bermuda cedar, was the victim of an introduced insect that reached the island in 1940. A resistant strain of the tree has been developed and reintroduced, and the cedar that provided the wood for the *Deliverance* and the *Patience* is today a protected species.

The Bermuda cahow was thought to be extinct for three centuries, but in 1951 ornithologists were delighted to discover that a small breeding population of the bird survived on remote islands. The birds—tame and vulnerable as ever—have been nurtured by conservationists ever since. Now numbering about two hundred, the small flock lives a precarious existence. An attack by a single snowy owl in 1986 killed five birds and was considered a serious blow to the colony. The rescue effort continues with guarded optimism, however, and the haunting night cries heard on the island in 1609 ring ever louder over rocky islets off the Bermuda coast.

Bermuda quietly relishes its role in the creation of *The Tempest*. One island entrepreneur in 1946 exploited Shakespeare's references to Prospero's cave by opening an island cavern to tourists, putting up a statue of the playwright, and promoting it as "Prospero's Cave, the scene of *The Tempest*." Many of the island's subterranean hollows feature sunken rivers that ebb and flow with the tide. In 1978 a scientist found a new species of marine creature in one of the rivers and named it for Shakespeare's cave-dwelling magician. George Somers received the same honor two years later. Thus did miniature Bermuda creatures become *Mesonerilla prospera* and *Somersiella sterreri*.

Somers' Day is celebrated each year in late July or early August on

Bermuda. In 1876 a new plaque was installed to mark the traditional burial place of the admiral's heart. A thirty-foot column of Bermuda limestone was added on the 1909 tercentenary of the wreck. In 1984 on the three hundred and seventy-fifth anniversary, a statue of Somers by sculptor Desmond Fountain was unveiled in the town of St. George's near a replica of the *Deliverance*. The same year, Bermuda issued postage stamps that bear portraits of Somers and Thomas Gates and a picture of the *Sea Venture* fleet departing Plymouth. Across the sea on the New England coast, another trace of George Somers may have been found. A gold signet ring reputed to bear his family crest was uncovered in the sand of a Connecticut beach in 1924. If the ring did indeed belong to Somers, the likely explanation is that he stopped there while awaiting a breeze to take him to Bermuda for the last time.

In the years that followed the *Sea Venture* wreck the ship yielded a little more of its cargo to Bermuda before finally being lost below the waves. In 1622 island colonists brought up a gun, an anchor, and bars of iron and lead when Governor Nathaniel Butler ordered divers "to make a discovery upon the rotten ribs of a ship called the *Sea Adventure*, which (as you formerly heard) had been wrecked about some thirteen years before. The which being found out, and his divers sent down to the bottom (which was three or four fathoms deep) to see what was to be done, at the very first proof there was by great chance discovered a very fair saker." The gun and other material, Butler said, greatly benefited the plantation.

The remnants of the *Sea Venture*—said by one historian to be "arguably the most important of Bermuda's many historic shipwrecks"—lay untouched for the next three hundred and thirty-six years until amateur diver Edmund Downing, a descendant of *Sea Venture* passenger George Yardley, spent the summer of 1958 searching for the historic hulk. On October 18 he and friend Floyd Heird dove to a wreck near the location described by the chroniclers. The first time down they sighted timbers and ballast of an old ship. A gun was raised to the surface and, perhaps fortuitously, dated by London experts to the eighteenth century. Interest in the wreck consequently waned for twenty years. Then—after Bermuda had passed new legislation protecting historic underwater sites—the Bermuda Maritime Museum undertook a new study of the Downing wreck. This time a painstaking analysis identified the remnants as those of the *Sea Venture*. Hundreds of artifacts were subsequently raised—a candlestick wedged between two boards, rat and cat bones, a dagger, intact Bartmann bottles, Chinese porcelain, and many others things that had not been touched since a tempest-tossed ship ran for the Bermuda shore on a stormy day in July 1609. The most important artifacts were put on display in an exhibition in the museum's Treasure House along with a scale model of the *Sea Venture*.

Across the Atlantic in Jamestown, archaeological remains have also been revealed. Many artifacts lay undiscovered there, too, on the mistaken assumption that the fort site had eroded into the James River. In 1994 archaeologist William M. Kelso and the Association for the Preservation of Virginia Antiquities initiated a dig to determine whether remnants of the fort might instead lay underground at the edge of the river. Kelso's work revealed that while the fort had indeed lost a guard tower to the scouring water, most of the palisade stood on what remains intact ground. Kelso and fellow archaeologists of his Jamestown Rediscovery project have since uncovered seven hundred thousand artifacts, a third of which date to the first four years of European occupation. In May 2006 a new museum at the site, the Historic Jamestowne Archaearium, was opened to display the artifacts. Among notable discoveries were Bermuda cahow bones and conch shells from refuse pits; Bermuda limestone blocks used as building material; butchered bones of horses, rats, and snakes from the Starving Time; and a skeleton Kelso and his team identified through forensic clues as being that of colonist Bartholomew Gosnold.

One of the most startling finds in the Jamestown earth was a brass signet ring embossed with an eagle. Research by Kelso's team at the College of Arms in London tentatively identified a family crest on the ring as belonging to a secretary of the colony whose writings inspired a London playwright to create an ethereal work. The ring apparently slipped from the hand of William Strachey into the dust of Virginia, to emerge in the present as a gleaming reminder of a Jamestown colonist who helped create William Shakespeare's New World masterpiece.

ACKNOWLEDGMENTS

My colleagues at the Adams Papers at the Massachusetts Historical Society have provided unfailing support throughout this project. Editor in Chief C. James Taylor is a mentor and always a friend; Gregg L. Lint demonstrates daily what it takes to be a professional historian; Margaret A. Hogan has taught me much about the artful use of language. My coworkers Karen N. Barzilay, Mary T. Claffey, Judith S. Graham, Robert Karachuk, Amanda Mathews, and Sara B. Sikes, and my former colleagues Nathaniel Adams, Jessie May Rodrique, and Paul Fotis Tsimahides have been great friends. I would also like to thank everyone at the Massachusetts Historical Society for their support during my project.

My agent, Patricia Moosbrugger, is a constant source of encouragement and a valued adviser. Alessandra Lusardi, my editor at Viking Penguin, has tirelessly helped me to make my book the best it can be. My thanks also to Wendy Wolf, Ellen Garrison, Hilary Redmon, Anna Sternoff, and Jacqueline Powers. I am grateful, too, for the support of Jeanne K. Hanson and Nicholas T. Smith.

I have been enormously assisted by input from colleagues and friends who read a draft of my manuscript: Karen N. Barzilay, Susan Beegel, Christy Law Blanchard, Kevin Blanchard, V. Powell Bliss, Sarah Bliss, Peter Cummings, David Gullette, Dr. Edward Harris, Margaret A. Hogan, Amy Johnson, Rosemary Jones, Karen Ordahl Kupperman, Gregg L. Lint, C. S. Lovelace, Dianne O'Donoghue, Nathaniel Philbrick, Laura Prieto, Gary Root, Mary S. Skinner, James Somerville, Renny Stackpole, C. James Taylor, Alden T.

Vaughan, Elizabeth Woodward, Stewart Woodward, and Walter Woodward. Any errors or omissions are mine alone.

This book would not have been possible without the assistance of librarians, archivists, and historians in the United States, Bermuda, and Great Britain. My thanks to the staffs of the Massachusetts Historical Society, the libraries of Harvard University, the Boston Public Library (especially Elise C. Orringer), the New England Historic Genealogical Society, the Newburyport Public Library, Beatley Library at Simmons College, the G. W. Blunt Library at Mystic Seaport, the Folger Shakespeare Library (especially Nicole Murray and William Davis), the Library of Congress, and the Caribbean Conservation Corporation (especially Rocio Johnson). My thanks also to Andrew Dobson and Clarence Maxwell.

In Virginia I was ably assisted by Katherine Wilkins, Jeffrey Ruggles, and Meg Eastman at the Virginia Historical Society; Dana Angell Puga and Paige Buchbinder at the Library of Virginia; William M. Kelso and Ralph Freer at Historic Jamestowne; Jay Templin at Jamestown Settlement; Howell W. Perkins at the Virginia Museum of Fine Arts; and the staffs at the John D. Rockefeller Jr. Library at Colonial Williamsburg, the Swem Library at William and Mary College, and the American Shakespeare Center.

Rosemary Jones and Paul Shapiro offered extraordinary assistance on Bermuda to a stranger from America. I received kind assistance also from Dr. Edward Harris, Elena Strong, and Mizzah Hunt at the Bermuda Maritime Museum; Karla Hayward, Kristy R. Warren, Mandellas A. Lightbourne, Roderick W. McFall, and Frances K. Marshall at the Bermuda Government Archives; Michelle Nearon Richardson at the Bermuda National Library; Andrew Bermingham at the Bermuda Historical Society; and the staff at the Bermuda College Library.

In Britain I received a cordial welcome at the British Library, the British Museum, the National Archives of Britain, the Bodelian Library of Oxford University, the National Portrait Gallery (especially Helen Trompeteler), and Shakespeare's Globe (especially Callum Coates). Seán Pòl Ó Creachmhaoil assisted me in locating a rare publication about Bermuda history.

This book would not have been possible without the work of the scholars whose research and writing provided the foundation on which it was constructed. S. G. Culliford's biography *William Strachey, 1572–1621*, is a tour de force of historical scholarship. My copy of the Arden *Tempest* has long been a dog-eared source of information and inspiration thanks to the insightful annotation of editors Virginia Mason Vaughan and Alden T. Vaughan. Alden T. Vaughan's work on the visits of Powhatans to England was an essential source. Edward Wright Haile, Philip L. Barbour, David B. Quinn, Mark Nicholls, W. Noel Sainsbury, Susan Myra Kingsbury, Wesley Frank Craven, David H. Flaherty, Louis B. Wright, and Alexander Brown provided invaluable access to seventeenth-century letters and accounts through their documentary editions. All but a few of the parallels between the Jamestown chronicles and *The Tempest* were identified before this book was written in the diligent work of Robert Ralston Cawley, Charles Mills Gayley, Geoffrey Bullough, Geoffrey Ashe, and David Kathman. Many works of Jamestown history have been relied upon, but the scholarship of Helen C. Rountree, William M. Kelso, Karen Ordahl Kupperman, and Frederick J. Fausz deserves special mention. The superb work of Allan J. Wingood, Jonathan Adams, Cyril H. Smith, Eric J. R. Amos, and Rosemary Jones in documenting the culture and history of Bermuda was indispensable in the composition of this work. Numerous books on Shakespeare were consulted, but those by Stephen Greenblatt, Peter Ackroyd, Marchette Chute, John G. Demaray, and Andrew Gurr were especially helpful. Finally, John Parker's *Van Meteren's Virginia, 1607–1612* provided decisive documentation of the presence of Powhatan voyagers on the *Sea Venture*.

Mentors have been a constant source of support and inspiration throughout my life, especially Donald W. Stokes, Benjamin Daise, Steve Sheppard, Elizabeth Shown Mills, C. S. Lovelace, Elizabeth Oldham, Laura Prieto, and C. James Taylor. George Sommers, Michael Muehe, Brian Calhoun-Bryant, Michael McHone, Nancy McHone, Peter Greenhalgh, Kevin Blanchard, Christy Law Blanchard, and Ran Baumflek have always been glad to talk about my latest discoveries. No one has been a greater encouragement to me than my family. Sarah Bliss, Dianne O'Donoghue, Barbara Bardenett, Amy Johnson, Greg Johnson, Gary Root, Christine Root, Paul Root, Alan Root, and Dennis Dickquist have offered support from the very beginning. My brother, Stewart Woodward, has been a lifelong friend and guiding presence. My mother, Mary S. Skinner, introduced me to history and has given me the sense of adventure and fortitude I needed to follow my aspirations. My father, V. Powell Bliss, has shared with me countless treasured adventures in pursuit of elusive ancestors and given me a sense of compassion that is the center of my life. My wife, Elizabeth Woodward, provides me unlimited love and patience and the good cheer of a best friend, for which I am eternally grateful. My daughters, Sadie and Sage, have endured two years of "Daddy's book" with loving words and good humor that always makes me smile.

NOTES

Abbreviations

ANC Ancient Planters. "A Breife Declaration of the Plantation of Virginia During the First Twelve Yeares." In *Journals of the House of Burgesses of Virginia 1619–1658/59*, edited by H. R. McIlwaine. Richmond, VA: Colonial Press, 1915.

ARD William Shakespeare. *The Tempest*. The Arden Shakespeare. Edited by Virginia Mason Vaughan and Alden T. Vaughan. London: Thomson Learning, 1999.

BER Nathaniel Butler. *The Historye of the Bermudaes or Summer Islands*. Edited by J. Henry Lefroy. London: Hakluyt Society, 1882.

DIS Silvester Jourdain. *A Discovery of the Barmudas, Otherwise Called the Ile of Divels*. London: Roger Barnes, 1610.

EST Virginia Company of London. *A True Declaration of the Estate of the Colonie in Virginia*. London: William Barret, 1610.

FIR Philip L. Barbour, ed. *The Jamestown Voyages Under the First Charter 1606–1609*. 2 vols. London: Cambridge University Press for the Hakluyt Society, 1969.

GEN Alexander Brown, ed. *The Genesis of the United States*. 2 vols. Boston: Houghton Mifflin, 1890.

HIS William Strachey. *The Historie of Travaile into Virginia Britannia*. Edited by R. H. Major. London: Hakluyt Society, 1849.

NAR Edward Wright Haile, ed. *Jamestown Narratives: Eyewitness Accounts of the Virginia Colony, The First Decade: 1607–1617*. Champlain, VA: Roundhouse, 1998.

NEW David B. Quinn, ed. *New American World: A Documentary History of North America to 1612*. 5 vols. New York: Arno Press, 1979.

PIL Samuel Purchas, ed. *Purchas His Pilgrimes*. 4 vols. London: Henrie Fetherstone, 1625.

REL Mark Nicholls. "George Percy's 'Trewe Relacyon': A Primary Source for the Jamestown Settlement." *Virginia Magazine of History and Biography* 113, no. 3 (2005): 212–75.

SMI   John Smith. *The Complete Works of Captain John Smith (1580–1631).* Edited by Philip L. Barbour. 3 vols. Chapel Hill: University of North Carolina Press, 1986.

TRU   Virginia Company of London. *A True and Sincere Declaration of the Purpose and Ends of the Plantation Begun in Virginia.* London: J. Stepneth, 1610.

VOY   Louis B. Wright, ed. *A Voyage to Virginia in 1609, Two Narratives: Strachey's "True Reportory" and Jourdain's "Discovery of the Bermudas."* Charlottesville: Association for the Preservation of Virginia Antiquities by the University Press of Virginia, 1964.

In *A Brave Vessel* I have modernized spelling, punctuation, and capitalization in quotations, with the exception of those from Shakespeare that follow the latest Arden editions. Citations of original works are followed by parenthetical references to the same material in recent documentary editions. Publications that do not have numbered pages are cited with supplied page numbers in brackets.

In the seventeenth century, Britain had not yet recalibrated the flawed "old-style" calendar, and to maintain the integrity of the original documents I have retained those dates. Therefore, every date cited is ten days behind the modern one. The only element of the old-style system that I have modernized is the date on which the year began (in seventeenth-century Britain the year began on March 25, but I have pushed the date back to the modern January 1). By 1609, Spain and the Netherlands had switched to the modern calendar, and so documents from those countries already carry new-style dates. To minimize confusion, those new-style dates are not cited in the text, and passages from those documents are silently placed at the appropriate points within the old-style timeline. Brown in *GEN* altered the dates of British documents to new style, and I have silently brought those dates back into sync with the old-style dates written on the originals.

Strachey in *HIS* copied without attribution long passages from the works of John Smith, and Smith himself appropriated passages written by other chroniclers. I have attempted to attribute quotations from the works of Strachey and Smith to the people who originally made them.

Chapter One

"Thou hast howled": 1.2.296, *ARD*, 170. Strachey's biography: Culliford, *Strachey*, 4–5, 22–38, 47–55, 57–60, 67; Sanders, *Family*, 10–27; Dorman, *Purse*, 3:251–57; *NAR*, 62–63; *GEN*, 2:1024; Wood, "Strachey"; Sheehan, "Strachey." *Sejanus* publication: Stationers' Company, *Registers*, 3:201. "Nothing violent," "swift lightning," "ruinous blasts": Jonson, *Sejanus* [11]. "My old companion": Foster, *Elegy*, 288. Trip to Turkey, "one Strachey": Culliford, *Strachey*, 61–96 (quotation: 93).

"Vaunt-courier," "hurricano": 3.2.2, 3.2.5, Shakespeare, *King Lear* (Arden, 2001), 263. Ashe, "Strachey," 509–11, proposes that Shakespeare used Strachey's sonnet in *King Lear*. Scholars continue to debate the question because it is uncertain whether Shakespeare's play came before or after the May 1605 publication of his main source, the earlier anonymous play *King Leir*. Knowles, "*King Leir*," 12–35, makes a compelling case that Shakespeare was inspired by the published version rather than an earlier direct knowledge of the play, and I have proceeded on that basis. Also considering the question are Foster, *Elegy*, 287 (accepts Shakespeare's use of Strachey); Taylor, "Source" (argues the playwright used additional post–May 1605 texts); Greenblatt, "King Lear" (notes general agreement on a post–May 1605 date for *King Lear*); Muir in Shakespeare, *King Lear* (Arden, 1972), xx–xxi (argues Shakespeare was first and Strachey copied *King Lear*); Kermode, "King Lear," 1297–98 (agrees that Strachey copied Shakespeare but says the evidence is not strong); Wells in Shakespeare, *King Lear* (Oxford), 14 (argues that the resemblance between the sonnet and the play is coincidental).

Origin of "hurricane": Emanuel, *Divine*, 18. Strachey familiar with Willes: Culliford, *Strachey*, 167–71. Strachey quotes Willes: *PIL*, 4:1738–41, (*NAR*, 391–92, 395, 396, 398, 400–401). "In time when": Willes, *Travayle*, 434 (verso), 435 (verso). "When we came in": Hakluyt, *Navigations*, 3:493.

Namontack overview: Vaughan, *Transatlantic*, 45–51, 276–78. While no document states that Strachey saw Namontack in London, Strachey's interest in Virginia and Namontack's notoriety make it likely that he did. Wahunsenacawh, Powhatan, and Tsenacomoco: *HIS*, 29, 47, 48 (*NAR*, 598, 613–14). I follow Rountree, *Pocahontas, Powhatan*, when spelling Powhatan words. Tsenacomoco population: Fausz, "Powhatan." "Trusty servant": *SMI*, 1:216. Namontack's first encounters: *SMI*, 1:63, 67, 91, 216, 240, 2:187, 290. Namontack's 1608 trip abroad: *NAR*, 451; *SMI*, 1:236–37, 2:183–84. "This Newport brought": *FIR*, 1:163 (in translation). Powhatan hairstyles, "some have chains," "I found not": *NAR*, 122–23. "Had gone naked": Crashaw, *Sermon* [39]. Plague symptoms and care: Aberth, *Brink*, 111, 118, 121–22. Epidemic dates: Bradbrook, *Shakespeare*, 207, 250.

"My good friend," "I dare boldly": Culliford, *Strachey*, 93. Countess of Bedford's patronage of Donne: Lawson, *Shadows*, 74, 86–111; Thomson, "Donne," 329–40; Stubbs, *Donne*, 221–24, 240–47, 300–306. "My Lady Bedford," "the best lady": Stubbs, *Donne*, 224, 241. No document states that Strachey visited the countess, but he surely did if she was the recipient of his Bermuda letter to the "Excellent Lady." See chapter eight notes below. Publicity drive unprecedented: Skura, "Discourse," 55; Linebaugh and Rediker, *Hydra*, 15; Fitzmaurice, *Humanism*, 63–64, and "Solution," 43–44, 47. "They have collected": *FIR*, 2:256. Virginia Company's early success: Fausz, "Blood," 29. "News here": *FIR*, 1:247. Donne's Virginia inquiry: Culliford, *Strachey*, 101; Lawson, *Shadows*, 107; Cooper, "Donne."

Donne's earlier expeditions: Stubbs, *Donne*, 47–79. Matthew Scrivener appointed Jamestown secretary: Culliford, *Strachey*, 102–3.

Strachey's acquisition of two shares Virginia Company stock: Culliford, *Strachey*, 101–2; *NAR*, 63. While Culliford proposes Strachey purchased shares, his agreement to travel abroad would have entitled him to a single share, and his elevated social status would have brought him additional value. Thus, he probably acquired them simply by signing on. Stock terms: Johnson, *Nova* [26]–[30] (*NEW*, 245–46). Present-day value: Officer, "Purchasing Power." Appearance of certificate: Quinn, "Pious," 553. Strachey kept a journal: Culliford, *Strachey*, 123, 185; Wright and Freund in Strachey, *Historie of Travell* (1953), xv.

Newport's January 1609 return to England: *FIR*, 1:246–47; *SMI*, 1:127. "The kind reception" and Namontack's return to England: *NAR*, 450–51. If Namontack rode home on the *Sea Venture* in May 1609, then he surely came to England with Newport on the only known voyage from Virginia in the winter of 1608 to 1609. The question of whether Namontack and Machumps were aboard the *Sea Venture* has long been a subject of inquiry, most comprehensively by Vaughan in *Transatlantic*. Two widely cited accounts place Namontack on the ship: John Smith in his 1624 *General Historie* in *SMI*, 2:350, claims Machumps murdered Namontack on Bermuda, and Purchas in 1625 referred to the alleged murder in *PIL*, 4:1771 (probably echoing Smith). Undermining Smith and Purchas (neither of whom were on the *Sea Venture*) is the fact that the Powhatans were not mentioned by anyone who was on board, most notably Strachey, who includes no Powhatan in a list of five people who died on Bermuda in *PIL*, 4:1746 (*NAR*, 413). What seems to be additional evidence against their claim is that in later writings Strachey mentions both Namontack (in a prevoyage context) and Machumps without stating that he had sailed with them. Smith was known to publish hearsay as fact, and the fifteen-year gap between the Bermuda sojourn and his claim suggests he may have been doing so in this case. Smith's macabre report seems more like an English cartoon of Powhatan behavior than a true account. Likewise, it seems unlikely that the English would not have punished Machumps if (as Smith alleges) he told them of the murder after his return to Virginia.

Despite the above evidence, an overlooked third record by a contemporary Dutch writer makes it clear that Namontack and Machumps were indeed on the *Sea Venture* and that the English did indeed believe that Machumps murdered Namontack on Bermuda. The passage appears in Dutch in Van Meteren's posthumous 1614 edition of *Historie der Neder-landscher*, portions of which Parker translates in *Van Meteren's*. In a passage on 66–67, 71, Van Meteren relays information provided by Gates in 1610 (whether directly from Gates or through an intermediary is unclear): "During all this time they lost only four men, of whom one was a *casicke*, or son of a king in Virginia who had been in England and who had been killed by an Indian, his own servant." Linebaugh and Rediker note this account in *Hydra*, 12, 356, without elaborating on its significance to this debate.

An additional overlooked clue further strengthens the case that Powhatans sailed on the *Sea Venture*. Strachey in *PIL*, 4:1741–47 (*NAR*, 400, 416), states that two canoes were in use on Bermuda. Though the English castaways built a small boat of European design on the island, as noted by Strachey in *PIL*, 4:1740 (*NAR*, 397), and Jourdain in *DIS*, 12–13 (*VOY*, 110), shipwrecked Englishmen whose labor was at a premium would surely not have experimented with the construction of dugout canoes of New World design. A pair of stranded Powhatans, however, with ample time, fire, and lumber and a pressing need to fish would almost certainly have done so. Thus, Strachey's mention of canoes on Bermuda constitutes significant circumstantial evidence that Powhatans were present.

Newport's presence on the *Sea Venture* also enhances the likelihood that Namontack was on board. Namontack guided Newport in Virginia, and Newport chaperoned Namontack on his first trip to England. Newport was at the helm of the ship that probably carried Namontack abroad a second time; it is likely the Powhatan envoy would have returned home with the same captain.

There are two post–*Sea Venture* references to Namontack, but neither indicates that he was living at the time. Strachey, in his one comment about him, in *HIS*, 131 (*NAR*, 687), notes that mines discovered by Namontack in 1608 were named for him. The other allusion is in a May 1614 account of a conversation between colonist Hamor and Wahunsenacawh in Hamor's *Discourse*, 38 (*NAR*, 831) (the same exchange is recounted in *SMI*, 2:248). The Powhatan leader told Hamor that he had sent Namontack into England (for a second time) and that many ships had returned without him. Hamor revealed nothing about Namontack's disappearance, undoubtedly for tactical reasons. The exchange suggests that when Machumps returned to Virginia without his companion he told Wahunsenacawh that Namontack had stayed behind in England.

A 1630 English narrative in *NAR*, 245, complicates the matter by mentioning a Powhatan traveler to England identified as "Nanawack," who is said to have come to England when Delaware was colonial governor (between June 1610 and March 1611), stayed "a year or two" and died in England. Despite the similarity in the names *Nanawack* and *Namontack*, the strength of the Van Meteren evidence forces the conclusion that either Nanawack was a different man or the account is a distorted version of Namontack's story. Vaughan, *Transatlantic*, 51–52, 278, argues that they were different people.

Machumps is mentioned as alive after the *Sea Venture* wreck by Strachey in *HIS*, 26, 54, 94 (*NAR*, 596, 619–20, 655). In one case, Strachey states that Machumps spent time in England, a significant point, since there were few opportunities for him to go abroad and return unless he rode the *Sea Venture*. Whitaker in *NAR*, 550, makes the last known allusion to Machumps in August 1611.

The most significant obstacle to the claim that Namontack and Machumps were on Bermuda is the absence of English prosecution of Machumps's alleged murder of Namontack. Crimes by Powhatans living among the English would likely have been prosecuted under English law. In light of this, I have depicted Namontack as disappearing on Bermuda, Machumps (whether innocent or guilty) claiming ignorance of his companion's fate, Gates assuming foul play but lacking evidence of a crime, and in 1624 John Smith (or one of his reporters) exaggerating details of Namontack's presumed death (perhaps confusing it with that of Samuel, who was murdered on the island by a fellow sailor). An enticing but speculative possibility is that whoever provided the bloody portrait of Machumps conflated the biography of the Powhatan castaway and Shakespeare's portrait of the fictional and monstrous Caliban.

Virtually all scholars to date who have addressed the question of Namontack's and Machumps's presence on the *Sea Venture* have been aware only of the Smith and Purchas passages. They include Malone, *Account*, 3–4 (published in 1808); Rountree and Turner, *Before*, 81 (accept Smith's statement); Horn, *Land*, 144 (places Machumps on the *Sea Venture* without mention of murder); Kelso, *Buried*, 36 (dates Namontack's death as 1610 without comment); and Vaughan, *Transatlantic*, 45–51, 276–78 (expresses doubt about Smith's story). The question must now be reevaluated in light of Linebaugh and Rediker's notice of the Van Meteren passage in *Hydra* and the overlooked circumstantial evidence of the presence of canoes, which together erase reasonable doubt that the Powhatan emissaries were on the *Sea Venture*.

Stracheys' Crowhurst residency: Culliford, *Strachey*, 32–33, 59. Household items described: Picard, *Elizabeth's*, 60–63, 127–31, 144–47. Items carried by colonists: Hughes, *Letter* [10]; *REL*, 215–16. "For the comfort": Hughes [10]. Writing implements described: Picard, *Elizabeth's*, 198; Kelso, *Buried*, 189. Strachey carried the books by Willes and Acosta: Culliford, *Strachey*, 165–71. Copy of Willes signed and dated by Strachey: James, *Dream*, 202–3. "You all know": Price, *Sauls* [44]. "The sickness increases": Brown, *Republic*, 83.

Chapter Two

"Though fools": 3.3.27, *ARD*, 236. Woolwich departure: Archer in *PIL*, 4:1733 (*FIR*, 2:279). Since Archer was on board, I have accepted his account over that of Londoner Powle, who claims a Blackwall departure in Quinn, "Pious," 554. Woolwich description: Weinreb and Hibbert, *London*, 971. Carriage transport: Picard, *Elizabeth's*, 31–35. Vessels' names: *PIL*, 4:1733 (*FIR*, 2:280). The vessel called "Catch" was either named *Catch* or was a ketch. Given the prevalence of the ketch class, as noted in Baker, *Vessels*, 119–44, I have called it an unnamed ketch. Fleet makeup: *PIL*, 4:1733 (*FIR*, 2:279); *PIL*, 4:1734 (*NAR*, 383); *DIS*, 4 (*VOY*, 105). Five hundred colonists. *TRU*, 7 (*NAR*, 360); *FIR*, 2:255, 276; *SMI*, 2:219; Bernhard

"Response," 668. One hundred and sixty mariners: estimate based on Lavery, *Merchantman*, 24; Mainwaring, *Dictionary*, 183; Barbour, *Pocahontas*, 97; Gill, *Plymouth: 1603*, 7; Camfield, "Worms," 654–55. The best formula is Lavery's inferred adjusted average of one crewman for every 8.6 tons burden of a ship.

Prevalence of figureheads on ships like the *Sea Venture*: Lavery, *Merchantman*, 18–19. *Sea Venture* dimensions based on wreck: Wright, *Story*, 24, 27; Mardis, *Wreck*, 47–57. Three hundred tons burthen: *PIL*, 4:1747 (*NAR*, 415); Craven, "Hughes," 75; *BER*, 11; Burrage, *Lost*, 3. *Sea Venture* a new ship: Stow, *Annales* (1615), 944. Wright, *Story*, 10; Raine, "Somers," 91; Peterson, "Sea Venture," 40–46, speculate about the origin of the *Sea Venture* based on records of vessels that shared the relatively common name. Wright proposes it was built in 1608 in Aldeburgh, England, based on Marsden, "Ships," 331, 336–37, whereas Peterson suggests that it was a textile ship launched in 1603. Vessel design based on wreckage: Wingood, "Report" (1982), 335; Adams, "Report" (1985), 297. London departure date: *PIL*, 4:1733 (*FIR*, 2:279); Quinn, "Pious," 554.

Early Jamestown: *NAR*, 3–38; Price, *Love*, 3–13. "We are fallen": *FIR*, 1:108. Virginia Company second charter: *NEW*, 205–12; *TRU*, 6–7 (*NAR*, 360). Shift from royal control, mineral profits to king: *FIR*, 2:270, 272. Charter revision, expanded territory claim: *FIR*, 2:249–51. Ranks of expedition officers, plan for later expedition: Quinn, "Pious," 554; *FIR*, 2:254–55; *SMI*, 1:268, 2:218. "Earthly paradise," "ravished with," "generally very loving," "most winds": Johnson, *Nova* [7]–[12] (*NEW*, 237–39).

"Petty commodities": *GEN*, 1:205. Natural resources as true treasure: Johnson, *Nova* [17]–[20], [26]–[27] (*NEW*, 241–42, 245); *HIS*, 133 (*NAR*, 688–89); Rich, *Newes* [8] (*NAR*, 378); *GEN*, 1:384–86. Virginia commodities replace Eastern European goods: *TRU*, 4, 18 (*NAR*, 359, 367) (marginal note on *TRU*, 4, is not in *NAR*). List of goods sought in Virginia: *GEN*, 1:384–86. Glassmaking at Jamestown: *PIL*, 4:1756 (*NAR*, 437); Harrington, *Glassmaking*; Kelso, *Buried*, 51–52, 183. Wine making: *HIS*, 120 (*NAR*, 678–79). Virginia furs and the Council of Jamestown: *NAR*, 121, 450. Medicinal plants: *FIR*, 1:79, 162. "This little northern": Johnson, *Nova* [27] (*NEW*, 245). Hunt for passage to East Indies: *FIR*, 1:81; Johnson, *Nova* [26] (*NEW*, 245); *SMI*, 1:49, 102, 165–66; *HIS*, 34, 104, 126 (*NAR*, 602, 665, 683). New World trade networks: Adams, *Best*, 33.

Preachers as promoters: *FIR*, 2:259; Wright, *Religion*, 84–114; Fitzmaurice, *Humanism*, 64; Horn, *Land*, 139; Knapp, *Empire*, 238–39. "If these objectors," "certainly our objector": Symonds, *Sermon*, 14–15. Analysis of Symonds's sermon: *HIS*, 17 (*NAR*, 588). "As for supplanting," "their children": Johnson, *Nova* [13]–[14], [32] (*NEW*, 239, 247). "To handle them": Neill, *History*, 28. Treatment of Powhatans compared to father's discipline: Symonds, *Sermon*, 14; *HIS*, 17 (*NAR*, 588). Lack of extant publications attacking Virginia Company: M. Fuller, *Voyages*, 90; Skura, "Discourse," 55. "Gold is more": Chapman, Jonson, and Marston: *Eastward* [36].

"Three most worthy": *DIS*, 3 (*VOY*, 105). Fleet officers' ranks: *TRU*, 12 (*NAR*, 364). Gates contends in *EST*, 19–21 (*NEW*, 252), that the three leaders had permission to ride together. Barbour in *SMI*, 2:219, rightly questions John Smith's 1624 statement that the three rode together because they "could not agree" to alternate ship assignments. The Virginia Company was disingenuous on the question of the three sealed boxes: in its instructions to Gates in *NEW*, 217–18, it says that the boxes should remain with him, but after the loss of the *Sea Venture* it says in *TRU*, 12 (*NAR*, 364), that they should have been placed on separate ships. Price, *Love*, 17, notes that on the first expedition to Jamestown similar boxes were carried on separate ships. Crashaw, *NAR*, 704, defends Gates's actions.

Somers meets fleet in Plymouth: *PIL*, 4:1733 (*FIR*, 2:279); *GEN*, 1:320. Newport biography: Andrews, "Newport," 28, 30–32, 37–38, 40; Quinn, "Newport"; Stow, *Annales* (1632), 1018; Ransome, "Newport," 354. "A mariner": *SMI*, 1:204. Whittingham is cape merchant: *PIL*, 4:1742 (*NAR*, 402). "Men of all": *SMI*, 3:28. Sailors feared by colonists: Greenblatt, *Shakespearean*, 149, 196. "Persons of rank": *TRU*, 12 (*NAR*, 364). "Their accustomed dainties": *SMI*, 1:175–76. "Common people," "hot bloods," "gentlemen of quality," "the idle," "the better sort": *PIL*, 4:1739, 1742–44 (*NAR*, 396, 402, 405, 407). Status of elite colonists: Canny, "Permissive," 37; Kelso, *Buried*, 186. Virginia Company stock policy, "go in their persons," "thither to remain": Johnson, *Nova* [26]–[30] (*NEW*, 245–46). Lists of tradesmen wanted: *TRU*, 26 (*NAR*, 371); Johnson, *Nova* [25] (*NEW*, 244). Established tradesmen reluctant to go: Harrington, *Glassmaking*, 6. Guilds support Virginia enterprise: *NEW*, 206, 233–34. Enclosure of farmland: Linebaugh and Rediker, *Hydra*, 15–20. Population growth in England: Holland in Shakespeare, *Tempest* (Pelican), vii; Picard, *Elizabeth's*, xxii; Adams, *Best*, 133–34. "Our land abounding": Johnson, *Nova* [21]–[22] (*NEW*, 243). Virginia Company accepts indigent laborers: *GEN*, 1:252–53; Canny, "Permissive," 25–27.

Chapter Three

"Calm seas": 5.1.315, *ARD*, 284. Plymouth details: Gill, *Plymouth: Ice*, 196, 199, 202, 205, 211, and *Plymouth: 1603*, 10. "From Woolwich": *PIL*, 4:1733 (*FIR*, 2:279). Somers with two vessels joins at Plymouth: Quinn, "Pious," 554; *PIL*, 4:1733 (*FIR*, 2:279–80). History of the pinnace *Virginia*: Neill *History*, 30; *GEN*, 1:197; Evans, *Shipping*, 4. "Three score years," "worthy and valiant": *DIS*, 22 (*VOY*, 115–16). "A man very": Stow, *Annales* (1632), 1018. "A gentleman": *PIL*, 4:1735 (*NAR*, 383). "Sir George Somers": T. Fuller, *Worthies*, 283. Somers's biography: Darrell, "Admiral," and *Links*, 4–6, 10. "Intending to pass": Broadley, "Will," 25. Matthew Somers on the *Swallow*: *PIL*, 4:1733 (*FIR*, 2:280). Life in Plymouth: Gill, *Plymouth: Ice*, 198, 210, and *Plymouth: 1603*, 7–8. Names of officers: *PIL*, 4:1733 (*FIR*, 2:280). "Expert captains": Stow, *Annales* (1632), 1018.

Number of people on *Sea Venture* (colonists *and* mariners): *PIL*, 4:1747 (*NAR*,

415); *EST*, 23 (*NEW*, 252); *SMI*, 1:268, 276, 2:219; *NAR*, 545; Craven, "Hughes," 57 (claims 140); Stow, *Annales* (1615), 943 (claims 160). Elizabeth Persons on *Sea Venture*: *PIL*, 4:1746 (*NAR*, 413). Rolfe biography: *NAR*, 55. Buck biography: Dorman, *Purse*, 1:427 (a flawed Buck biography in the 1987 3rd ed. of *Purse* was corrected in the 4th ed.); Chorley, "Planting," 200. "An able": *NAR*, 707. Hopkins biography: Johnson, "Origin," 164–66, 169–70; Christensen, "Parentage," 243–46. "A fellow": *PIL*, 4:1744 (*NAR*, 406).

Ballast characteristics: Mainwaring, *Dictionary*, 92–93; Wingood, "Report" (1982), 335; Adams, "Report" (1985), 280, 282, 284; Bermuda Maritime Museum, "*Sea Venture*." Cargo layout: Lavery, *Merchantman*, 88. Food storage: Mainwaring, *Dictionary*, 237; Bermuda Maritime Museum, "*Sea Venture*." Cod bones found in wreck likely from Plymouth: Armitage, "Rats," 145, 159. "Butter, cheese": Strachey, *For the Colony* (1612), 9 (1969 ed., 16). Food on voyages, "the juice of lemons," "suckets," "comfits": *SMI*, 3:28–29. Devonshire pottery in wreck: Wingood, "Report" (1982), 341, and "Artefacts," 151; Bermuda Maritime Museum, "*Sea Venture*." Chinese porcelain: Wingood, "Report" (1982), 341, 344. German casting counter: Wingood, "Artefacts," 156. Bartmann bottles and Spanish olive jars: Wingood, "Report" (1982), 341–42; Bermuda Maritime Museum, "*Sea Venture*." Other items found in wreck: Wingood, "Report" (1982), 337, 341–45, and "Artefacts," 151–55; Adams, "Report" (1985), 279, 281. "Quarter cans": *SMI*, 3:15–17.

"Many oxen," "a number": *FIR*, 1:212. "Some stallions," "bucks," "hogs": *FIR*, 2:277. Hogs and dog on *Sea Venture*: *PIL*, 4:1741 (*NAR*, 399–400). Pens on deck and bones of cows (carried as beef), hogs, sheep, cat, and rats in wreck: Armitage, "Rats," 145–46, 148–49, 152, 157, and "Victuals," 8–10. *Sea Venture* dog: Rich, *Newes* [4] (*NAR*, 375). Dog bones found at Jamestown: Kelso, *Buried*, 92–93. *Sea Venture* guns: Mardis, *Wreck*, 29; Wingood, "Report" (1982), 334–35, 339–41, and "Artefacts," 149–51; Bermuda Maritime Museum, "*Sea Venture*." Weights of guns: *SMI*, 3:26, 109. Duties of cape merchants: *SMI*, 3:15, 83. "Some superstitious": Mainwaring, *Dictionary*, 163. Sleeping arrangements: Lavery, *Merchantman*, 24–26, 82–85; Baker, *Vessels*, 20, 42; Mainwaring, *Dictionary*, 86–87, 138–39, 253–54; Price, *Love*, 16.

"The coming hither," "Sir George": *GEN*, 1:320. Second charter dated May 23, 1609: *NEW*, 205–12. Gates at charter signing May 29: *GEN*, 1:316–18. Treaties between Britain, Spain, Netherlands: Davenport, *Treaties*, 246, 258. Delay in departure of fleet: *FIR*, 1:212. Expedition held back to allow soldiers to join: *FIR*, 2:255, 258–59, 261. "A grave": Stow, *Annales* (1632), 1018. "Very remarkable": *FIR*, 2:255. Gates's biography: Prince, *Devon*, 403–5; Horn, *Land*, 132–33; *SMI*, 1:xxxv; *NAR*, 46–47; *GEN*, 2:894–96. Gates stopped at Roanoke: Sheehan "Gates," 792. Gates's military record: *FIR*, 1:235, 2:277.

"Upon Friday": *PIL*, 4:1734 (*NAR*, 383). "Crossed by": *PIL*, 4:1733 (*FIR*, 2:279).

Departure of fleet: *TRU*, 12 (*NAR*, 364); *SMI*, 1:127. Procedure when putting to sea, "yea, yea": *SMI*, 3:17, 85. "God bless": Stern, *Powle*, 142. "Kept in friendly": *PIL*, 4:1734 (*NAR*, 383). Pinnace turns around: *PIL*, 4:1733 (*FIR*, 2:280). Returning pinnace is *Virginia*: Horn, *Land*, 305. Pierce family separated: Dorman, *Purse*, 1:30, 31, 2:797–800, 3:24. "A quarter can," "a dish," "a little poor," "the men leap": *SMI*, 3:86, 92, 113. Use of gallery balconies: Bermuda Maritime Museum, "*Sea Venture*"; Lavery, *Merchantman*, 19. Smoking pipes: Wingood, "Artefacts," 152; Bermuda Maritime Museum, "*Sea Venture*"; Kelso, *Buried*, 88–89. Ships' heads: Lavery, *Merchantman*, 27.

"Prosperous winds": *REL*, 243. *Sea Venture* route: C. Smith, "Course," based on *TRU*, 12–13 (*NAR*, 364–65); *EST*, 19–21 (*NEW*, 252); *PIL*, 4:1733 (*FIR*, 2:281); *PIL*, 4:1734–35 (*NAR*, 383); *DIS*, 3–4 (*VOY*, 105); *NAR*, 453. Atlantic currents: Waters, *Navigation*, 2: plate 65. Wind science: Emanuel, *Divine*, 41–47. Log line: Mainwaring, *Dictionary*, 181–82. Meeting of officers at sea: *TRU*, 12–13 (*NAR*, 364); *EST*, 19–20 (*NEW*, 252); *FIR*, 2:277–78. Fleet advised to avoid Caribbean: *NEW*, 212. Instructions to meet at Barbuda if separated: *TRU*, 13 (*NAR*, 364). Archer in *PIL*, 4:1733 (*FIR*, 2:280), claims Bermuda was the rendezvous spot, but *FIR* editor Barbour shows that Archer was surely in error: Bermuda was off course, surrounded by dangerous shallows, and feared as the "Devil's Isle," while Barbuda was near the planned route and unclaimed by the Spanish. "We ran," "tracing through": *PIL*, 4:1733–34 (*FIR*, 2:280–81). Diseases on tropical voyages: *TRU*, 13 (*NAR*, 364); *EST*, 19–21 (*NEW*, 252); *NEW*, 287. "In all hot": Mainwaring, *Dictionary*, 91–92, 191. Calenture is heatstroke: Barbour, *Three*, 272. "But in the *Blessing*," "in the *Unity*": *PIL*, 4:1733–34 (*FIR*, 2:280–81).

Chapter Four

"Ride on the curled": 1.2.191–92, *ARD*, 162. C. Smith, "Course," estimates that when the hurricane struck the *Sea Venture* was at a point 500 to 600 nautical miles (or 575 to 690 land, or statute, miles) southeast of Virginia and 240 to 300 nautical miles (or 275 to 345 statute miles) southwest of Bermuda, which places it at roughly latitude thirty degrees north, longitude sixty-eight degrees west. At onset of storm *Sea Venture* seven or eight days from Virginia: *PIL*, 4:1735 (*NAR*, 383–84). At onset, ship 100 leagues (300 nautical miles, or 345 statute miles) from Bermuda: *NAR*, 445. At onset, fleet 150 leagues (450 nautical miles or 520 statute miles) from West Indies: *TRU*, 13 (*NAR*, 364). At onset, vessels at latitude thirty degrees north: Stow, *Annales* (1615), 943. At onset, fleet at latitude of Azores (which span thirty-six to thirty-nine degrees north): *BER*, 11.

Identifying the date on which the storm began is complicated by the chroniclers' reference to St. James Day. Strachey in *PIL*, 4:1734–36 (the punctuation is altered in *NAR*, 383–84, 387), says the ships "unto the twenty-three of July, kept in friendly consort together" and, a few lines later, "When on S. *James* his day, July

24. being Monday (preparing for no less all the black night before) the clouds gathering thick upon us" (the period after "24" marks the completion of the numeral rather than the end of a sentence). Strachey also says the leak was discovered "upon the Tuesday morning." In another account Somers says the storm began "on St. James' eve, being the 23 of July," and adds later that the pumpers and bailers worked "from the 23 of until the 28 of the same July, being Friday" (National Archives of the United Kingdom, co 1/1, No. 21, 84–85; *NAR*, 445–46). Jourdain in *DIS*, 4 (*VOY*, 105), says the storm began "upon the five and twentieth day of July"; Archer in *PIL*, 4:1733 (*FIR*, 2:281), says it began "upon Saint James Day" without giving a date; the Virginia Company in *TRU*, 13 (*NAR*, 364), reiterates that it began "on S. *James* day." The designation of July 24 as St. James Day by Somers (and seemingly by Strachey as well) is difficult to explain. Chambers, *Book of Days*, 2:120–22, and Blackburn and Holford-Strevens, *Oxford Book of Days*, 306–7, indicate that St. James Day has been firmly anchored to July 25 for centuries. Numerous records of the early seventeenth century confirm that it was observed on July 25, perhaps none more definitively than accounts of the July 25, 1603, coronation of King James on the feast day of the monarch's namesake saint, see for example Wilbraham, *Journal*, 61. Two instances have been found of St. James Day being marked on July 24: Baker, *Records*, 136 (a paraphrase of a 1584 agricultural journal), and Linschoten, *Voyages*, 179 (a 1598 travel account by a Dutch explorer). Those instances suggest some variability in the date of the feast day and may explain why Somers and Strachey apparently observed it on July 24, 1609. I have thus interpreted the *Sea Venture* sources to mean the following: the fleet was together until the evening of Sunday, July 23, when signs of a storm prompted preparations through that night; the hurricane hit on Monday, July 24; the leak was discovered early on Tuesday, July 25; and the storm lasted until Friday, July 28.

Lashing of guns: Lavery, *Merchantman*, 39, 119. "A dreadful storm": *PIL*, 4:1735 (*NAR*, 384). Hurricane characteristics: *PIL*, 4:1735, 1737 (*NAR*, 384, 389); Smith, "Course." African weather patterns spawning hurricanes: Emanuel, *Divine*, 98–100. Scattering of the fleet: *EST*, 34 (*NEW*, 255); *PIL*, 4:1733 (*FIR*, 2:281). Methods of towing small vessels: Harland, *Seamanship*, 207–8. Casting off of the ketch, "Michael Philes": *PIL*, 4:1735, 1748 (*NAR*, 384, 418). I have used Strachey's spelling of "Philes" instead of Archer's "Fitch," *PIL*, 4:1733 (*FIR*, 2:280). Thirty people on ketch: Bernhard, "Men," 606, based on *FIR*, 2:283, and *PIL*, 4:1747 (*NAR*, 415). Daily rain production of hurricanes: Emanuel, *Divine*, 187. "It works upon," "the sea swelled," "the glut of water": *PIL*, 4:1735 (*NAR*, 384–85).

Heavy-weather steering options: Mainwaring, *Dictionary*, 169, 179–80, 232, 249, 255; *SMI*, 3:88; Harland, *Seamanship*, 209–20. Somers's decision to "run before" the storm or "spoon afore": C. Smith, "Course," based on Strachey's statements that the wind came from northern points and Somers steered toward southern points, *PIL*, 4:1735, 1737 (*NAR*, 384, 389), and the stern (rather than the bow) of the ship was hit by a breaking sea, *PIL*, 4:1736 (*NAR*, 387). "Sir George Somers sitting": *DIS*, 5–6 (*VOY*, 106).

Causes of leaks: Harland, *Seamanship*, 303. "It pleased God," "this imparting," "there might be seen": *PIL*, 4:1735–36 (*NAR*, 386–87). Empty pots used to find leaks, traditional use of beef plugs, "in some cases": Butler, *Dialogues*, 22–23; Mainwaring, *Dictionary*, 177. Candlestick found still wedged between boards of wreck: Wingood, "Report" (1982), 337, 343, 345. "Many a weeping leak": *PIL*, 4:1736 (*NAR*, 386). Depth of water in hold: *NAR*, 445 (nine feet); Burrage, *Lost*, 3 (seven to eight feet). Keel most dangerous place for leak: Mainwaring, *Dictionary*, 154. "The waters still": *PIL*, 4:1736 (*NAR*, 386–87). Improvised pump-intake strainer found in wreck: Wingood, "Artefacts," 156. Pump technology: Harland, *Seamanship*, 304–5.

"To me this leakage," "the men might": *PIL*, 4:1736 (*NAR*, 387). Pierce family details: Dorman, *Purse*, 1:30, 31, 2:797–800, 3:24. Number, location, volume of pumps and bailing lines: *PIL*, 4:1737 (*NAR*, 390). Strachey's "gallon" predates Britain's imperial gallon and is roughly equivalent to today's U.S. gallon. I have relied on Strachey's count of three pumps over Somers's use of two hash marks to indicate two pumps in *NAR*, 445. Pumping and bailing methods and technology: Mainwaring, *Dictionary*, 92, 203–4, 218, 229–30; Lavery, *Merchantman*, 22–23. "We kept one hundred": *NAR*, 445. "Sharp and cruel," "with the violent": *DIS*, 4 (*VOY*, 105). Lack of food during storm, "we much unrigged": *PIL*, 4:1737 (*NAR*, 389–90). Wright, *Story*, 22, interprets Strachey's "heaved away all our ordnance on the starboard side" to mean that *all* guns on the ship went over the starboard side, but guns remained on the ship, as indicated by Wingood, "Report" (1982), 334–35 (gun found at the wreck site); *PIL*, 4:1747 (*NAR*, 414) (guns from *Sea Venture* placed on Bermuda-built ships); *BER*, 26, 290, and *SMI*, 2:355, 387 (guns salvaged from *Sea Venture* wreck by Bermuda colonists). "Sometimes strikes": *PIL*, 4:1735 (*NAR*, 385). Powhatan canoes carry forty people: *HIS*, 75 (*NAR*, 638–39). *Sea Venture* probably passed through eye of hurricane: Smith, "Course." Characteristics of hurricane eyes: Emanuel, *Divine*, 8–13, 165; Elsner, *Hurricanes*, 3–4. Clouds block sun and stars from navigators, "for four and twenty," "ran now": *PIL*, 4:1735–37 (*NAR*, 385, 388–89).

Chapter Five

"We all were": 2.1.251, *ARD*, 202. Remora story, "so huge a sea," "it struck him," "it so stunned": *PIL*, 4:1736 (*NAR*, 387–88). Science of overtaking wave: Harland, *Seamanship*, 214–15. Canvas hatch covers: Baker, *Vessels*, 43. *Sea Venture* incident a rogue wave: Mountford, "Storms," 22–23. Contemporary source for remora tale: Deacon and Walker, *Discourses* (1601), 204–5. "There was not," "upon the Thursday," "towards the morning," "purposed to have cut," "it being now Friday": *PIL*, 4:1736–37 (*NAR*, 388–90). "They were so overwearied," "some of them having": *DIS*, 5–6 (*VOY*, 106–7).

Date and time of Bermuda landing, lack of food and drink during storm: *PIL*, 4:1737, 1747 (*NAR*, 390, 415); *DIS*, 5–6, 10–11 (*VOY*, 106, 109). "See the goodness," "it being better surveyed": *PIL*, 4:1737 (*NAR*, 390). "Most wishedly": *DIS*, 6 (*VOY*, 106). Precolonial history of Bermuda: Jones, *Bermuda*, 10, 12, 14. Bermuda has most early shipwrecks in Western Hemisphere: Armitage, "Rats," 155. Gates rather than Somers gives order to ground ship: *PIL*, 4:1737 (*NAR*, 390). Danger of overthrowing in shallows: Mainwaring: *Dictionary*, 194. Call for continued bailing, "hearing news": *DIS*, 6–7 (*VOY*, 106–7).

"The morning now," "we had somewhat": *PIL*, 4:1737 (*NAR*, 390). "It pleased God": *DIS*, 7 (*VOY*, 107). "The boatswain": *PIL*, 4:1737 (*NAR*, 390). Dimensions of ship based on wreck: Wright, *Story*, 24, 27. "Neither did": *DIS*, 7 (*VOY*, 107). Location of wreck: *PIL*, 4:1737 (*NAR*, 390); Wingood, "Report" (1982), 346. Single point of entry to Bermuda: *PIL*, 4:1739 (*NAR*, 394). Use of longboat and skiff: *DIS*, 7 (*VOY*, 107). Use of boats, description of bay, "under a point," "a goodly bay": *PIL*, 4:1737–40, 1747 (*NAR*, 390–91, 394, 397, 415). Commanding officer last to leave distressed ship: Harland, *Seamanship*, 310. "By the mercy": *PIL*, 4:1737 (*NAR*, 390). Palmetto leaves as blankets: Jourdain, *Plaine*, 22; Collett, *Plants*, 78.

Chapter Six

"The still-vexed": 1.2.229, *ARD*, 165 (editors Vaughan and Vaughan modernize "Bermoothes" to "Bermudas"). Temperate air of Bermuda: Burrage, *Lost*, 16–17. "Gushings and soft": *PIL*, 4:1740 (*NAR*, 396). Early history of Bermuda: Jones, *Bermuda*, 12, 14. "We found it," "because they be": *PIL*, 4:1737 (*NAR*, 390–91). "As they would shun," "the islands of": *DIS*, 8–9 (*VOY*, 108). Powell identification, "fens, marshes": *PIL*, 4:1740, 1746 (*NAR*, 398, 413). Fear of contagion from marshes: Kupperman, "Climates," 224. Tradition that well dug by castaways still exists as Lunn's Well: Hayward, *Bermuda*, 177; Kennedy, *Isle*, 37, 258. "Drinks always sweet": Hughes, *Letter* [6].

"We saved all": *NAR*, 445. Salvage brought to island, "nothing but bared ribs": *PIL*, 4:1741 (*NAR*, 399); *DIS*, 7–8 (*VOY*, 107); *EST*, 23 (*NEW*, 252). "Many kind of fishes": *DIS*, 11–12 (*VOY*, 109–10). Fish caught near camp: *PIL*, 4:1740 (*NAR*, 396–98). Bermuda fish species: Hughes, *Letter* [6]. "We had knowledge," "at night was watched," Oviedo quoted on Spanish leaving hogs on Bermuda: *PIL*, 4:1738, 1741 (*NAR*, 391–92, 399–400). Diego Ramirez's visit: Wilkinson, *Adventurers*, 22; Jones, *Bermuda*, 11, 16. Bermuda hogs compared to modern breeds: Armitage, "Rats," 147. "Our people would go": *PIL*, 4:1741 (*NAR*, 400).

Palmetto fronds described: Stamers-Smith, "Flora," 120. "With these leaves," "so broad are": *PIL*, 4:1739 (*NAR*, 396). Consumption of palmetto berries and leaf heads: *DIS*, 15–16 (*VOY*, 112). "Roasting the palmetto," "a kind of peas," prickly pear description: *PIL*, 4:1739–40 (*NAR*, 396); *HIS*, 119 (*NAR*, 678). The *Oxford English Dictionary* says the first published use of "prickle pear" is *EST* (1610), 24 (*NEW*, 253). Bermuda a defensive stronghold: *DIS*, 17–18 (*VOY*, 113). "Desolate and not inhabited": *PIL*, 4:1739 (*NAR*, 394). "The best of it was": Beverly, *History*, 33. "They were long": *PIL*, 4:1739 (*NAR*, 394). "They are here": *BER*, 6. "Sir George Somers in" (with parenthetical aside silently omitted): *PIL*, 4:1739 (*NAR*, 394). "The mosquitoes": *BER*, 6. "Whereas it is reported," "no, nor any": Jourdain, *Plaine*, 19. "My opinion sincerely": *DIS*, 10 (*VOY*, 109). "I hope to deliver," Samuel murder described, "disdain that justice," "afterward by the mediation": *PIL*, 4:1737–38, 1746 (*NAR*, 391, 412, 413).

Chapter Seven

"Had I plantation": 2.1.144, *ARD*, 193. Migration of birds and insects, monthly temperatures: Amos, *Birds*, 18-19, 22, 23. "Many an ancient," "a round blue": *PIL*, 4:1739–40 (*NAR*, 396). Strachey's blue berry is bay grape: Sterrer and Cavaliere, *Seashore*, 22–24. Palmetto bibby: Stamers-Smith, "Flora," 119; Collett, *Plants*, 78. "The berries whereof": *PIL*, 4:1739 (*NAR*, 395). Strachey's "corynthes" are currants: *Oxford English Dictionary*. "There are an infinite": *DIS*, 16 (*VOY*, 112). Tobacco found on Bermuda: *DIS*, 18 (*VOY*, 113); Stamers-Smith, "Flora," 120. Olives and pawpaws introduced circa 1593: Collett *Plants*, 96. Mulberries and silkworms found: *DIS*, 15 (*VOY*, 111–12).

Summer food storage difficult: Jourdain, *Plaine*, 19. "Kept three or four": *PIL*, 4:1740 (*NAR*, 397). Salt making on Bermuda: *HIS*, 61 (*NAR*, 626); *DIS*, 19 (*VOY*, 119); Craven, "Hughes," 75–76. Volume of wood to make sea salt: LeConte, *Salt*, 10. Continuous fires: *PIL*, 4:1740 (*NAR*, 397). Spanish use of Bermuda cedar: Jones, *Bermuda*, 12. Size of largest cedars: Stamers-Smith, "Flora," 117. Island-built gondola: *DIS*, 12–13 (*VOY*, 110). Gondola construction, "we have taken": *PIL*, 4:1740 (*NAR*, 397). Strachey's "gundall" and "skulles" are gondola and schools: *Oxford English Dictionary*. Canoes used on Bermuda: *PIL*, 4:1741, 1747 (*NAR*, 400, 416). Namontack and Machumps were on Bermuda: *SMI*, 2:350; Parker, *Van Meteren's*, 67. I have assumed that only Powhatans would have exerted the time and effort necessary to construct canoes. Powhatan canoe construction and fishing: *SMI*, 1:163–64. "A kind of boat": *NAR*, 494. "Enclosures made": *HIS*, 68 (*NAR*, 633).

Typical length of longboats: Lavery, *Merchantman*, 23. Outfitting of longboat, pinnace construction, naming of Frobisher's Building Bay, "a painful," "we made up" (with a parenthetical aside silently omitted), "the twenty-eighth," "promising if he": *PIL*, 4:1740, 1742–43 (*NAR*, 397, 401–4). Frobisher's Building Bay is universally identified with the modern Building Bay on St. George's Island just north of Town Cut. The Somers map in the Bermuda Archives, however, places Frobisher's Building Bay farther north, at a notch in the shoreline at the modern intersection of Coot Pond and Barry roads. That notch, however, is too small and its sides too steep (at least in its present configuration) to be used as a site for the construction of a pinnace. Also, Strachey's description of fishing in Frobisher's Building Bay seems to better match the configuration of the modern Building Bay. The persistence of the name on continuously occupied Bermuda is additional evidence that the two are one and the same. Therefore, despite the label on the map, I have located Frobisher's Building Bay at the modern Building Bay. Date of laying of keel, pinnace specifications: *PIL*, 4:1746–47 (*NAR*, 413–15). Boat-building methods, "first lay the keel," "the lengths": *SMI*, 3:17–18, 57–58. "The governor dispensed": *PIL*, 4:1743 (*NAR*, 403–4).

"I am persuaded," "some dangerous," "in Virginia nothing," "there being neither" (with a parenthetical aside silently omitted), "a mutinous," "they were condemned": *PIL*, 4:1743 (*NAR*, 404–5). Mutineers' desire to stay: *BER*, 13. Conflicting motivations of Gates and the mutineers: Greenblatt, *Shakespearean*, 151–53. Early autumn weather conditions: Amos, *Birds*, 25. "Our governor (not easy)": *PIL*, 4:1743 (*NAR*, 406).

Strachey's interviews with Machumps and other Powhatans (in Jamestown; there is no record of Bermuda interviews, but I have assumed they occurred): *HIS*, 26, 53–54, 94 (*NAR*, 596, 619–20, 655). Namontack's knowledge of English: Vaughan, *Transatlantic*, 47. Strachey's record of Powhatan words: *HIS*, 183–96; Strachey, *Dictionary*. Powhatan bows and hunting methods: Rountree, *Powhatan Indians*, 39–40, 42. Bermuda's cave system: Sterrer and Iliffe, *"Mesonerilla,"* 509. "Some such differences": *SMI*, 2:350. Smith, and Van Meteren in Parker, *Van Meteren's*, 67, allege that Machumps murdered Namontack on Bermuda. Because there is no indication that the English punished Machumps, I have assumed that Namontack disappeared, the English were suspicious but could not prove murder, and the story of the disappearance was exaggerated by returning voyagers.

Chapter Eight

"'Twas a sweet": 2.1.73 *ARD*, 189. Autumn weather conditions, cahow arrival and laying timetable: Amos, *Birds*, 25, 28, 31, 40. "At dusk, such": Wilkinson, *Adventurers*, 23; Jones, *Bermuda*, 10, 16. "Birds Ilands" are labeled on the Somers map in the Bermuda Archives (now Cooper's Island and Castle Islands nature reserves south of Bermuda International Airport). "A kind of web-footed," "there are thousands": *PIL*, 4:1740–41 (*NAR*, 398–99). Oviedo use of "sea-mew" (a possible source for Strachey): Jones, *Bermuda*, 13.

Naming of features, identifications of Gates Bay and Somers Creek, description (without naming) of Strachey's Watch: *PIL*, 4:1738–39, 1742 (*NAR*, 391–92, 394, 402). Strachey's Watch is named on the Somers map in the Bermuda Archives. Strachey's Watch is probably the bluff where St. David's Lighthouse now stands: Zuill, "Cast Away," 55.

Somers's mapping of Bermuda, "Sir George Somers, who coasted," Strachey sending the map and a report to the "Excellent Lady": *PIL*, 4:1738, 1742 (*NAR*, 391, 403). A map identified as Somers's map is owned by the Bermuda National Trust and on deposit in the collection of the Bermuda Archives, and an incomplete duplicate of that map is in the British Library (Cotton Charter XIII.45). The outline of the island in the two versions differs minutely, as if one is a freehand copy of the other. The two versions share illustrations that also vary in small ways—a whale, a depiction of two hunters and a dog chasing hogs, a compass rose, and the Harrington family coat of arms. On the Bermuda Archives copy a cherub on the back of a sea turtle carries a banner identifying the Bermuda archipelago as the "Sumer Iles" (i.e., Summer or Somers Islands), a name not coined until 1612, evidence that dates the illustration to that year or later. The Bermuda Archives version also has unique labels that identify features of the *Sea Venture* era: Gates Bay, Frobisher's Building Bay, Somers Creek, the Bird Islands, Strachey's Watch, and Ravens Sound (the map is the only known source of the last two names). The named features closely match those described by Strachey, demonstrating that the author of the labels was familiar with the geography of the *Sea Venture* era. A complication is that while the notch of Frobisher's Building Bay is accurately depicted on the map, the label naming it is placed too far north. Thus, it seems the author of the labels may have had a degraded memory or imperfect knowledge of the early geography of the island. Two other named features on the Bermuda Archives version, "Baylysses house" and "Waltons house," certainly date to the settlement period following 1612. Wilkinson, *Adventurers*, plate facing 47, calls the Bermuda Archives document "an early map, probably a copy of Sir George Somers's map." While it is possible that both maps are copies of a lost original, a perhaps more likely scenario is that one of the two is the original (with added information of a later date) and one is a copy. Quinn, "Bermuda in the Age," 22–23, suggests that the British Library map is more likely the original, but definitive evidence is lacking.

Both maps also carry the coat of arms of the Harrington family, as noted in the British Library catalog entry for Cotton Charter XIII.45; Wilkinson, *Adventurers*, plate facing 47; and Tucker, *Bermuda Today and Yesterday*, 35. As Wilkinson and Tucker note, the presence of the Harrington coat of arms on the maps suggests they were once owned by the daughter of the first Lord Harrington, Lucy, Countess of Bedford, and that therefore she was probably the anonymous "Excellent Lady" to whom Strachey sent the map and his report of the wreck. Wingood, Wingood, and Adams, *Tempest Wreck*, 10, and Rowse, *Southampton*, 239, also argue that the countess was Strachey's "Excellent Lady" without noting the evidence of the coat of arms on the maps. The countess was a shareholder in the Virginia Company, a patron of the literary arts, close to Strachey's friend John Donne, and later an owner of large landholdings on Bermuda (the island's

Harrington Sound was named after her). Those factors all support the identification of her as the likely recipient of Strachey's letter. Furthermore, her continuing interest in Bermuda from the early years of the Virginia Company through the post–settlement era explains why a map in her possession would carry labels from both eras. The Countess of Bedford's post–settlement real estate activities are described in Craven, "Introduction," 338–40. Her friendship with Donne is detailed in Lawson *Shadows*, 74, 86–111; Thomson, "Donne"; Stubbs, *Donne*, 221–24, 240–47, 300–306. Several other "Excellent Lady" candidates have been proposed: Culliford, *Strachey*, 152–54, and Foster *Elegy*, 279, suggest she was Sara Blount Smith; Gayley, *Shakespeare*, 231–32, argues that she was Elizabeth Hume Howard.

Gayley, *Shakespeare*, 18–20, 70–76, recounts what is known about Strachey's "True Reportory" manuscript, which is no longer extant. Noël Hume in "Unrecorded First Draft" proposes that a late nineteenth or early-twentieth-century transcript discovered on Bermuda reflects the existence of a second variant of Strachey's letter. My reading of the evidence is that the transcript is more likely a rough and selective transcription of the *PIL* text. Vaughan, "Evidence," 256–59, agrees with Noël Hume.

The editor of *PIL*, 4:1738 (*NAR*, 391), in a 1625 marginal note next to Strachey's discussion of Somers's map, says "Sir George Summer's diligent survey; his draught which we have not. M. Norgate hath since published an exact Map." As editor, Wright notes in *VOY*, 17, the allusion to an "M. Norgate" map is likely a misspelled reference to "Mr." Richard Norwood's later map of Bermuda that was published in 1622.

Powell and Persons wedding: *PIL*, 4:1746 (*NAR*, 413); *DIS*, 17 (*VOY*, 113). English wedding traditions: Monger, *Marriage*, 34, 38, 46, 53, 98, 115, 293. "Amongst all those": *SMI*, 2:349. "There is great": *DIS*, 16–17 (*VOY*, 112). Pearls on Bermuda: *PIL*, 4:1738, 1745 (*NAR*, 393–94, 410). "In the bottom": *SMI*, 2:341. "There is one": Jourdain, *Plaine*, 21.

Strachey in *PIL*, 4:1742–43 (*NAR*, 403–4), and Jourdain in *DIS*, 13 (*VOY*, 110–11), note the fractured relationship between Gates and Somers. Butler (who was not among the castaways) in *BER*, 14, followed by Smith, in *SMI*, 2:349, and Irving in *Wolfert's*, 66, exaggerate the antagonism between the two leaders. I have followed Jones, *Bermuda*, 25, who characterizes the split as the two leaders "demonstrating traditional rivalry, Somers, the sailor, and Gates, the soldier."

Indentured castaways fear abandonment, leaders communicate by letter, Communion on Christmas eve, "two moons," "the seven and twentieth," "twenty of the ablest": *PIL*, 4:1742, 1745–46 (*NAR*, 402–3, 410–13). No frost on Bermuda: Phillips-Watlington, *Botanical*, 15. Breakwater construction, "at Christmas," "these islands are often," "the three winter": *PIL*, 4:1738, 1747 (*NAR*, 392–93, 414). Hopkins biography: Johnson, "Origin," 164–66, 169–70; Christensen, "Parentage," 243–46.

Hopkins's arguments justifying mutiny, "full of sorrow" "so penitent": *PIL*, 4:1744 (*NAR*, 406–7).

Births of babies: *PIL*, 4:1746 (*NAR*, 413); *DIS*, 17 (*VOY*, 113); Rich, *Newes* [5] (*NAR*, 375); Hughes, *Letter* [4]; *SMI*, 2:349. Only married women assist with childbirth: Picard, *Elizabeth's*, 182–83. Childbirth methods, "the time of delivery," "sometimes the midwife," "to give her women," "the child being": Sermon, *Companion* (1671), 92–95, 99–101, 106–8, 120. Sermon's "mummy" is human remains used as medicine: *Oxford English Dictionary*. Cedar compress on cord stump: Stamers-Smith, "Flora," 117; Collett, *Plants*, 57. "The eleventh": *PIL*, 4:1746 (*NAR*, 413). "All intents and purposes": *NEW*, 210. "Young children": Hughes, *Letter* [7].

Cahows' and hens' eggs similar: *PIL*, 4:1741 (*NAR*, 399). Sea turtle nursery, average weight of green sea turtle: Bermuda Turtle Project, "Species." Palmetto berry season, sea turtle hunting: *PIL*, 4:1741 (*NAR*, 400). Sea turtle hunting, "we take them," "they will live," "the flesh that cleaveth": Burrage, *Lost*, 20, 22. Use of turtle oil: *DIS*, 15 (*VOY*, 111). Bermuda birds, "the mornings," "fowl there": *PIL*, 4:1738, 1740 (*NAR*, 393, 398).

Chapter Nine

"I do begin": 4.1.220–21, *ARD*, 258. "Deadly and bloody," "the life of our," "pass the act," "evil language," "Paine replied," "with the omitted," "our governor who," "whether mere rage," "so weak and unworthy," "of that ancient love," "Sir George Somers did," "of a mighty compass," "the mightiest blast": *PIL*, 4: 1738, 1744–46 (*NAR*, 393, 408–12). "A place heretofore": Prince, *Devon*, 403–4. Death of Bermuda Rolfe, "the five and twentieth": *PIL*, 4:1746 (*NAR*, 413). Pierce family information: Dorman, *Purse*, 1:30, 31, 2:797–800, 3:24.

Five hundred salted fish put on ships: *PIL*, 4:1740 (*NAR*, 397). Live turtles and salted birds, pork, and fish taken: Craven, "Hughes," 75–76; *BER*, 14. Bermuda grouper, snapper, sea turtle, cahow, and pork remains in Jamestown digs: Kelso, *Buried*, 89–90; Bowen and Andrews, "Starving," 48–50, 58–59, 72–73. "They come and lay," "very fat and sweet": *DIS*, 13 (*VOY*, 110–11). "Egg bird" described: *BER*, 4; *SMI*, 2:342. Egg bird probably common tern: Verrill, *Bermuda*, 254–56. Common tern described: Amos, *Birds*, 33. Spring weather, April humpback whale migration: Amos, *Birds*, 33. Whales seen and heard off shore: *DIS*, 17 (*VOY*, 112–13). Strachey (citing Oviedo) on thresher and swordfish attacks on whales: *PIL*, 4:1740 (*NAR*, 398). Similar passages by Percy and an anonymous early colonist of Bermuda: *NAR*, 86; Jourdain, *Plaine*, 22. Barbour, "Honorable," 10–11, proposes Strachey copied the passage from Percy, but the similarity is more likely due to the common use of Oviedo. Donne's use of the same image in 1601: Donne, *Poems*, 188; Stubbs, *Donne*, 151–52. Historical confusion between swordfish and thresher and killer whales: Martin, "Thresher." Tropic birds and pimlicos on

Bermuda: *BER*, 4–5; *SMI*, 2:343. Tropic bird behavior: Amos, *Birds*, 31, 41. Pimlico is Audubon's shearwater: Verrill, *Bermuda*, 265–67.

Caulking of Bermuda vessels: *PIL*, 4:1746–47 (*NAR*, 414). Hull sealing methods: *SMI*, 3:66–67. Launch of *Deliverance*, vessel specifications, "when she began," "the thirtieth of March," "we launched her," "the most part," "her beams": *PIL*, 4:1747 (*NAR*, 414–15). *Deliverance* specifications: Hardy, *Voyage* [vi]; Sams, *Conquest*, 717–18. Bermuda limestone ballast in Jamestown digs: Kelso, *Buried*, 90, 107. "God in the": *DIS*, 20 (*VOY*, 114). Launch of *Patience*, vessel specifications: *PIL*, 4:1747 (*NAR*, 415–16). Somers's work on *Patience*, single bolt in vessel: *DIS*, 23 (*VOY*, 116). Frobisher's inscription in Latin: Hardy, *Voyage* [vi]. Frobisher translated as "there was built": Sams, *Conquest*, 717–18. "In memory of our" (memorial is no longer extant), "from this time," "about ten of": *PIL*, 4:1747–48 (*NAR*, 415–16).

Chapter Ten

"O brave new": 5.1.183, *ARD*, 275. "Had it not been," "we buried five": *PIL*, 4:1746, 1748 (*NAR*, 413, 416–17). Rich, *Newes* [5] (*NAR*, 375), says two died, apparently understating the number to exactly offset the two births. Machumps suspected in Namontack's disappearance: Parker, *Van Meteren's*, 67; *SMI*, 2:350. Machumps circulated freely among the English after Namontack's disappearance: *HIS*, 26, 54, 94 (*NAR*, 596, 619, 655); *NAR*, 550. "The body of": *PIL*, 4:1746 (*NAR*, 412).

Voyage to Virginia: *PIL*, 4:1748 (*NAR*, 417). Speed of pinnaces: Smith, "Course." "The twentieth about": *PIL*, 4:1748 (*NAR*, 417). "A well-bowed": *SMI*, 3:64. "In the morning," "about seven," "the one and," "being Monday": *PIL*, 4:1748 (*NAR*, 417–18). "We espied two": *REL*, 250. "The good news," "from hence": *PIL*, 4:1748 (*NAR*, 418–19). Soldiers at fort report famine: *NAR*, 445–46. Deep water off Jamestown: *NAR*, 94. Jamestown description: *PIL*, 4:1752–53 (*NAR*, 429–30). Sixty survived famine in Jamestown palisade: *SMI*, 1:275–76, 2:232; *DIS*, 20–21 (*VOY*, 114–15); *ANC*, 29; *REL*, 271. Twenty-five to forty more survived at Point Comfort fort: Bernhard, "Men," 599, 612, 613; Camfield, "Worms," 659. Two hundred forty-five total were reduced to ninety: Kelso, *Buried*, 90. Women were among the starving: Bernhard, "Men," 614. "Great pain": *NEW*, 210. "Sloth, riot," "factionaries," "their ignoble," "no story can remember": *PIL*, 4:1749 (*NAR*, 420). "Tempest of dissension": *EST*, 34 (*NEW*, 255). "The happiest day": Neill, *History*, 408.

Drought of 1606 to 1612: Blanton, "Drought," 76, 77; Stahle, "Lost"; Fagan, *Ice Age*, 96–97; Kelso, *Buried*, 122–23, 178. Health problems caused by saltwater consumption: Earle, "Environment," 99–105, 109–11, 116–17, 122–25; Price, *Love*, 48; Adams, *Best*, 164–67. "Had not now," "true it is": *PIL*, 4:1751, 1753 (*NAR*, 425, 430–31). Concern about water quality: *EST*, 32–33, 42 (*NEW*, 254–55, 257). Mosquitoes at Jamestown: Noël Hume, *Here Lies*, 68–69. Health threats during drought: Rutman and Rutman, "Agues," 33–34, 38, 50; Kupperman, "Apathy," 24–25, 28–34, 36 (prisoner of war comparison), and "Climates," 213–14, 228–29, 231–33; Blanton, *Medicine*, 47–55, 62–69; Adams, *Best*, 164–67; Bernhard, "Men," 605, 615, and "Bermuda," 58–59; Price, *Love*, 55–56 (concentration camp comparison).

Reunited fleet disobeyed Gates's Barbuda order: Glover and Smith, *Shipwreck*, 98. "The *Unity*," "having cut her": *PIL*, 4:1733–34 (*FIR*, 2:281, 282). "In the tail": *SMI*, 2:219–20. "Houses few": *ANC*, 29. Argall's voyage to Jamestown: *SMI*, 1:267, 2:216–17; *FIR*, 2:285; Eaton, "Voyage"; Connor, "Argall," 163–64. Wounding of John Smith, arrival of the *Virginia*, Smith's departure for England: *SMI*, 1:128, 272–73, 2:223–25, 231–32; *FIR*, 2:253; *REL*, 245–46; *TRU*, 14 (*NAR*, 365); Bernhard, "Men," 608–9; Brown, *Republic*, 109. "Sir Thomas Gates": *NEW*, 287. Starving Time details, "famine beginning," "to do those things": *REL*, 247–51. Events during Jamestown famine: *EST*, 36–43 (*NEW*, 255–57); Neill, *History*, 408; *ANC*, 29; *SMI*, 2:232–33; Sainsbury, *State Papers: Colonial*, 1:39; *FIR*, 1:150; Fausz, "Blood," 25–27.

Chapter Eleven

"Our royal": 5.1.237, *ARD*, 279. Pierce family details: Dorman, *Purse*, 1:30, 31, 2:797–800, 3:24. Reuniting of the Pierces: Bernhard, "Men," 616–17. "Our much-grieved": *PIL*, 4:1748–49 (*NAR*, 419). "A homely thing": *SMI*, 3:295. Church building details: Lounsbury, *Church*, 3–4. "Viewing the fort": *PIL*, 4:1749 (*NAR*, 419). "Our governor Sir": *NAR*, 446. "There was a general": *PIL*, 4:1749–52 (*NAR*, 419–27). "Every man glad": *ANC*, 29. "Most of our men": *REL*, 251. Careening of ships: Mainwaring, *Dictionary*, 117–19.

Gates's posting of laws (an editor's note not reprinted in *NAR* says they numbered 21): *PIL*, 4:1749 (*NAR*, 420). Flaherty in commentary in Strachey, *For the Colony* (1969), xvi, xviii, xxiii, argues that based on language style the first nineteen laws published later by Strachey may safely be attributed to Gates. Because the language of the nineteenth is ambiguous, I have attributed the first eighteen to him. Laws rooted in military code and more severe than civil law: Flaherty in Strachey, *For the Colony* (1969), ix, xv, xxvi–xxviii, xxxii; *GEN*, 2:529; Linebaugh and Rediker, *Hydra*, 18. "Have a bodkin," "disgraceful words," "tied head and feet," "no man shall ravish": Strachey, *For the Colony* (1612), 3, 5, 7 (1969 edition, 10–14).

Virginia departed in advance for Point Comfort: *NAR*, 456, 458. Date of departure, "he commanded," "his own company": *PIL*, 4:1752 (*NAR*, 427). "Quitted Jamestown": *ANC*, 29. "About an hour": *PIL*, 4:1752 (*NAR*, 427). Longboat meets Jamestown vessels: *NAR*, 458; *EST*, 45–46 (*NEW*, 257). Delaware in *NAR*, 466, says Gates intended to wait ten days at Point Comfort for Delaware's fleet before leaving for Newfoundland. The contention lacks credibility, given Gates's precarious food supply, and I have attributed it to an attempt by Delaware to deflect criticism from Gates for deciding to abandon the colony. Alternately, Kelso, *Buried*, 40, 91–92, notes that Point Comfort was rich in shellfish that could have sustained the colonists if they had waited there for Delaware.

Delaware expected to follow Gates fleet with a thousand people in nine ships: Brown, *Republic*, 101; *GEN*, 1:358. Delaware actually carried 150 colonists plus crew in three ships: *NAR*, 465; *NEW*, 219. Higher estimates of Delaware contingent: Rich, *Newes* [6] (*NAR*, 376) (170); *ANC*, 30 (250); *REL*, 251–52 (300). Names of Delaware's ships: *NAR*, 454–55. "Made our hearts": *NAR*, 446. "Revived all": *DIS*, 21–22 (*VOY*, 115). "The great grief": *ANC*, 30. I have reconciled conflicting statements about Gates's location in *PIL*, 4:1752 (*NAR*, 427), and *ANC*, 30, by presuming that Gates sent most of his fleet back to Jamestown immediately and later rode the *Virginia* up river in convoy with Delaware's ships. "It was seasoned": *NAR*, 456.

Argall brought news of the loss of the *Sea Venture* to England by November 9, 1609: *FIR*, 2:285–86. "Were dashed": *FIR*, 2:278. Ships lost off France, "they tell me": *FIR*, 2:286, 289. "Unruly youths," "vile and scandalous," "color their own," "cheer themselves," "these devices infused," "lascivious sons": Virginia Company, *Publication* (*GEN*, 1:354–55). *TRU* registered for publication December 14, 1609: Barbour, *Three*, 284. *Sea Venture* wreck widely discussed in London: Bristol, *Shakespeare*, 63. "Ignorant rumor," "we will call," "is he fit," "so small a root," "blessed and unexpected," "perhaps bound in," "the loss of him," "against some doubt": *TRU*, 2, 5, 14, 15, 17 (*NAR*, 358–59, 365–67). "Some say that": *FIR*, 2:288. "Loose, lewd," "the very excrements," "such fellows," "let no wise man": Crashaw, *Sermon* [38], [44]–[45]. Delaware's voyage preparations: Quinn, "Pious," 554. Departure date, number of ships and passengers: *NAR*, 465.

Chapter Twelve

"Savages and men": 2.2.57, *ARD*, 210. Date of Delaware's arrival in Jamestown, his entry into the palisade, newly appointed officers, "his lordship landing fell": *PIL*, 4:1752, 1754 (*NAR*, 427, 432–33). The rank Strachey attributes to Scot, "ancient" (i.e., bearer of the ancient colors), is "ensign": *Oxford English Dictionary*. Weynman is Delaware's first cousin: Barbour, *Pocahontas*, 76. "I delivered some": *NAR*, 458–59. Delaware's report home: *NAR*, 454–64. Strachey calls recipient of his letter "Excellent Lady": *PIL*, 4:1734, 1742, 1756 (*NAR*, 383, 402, 438). Recipient was likely Lucy Harrington, Countess of Bedford: Wilkinson, *Adventurers*, plate facing 47; Tucker, *Bermuda Today and Yesterday*, 35 (see full analysis above in notes to chapter eight).

"I set the sailors": *NAR*, 466. Virginia Company thought colony had livestock: *PIL*, 4:1754 (*NAR*, 433). "I dispatched Sir": *NAR*, 466–67. Somers's departure date:

NAR, 459–60. Silvester Jourdain in *DIS*, 23 (*VOY*, 116), gives the same date. "Now we are": *NAR*, 446. Sheltering from a rainstorm, to sea June 23: *NEW*, 303. Butler's contention in *BER*, 15, that Somers had a secret pact with the men left behind to return to Bermuda is not credible. Refurbishing of Jamestown: *NAR*, 466. "Pretty chapel," "shall have a chancel": *PIL*, 4:1752–53 (*NAR*, 429). Delaware brought four preachers: *FIR*, 2:279. Church schedule, "every Sunday when" (Strachey meant that the total number of gentlemen and halberdiers was fifty rather than that there were fifty halberdiers): *PIL*, 4:1753 (*NAR*, 429). Jamestown artifact cache probably dates to Delaware's cleanup: Kelso, *Buried*, 101, 103.

Physical seasoning of colonists fresh from England: Kupperman, "Climates," 215, 220, 232. Delaware's illnesses, "presently after my," "I was upon": *NEW*, 263. Alleged fate of Ravens's expedition, diplomatic emissaries, "Powhatan returned no": *PIL*, 4:1748, 1755–56 (*NAR*, 418, 435–37). Negotiations with the Powhatans: *REL*, 253. Strawberries outside the palisade: *FIR*, 1:161. Colonists killed gathering strawberries, "certain Indians," "now being startled": *PIL*, 4:1755 (*NAR*, 434–35, 437). Strachey at Kecoughtan attack (I have presumed him to be at Jamestown unless explicit evidence places him outside the palisade): *PIL*, 4:1755 (*NAR*, 435). "Being landed he," "fell in upon": *REL*, 252. Kecoughtan attack, construction of English fort: *ANC*, 30; Fausz, "Blood," 6, 32. Kecoughtan description, "many pretty copses," "maracock apple" (editor Major identifies the maracock apple as the passionflower): *HIS*, 60 (*NAR*, 626–27). French vintners sent to Jamestown: *EST*, 58–59 (*NEW*, 260). "We proposed to set": *PIL*, 4:1755 (*NAR*, 435). "Behold the goodly": *HIS*, 120 (*NAR*, 678–79). Hostage's hand severed: *PIL*, 4:1756 (*NAR*, 437); *REL*, 255.

Gates's return to England: *SMI*, 1:277, 2:236. Returning ships are *Blessing* and *Hercules*: *GEN*, 1:455. Delaware's report home: *NAR*, 454–64. Capture of Tackonekintaco and Tangoit, "the Indians of Warraskoyack": *PIL*, 4:1756 (*NAR*, 437–38); *HIS*, 58–59 (*NAR*, 624–25). Analysis of Strachey's conflicting accounts of the incident: Townsend, *Pocahontas*, 98–99, 196; Vaughan, *Transatlantic*, 51, 278. Percy's attack on Paspahegh, participation of "Master Stacy": *SMI*, 2:236. "Master Stacy" is Strachey: Culliford, *Strachey*, 121. "We fell in upon," "my soldiers did," "marching about fourteen," "I replied that," "although Captain Davis": *REL*, 253–54.

Chapter Thirteen

"To see a dead": 2.2.32, *ARD*, 208. Argall's Sagadahoc expedition: *NEW*, 302–7. Argall's return to Jamestown: *REL*, 252. Argall names Delaware Bay: Fausz, "Argall," 588; Barbour, *Pocahontas*, 83. "Fell upon two": *HIS*, 59 (*NAR*, 625). Warraskoyack raid description: *REL*, 254–55. Arrival of the *Dainty*: *ANC*, 30. *Dainty* left England soon after arrival of *Swallow*: GEN, 1:393; Brown, *Republic*, 125. "The Indians hold," "thus it looks": *GEN*, 1:392. Return of the *Swallow*, "these are that scum": *EST*, 36–38 (*NEW*, 255–56). "My lord for an," "the party being thrown": *REL*, 255. Expedition upriver, conflict at Appomattox: *HIS*, 56 (*NAR*, 622); *NAR*, 521; *ANC*, 30; *REL*, 255–56; *NEW*, 301.

Argall's Patawomeck expedition: *NEW*, 264–65; *HIS*, 38–39 (*NAR*, 606). Spelman biography: *NAR*, 62; Fausz, "Middlemen," 45. "With this King": *NAR*, 485–86. "About Christmas," "sitting (the weather)," "we have five," "a man and," "after they are dead," "they find their forefathers" (asides identifying Iopassus as the speaker have been silently removed): *HIS*, 98–100 (*NAR*, 658–61). Death of Wowinchopunck: Rountree, *Pocahontas, Powhatan*, 153–54. Attack on the blockhouse: *REL*, 256. Blockhouse attack, "overthrew him": *HIS*, 59–60 (*NAR*, 625–26). Expedition upriver: *NEW*, 264; *HIS*, 131–32 (*NAR*, 687–88); *ANC*, 30. Death of Kemps: *HIS*, 53 (*NAR*, 619). Death of Weynman, "death was much": *REL*, 252. Weynman biography: *GEN*, 2:1049. Delaware's departure and voyage home: *NEW*, 263–64; *SMI*, 1:277, 2:237; *REL*, 257; Stow, *Annales* (1632), 1018. "At his going": *ANC*, 30–31. "Showing more valor," "where being five," "Paspahegh, Paspahegh": *REL*, 257–58. Second blockhouse battle: Fausz, "Blood," 6, 36–37.

Arrival of the *Hercules*: *ANC*, 31; *NAR*, 521. Arrival of the same ship (mistakenly called the *Blessing*): *REL*, 258. "I am much grieved," "I am going": Scull, *Evelyns*, 63–65 (*GEN*, 1:441–42). *EST* registered for publication November 8, 1610: Stationers' Company, *Registers*, 3:202. Virginia Company shifts focus with news of castaways' survival: Sievers, "Evidence," 143–44. Rich's biography: *NAR*, 54, 372. "Soldier blunt": Rich, *Newes* [1] (*NAR*, 373). "A *casicke* or son": Parker, *Van Meteren's*, 67. Machumps under suspicion in the disappearance of Namontack: *SMI*, 2:350. Machumps circulates freely in Jamestown after the Bermuda episode: *HIS*, 26, 54, 94 (*NAR*, 596, 619, 655); Whitaker, *NAR*, 550.

Elements seemingly transferred from Strachey's letter to the "Excellent Lady" (later "True Reportory") to *EST* include the description of passengers lamenting the pounding of the ship, the statement that two thousand tons of water was bailed and pumped during the storm, the exaggerated suggestion that the bailers nearly drowned as they labored, the phrasing of the description of the landing of the hundred and fifty voyagers, and the account of bellowing castaways attracting cahows and selecting the heaviest for killing: *PIL*, 4:1735–37, 1741 (*NAR*, 385, 387, 390, 399); *EST*, 21–22, 23, 24 (*NEW*, 252–53). Despite how it may appear to readers of *PIL*, however, Strachey does not quote *EST* in "True Reportory" (that would not be possible, since *EST* was written after "True Reportory" reached England). "True Reportory" ends in *PIL* at line 55 on 4:1756; the line beginning "after Sir Thomas Gates his arrival" (*NAR*, 438) is the voice of the editor of *PIL* introducing a reprint of *EST*. As Ashe notes in "Strachey," 509, this misconception has prompted some commentators to exaggerate the echoes of "True Reportory" in *EST*. Nevertheless, the echoes between the two texts constitute compelling evidence that "True Reportory" was used in crafting *EST*.

List of fortuitous events of the Gates expedition: *EST*, 46–48, 68 (*NEW*, 257–58, 262). Martin's letter to Strachey: Culliford, *Strachey*, 123–25. Dale's biography: Rutman, "Historian," 285, 289–94.

Chapter Fourteen

"I fear a madness": 5.1.116, *ARD*, 270. Dale's arrival in Virginia: *GEN*, 1:442–43; *ANC*, 31. "The twelfth of May": *NAR*, 520–23. "Their daily and usual": Hamor, *Discourse*, 26 (*NAR*, 821) (repeated in *SMI*, 2:239). "Sir Thomas Dale, at his": *ANC*, 35. "Sir Thomas Dale immediately": *ANC*, 31. Strachey, *For the Colony*, 1 (1612) (1969 edition, 9), says Delaware merely "exemplified and approved" the laws of Gates, thereby indicating that Gates and Dale were the only authors. The language shifts distinctly after the first eighteen laws, see Flaherty in Strachey, *For the Colony* (1969), xvi, xviii, xxiii. Therefore, I have attributed all but the first eighteen published laws to Dale. June 22 date, content of the laws, "to do the necessities," "be whipped," "outrage or injure": Strachey, *For the Colony* (1612), 1, 10–12, 13, 16–17, 23, 27–28, 29, 44 (1969 edition, 15, 17–19, 22–23, 29, 32–34, 49–50). Passing the pikes defined: Dean, "Polearms," 111.

Strachey on close terms with Dale (Strachey carries Dale's laws and hawks to England): Strachey, *For the Colony* (1612) [v]–[vi] (1969 edition, 3–4); *HIS*, 125 (*NAR*, 682). Dale's construction projects: *REL*, 258. Well found by Jamestown archaeologists may date to Dale's construction period: Kelso, *Buried*, 116, 119, 123–24. "Severe and strict," "with all severity": Hamor, *Discourse*, 27 (*NAR*, 822). Strachey participation in upriver expedition: *HIS*, 124 (*NAR*, 682). Upriver expedition plans, Namontack's fate a mystery to Wahunsenacawh: Hamor, *Discourse*, 26–27, 38 (*NAR*, 822, 831). "Comes to and fro," "before their dinners" (with aside silently removed), "the people have houses," "preserved seven": *HIS*, 26, 54, 94 (*NAR*, 596, 619, 655). Roanoke colony background: Price, *Love*, 8–9.

"In these conflicts": *REL*, 258–59. "As our men," "otherwise he threatened," "one night our men," "thanks be to God": *NAR*, 549–50. General use of poisons and drugs by Powhatans: *NAR*, 110, 121; Barbour, *Three*, 256; Fausz, "Middlemen," 55. "A fantasy possessed" (despite Percy's placement of the episode "in an Indian's house," it is clear he is describing the same event): *REL*, 259. Episode probably is jimsonweed poisoning: Noël Hume, *Adventure*, 301–5. New World use of jimsonweed as hallucinogen: Cichoke, "Herbal," 85. "I found in an," "they are assured": *HIS*, 124 (*NAR*, 682).

Background on Spanish claims: Wright, "Spanish," 452–55, 458, 470; *FIR*, 1:114–16. Details of Spanish ship episode, "Don Diego said": *NAR*, 534–37. "One of the mariners": *NAR*, 546. "Their intent was": *REL*, 259–60. "Are here so few": *NAR*, 558. Background on Gates's arrival: *REL*, 260–61; *SMI*, 1:277, 2:241; *ANC*, 31; *NEW*, 264. War preparations, "it was an English": Hamor, *Discourse*, 28–29 (*NAR*, 823–24). "The choicest persons," "it is not intended": *GEN*, 1:445, 463.

Delaware's stop in the Azores: *NAR*, 525–26. "I found help": NAW, 264. Death of Gates's wife, names of his daughters: *GEN*, 2:895. "His lady died": *GEN*, 2:532. Dale's departure upriver, Gates's plans to develop Jamestown: Hamor, *Discourse*, 29–30 (*NAR*, 823–25).

Strachey probably returned to England on *Prosperous*: Culliford, *Strachey*, 126. Last record of Strachey in Virginia (interrogation of Spanish prisoners, June or July 1611): *REL*, 259–60; Wright, "Spanish," 455, 473. First record of Strachey back in England (registering *For the Colony* for publication, December 13, 1611): Culliford, *Strachey*, 126. Only one ship known to have gone from Jamestown to England during period departed after August 17 date of Dale report to England (*NAR*, 552–58) and arrived before November 5 when Velasco reported it at port (*GEN*, 1:523–24, 527). Ship identified as *Prosperous* (*GEN*, 1:497; Brown, *Republic*, 161). Brown mistakenly places Strachey aboard a ship that left before the Spanish interrogation: Brown, *Republic*, 154–55, 160–61. Brown tacitly acknowledges error by stating elsewhere Strachey arrived home late October or early November 1611: *GEN*, 1:529, 2:1024. Letters dated August 9 and 17, 1611, likely carried home by Strachey: *NAR*, 548–59. Strachey carried the laws to England: *ANC*, 31. "I brought home," Strachey finds cat's claws: *HIS*, 124, 125 (*NAR*, 682).

Chapter Fifteen

"Carry this island": 2.1.91–92, *ARD*, 190. Virginia ship arrived during week previous to November 5 (i.e., a few days before or after November 1): *GEN*, 1:523–24, 527. Ship was *Prosperous*: *GEN*, 1:497; Brown, *Republic*, 161. Strachey lodging in Blackfriars, "during the time": *For the Colony* (1612) [v]–[viii] (1969 edition, 3–7). *For the Colony* registered for publication December 13, 1611, Tien lawsuit: Culliford, *Strachey*, 126, 128, 132–33. Donne's new patron, death of Countess of Bedford's infant: Lawson, *Shadows*, 110–13. Strachey carries hawks from Virginia: *HIS*, 125 (*NAR*, 682).

Documentary evidence of Whitehall debut of *Tempest*: Cunningham, *Extracts*, 210; *ARD*, 1, 6; Bullough, *Sources*, 8:237; Demaray, *Spectacles*, 4. Nineteenth-century charge that the record of the debut is a forgery is false: Bender, "Day," 254; Law, "Produced," 151–52. Cunningham, *Extracts*, 225–26; Law, "Produced," 153–54; Marshall, "Imperium," 376, argue that *Tempest* would have appeared before the public in advance of a royal performance, but no documentary evidence supports this view, which runs counter to theatrical tradition that places great value on debuts. Demaray, *Spectacles*, 76–79, 81–83, 88–91, argues convincingly that the stage directions in *Tempest* were written for the Masquing House rather than the Blackfriars Theater—evidence that Shakespeare expected a Masquing House debut.

History and layout of Masquing House: Thurley, *Whitehall*, 68–82; Law, "Produced," 150, 152–53, 159, 162–63; Demaray, *Spectacles*, 8–9, 75–77, 95, 153.

Likely composition of *Tempest* cast: Sturgess, *Jacobean*, 76; *ARD*, 8. "The imagination," "had in her hair": Law, "Produced," 163. "Waves capering," "a tempest so artificial": Demaray, *Spectacles*, 92–93. Strachey visited Blackfriars Theater up to three times a week as a shareholder: Culliford, *Strachey*, 54–55.

Shakespeare's life during the time when he wrote *Tempest*: Greenblatt, *Will*, 361, 366, 370, 373, 377. Closures of London theaters during plague epidemics: Chute, *Shakespeare*, 290; Holland in Shakespeare, *Tempest* (Pelican), viii–ix; Bradbrook, *Shakespeare*, 207, 250. Popularity of the London theater: Gurr, *Playgoing*, 64–69; Holland in Shakespeare, *Tempest* (Pelican), vii–viii, xiii. Document that places Shakespeare in Stratford in June 1609, stage directions in *Tempest* suggest Shakespeare was away from London and did not expect to attend rehearsals: Ackroyd, *Shakespeare*, 471–72, 477–78.

Similarity of names in Thomas's *Historie of Italie* and *Tempest*: Nosworthy, "Narrative," 282–83; Chambers, *Study*, 1:494; Orgel in Shakespeare, *Tempest* (Oxford), 42–43. England's Mediterranean trade may have inspired *Tempest* setting: Cawley, *Unpathed*, 237. Shakespeare's fondness for Mediterranean settings: Bullough, *Sources*, 8:245. Shakespeare's overlay of New World story on Old World setting in *Tempest*: Hulme, *Encounters*, 107–9, and "Hurricanes," 71–72.

Complexity is mark of Shakespeare's work: Bullough, *Sources*, 8:247, 271–72. Shakespeare often drew material from books and contemporary events: Wood, *Search*, 354–78. Literacy of Shakespeare's audience: Gurr, *Playgoing*, 64–65. Shakespeare's use in *Tempest* of Virgil, Ovid, Montaigne: Holland in Shakespeare, *Tempest* (Pelican), xxix–xxx; Dymkowski, "Production," 3. Montaigne's Golden Age theme in *Tempest*: Bullough, *Sources*, 8:243, 255; *ARD*, 193, 196; Fitzmaurice, "Every," 32–35, 41; Ebner, "Ideal," 161, 165, 167, 173. Shakespeare's use of Montaigne shows New World focus: Hart, *Columbus*, 137. Shakespeare characters frequently debate topical issues: Ackroyd, *Shakespeare*, 468–69, 472–74; Hamlin, "Inde," 34–35; Willis, "Shakespeare's," 258, 265; McDonald, "Reading," 15.

Shakespeare's use of travel narratives in earlier plays: Bullough, *Sources*, 8:240, 242, 249, 255; Hamlin, "Inde," 16, 38. Gonzalo Fernández de Oviedo ("Gonzalus Ferdinandus Oviedus"): Willes, *Travayle*, 185. Shakespeare's possible use of Oviedo's name: Gayley, *Shakespeare*, 62; Cawley, "Use," 715; Brockbank, "Conventions," 193. Patagonian deity Setebos: Pigafetta in Willes, *Travayle*, 434 (verso), 435 (verso). Shakespeare's use of Pigafetta's narrative: *ARD*, 40–41, 176. Caliban's references to Setebos: 1.2.374, 5.1.261, *ARD*, 176, 280.

Bermuda sea monster: Hartop in Hakluyt, *Navigations*, 3:493. Hartop biography: Mancall, *Hakluyt's*, 232–33. Shakespeare's possible use of Hartop's account: Bristol, *Shakespeare*, 83; Mathew, *Image*, 53; Payne, *By Me*, 370. Other uses of Hakluyt's *Navigations* in *Tempest*: *ARD*, 49. Bremo in *Mucedorus* as model for Caliban: Vaughan, *Caliban*, 69; *ARD*, 60; Hamlin, "Inde," 28–29, 31–33, 37, 42; Demaray, *Spectacles*, 21. Thirty-five New World people displayed in England during Shakespeare's lifetime: Vaughan, "Trinculo's," 50, 51, 58, 59. Dates of Namontack's visits to England, Jonson's allusion to Namontack in *Epicoene*: Vaughan, *Transatlantic*, 46–48. "Shrewd, subtle": *SMI*, 1:216. Namontack's positive report about England: *NAR*, 450–51.

Public enthusiasm for the Virginia enterprise: Marx, *Machine*, 34, 68; Rowse, *Southampton*, 238; Bullough, *Sources*, 8:240; Bradbrook, *Shakespeare*, 228–29. Shakespeare's connection to men affiliated with the Virginia Company: Gayley, *Shakespeare*, 18, 20–22, 24, 27–30, 37; Ebner, "Ideal," 166; Bullough, *Sources*, 8:239; Fitzmaurice, *Humanism*, 62. Earl of Southampton's connections to Shakespeare and the Virginia Company: Rowse, *Southampton*, 234–62; Ebner, "Ideal," 166; Bailey, "Founders," 10. Earl's name first on list in second charter: *NEW*, 207. King James's skeptical interest in Jamestown: *FIR*, 1:119. James's interest important for the success of any London play: Brown, "Darkness," 48. Number of King's Men royal performances: Demaray, *Spectacles*, 10, 74–75. King's Men perform for king during plague epidemic: Ackroyd, *Shakespeare*, 465. Vetting of plays by court officials, "rehearsed, perfected": Demaray, *Spectacles*, 7–8, 50, 75.

"Nothing that is good": Crashaw, *Sermon* [61]. Earlier references to Virginia in London plays: Demaray, *Spectacles*, 5–7; Gayley, *Shakespeare*, 76–80. *Tempest* audience would have recognized New World elements: Demaray, *Spectacles*, 14–16, 57–58, 101–9, 142; Gillies, "Masque," 676. Shakespeare may have had Princess Elizabeth's engagement in mind when he wrote *Tempest*: Srigley, *Images*, 116–22; Demaray, *Spectacles*, 10–11, 13, 20, 145. "Tragical comedy": *EST*, 26 (*NEW*, 253). Shakespeare's experiment with tragicomedy late in his career: Demaray, *Spectacles*, 18–19, 46–47, 64–65.

Vaughan, *Caliban*, 118, and Chalmers, *Account*, 20, note that in 1797 modern scholars first proposed parallels between *The Tempest* and the Virginia chronicles. The question of whether the correlations are legitimate has been debated ever since, most actively in the early twentieth century. Cawley was an ardent proponent from 1926 to 1940, and contends in *Elizabethan*, 339, that "nobody in his right mind" can deny the parallels. Stoll in "Fallacies," 487, takes the opposite point of view, arguing "this proof rests upon a few slight verbal parallels, most precariously." While a few scholars still dispute the point (Bergeron, *Romances*, 178, for example, admits only "an occasional parallel"), the prevailing opinion today is that the play is indeed based on the narratives. To Ebner, "Ideal," 166, it is "universally agreed"; to Bullough, *Sources*, 8:271, "the adventures of the Virginian voyagers suggested both his title and setting"; to Marx, *Machine*, 34–35, there are "unmistakable echoes"; to Vaughan and Vaughan in *ARD*, 1, 40–42, 54, 73, 100–101, 287, scholars are "almost unanimous" in agreeing that the parallels exist, though their importance remains open to question. The most recent treatments are Stritmatter and Kositsky, "Revisited" (dispute connection), and Vaughan, "Evidence" (favors connection).

Phrases from four Virginia narratives echo unmistakably in *Tempest*—Strachey's "True Reportory" in *PIL*; Jourdain's *DIS*; Virginia Company's *TRU* and *EST*: Bullough, *Sources*, 8:238–39; Gayley, *Shakespeare*, 45–46, 49; Gillies, "Masque," 681, 703; editor Haile in *NAR*, 381–82; Culliford, *Strachey*, 151–52. Shakespeare may also have used Rich's *Newes* and John Smith's *True Relation* (*SMI*, 1:23–117): editors Vaughan and Vaughan in *ARD*, 42–43. Shakespeare may also have used Crashaw's *Sermon*: Gillies, "Masque," 704. Beyond specific language parallels, Shakespeare drew the general theme of colonial expansion from the travel narratives: Marx, *Machine*, 68; Brown, "Darkness," 48; Bullough, *Sources*, 8:240; Holland in Shakespeare, *Tempest* (Pelican), xxix; editors Vaughan and Vaughan in *ARD*, 47; Salingar, "World," 209, 212.

Shakespeare's most important source, Strachey's "True Reportory," was not published until 1625 in *PIL* (no manuscript is extant). The 1625 published work carries a date of July 15, 1610, and was evidently circulating in England at the time Shakespeare was writing *The Tempest* (a common practice of the day). Schmidgall, "*Primaleon*," 433–35, proposes Welby as Shakespeare's source for Strachey's manuscript. Welby in Jourdain, *Plaine*, 8, says "more full." Hotson, *I, William*, 217–26, proposes that Shakespeare's associate Dudley Digges was the source. Sanders, "Colony," 119, reports a tradition among Strachey's descendants that his accounts were a *Tempest* source.

Capacity of the Blackfriars and similar theaters: Greenblatt, *Will*, 368; Holland in Shakespeare, *Tempest* (Pelican), xi. Onstage seating: Ackroyd, *Shakespeare*, 466. Estimate of weekly theater attendance, capacity of circular playhouses: Holland in Shakespeare, *Tempest* (Pelican), viii. Parallel history of open-air and enclosed theaters: Gurr, *Playgoing*, 14. Globe and Blackfriars ticket price comparison: Gurr, "*Tempest*'s," 101. All classes mixed in both theaters: Chute, *Shakespeare*, 291. "A man shall not be": Gurr, *Playgoing*, 45. History of the Blackfriars: Greenblatt, *Will*, 367; Ackroyd, *Shakespeare*, 465–66; Seltzer, "Last," 127; Chute, *Shakespeare*, 290. Blackfriars religious exemptions persisted: Bradbrook, *Shakespeare*, 205; Gurr, *Playgoing*, 27. Changes in playwriting caused by rise of enclosed venues: Seltzer, "Last," 127, 130, 152, 158; Dymkowski, "Production," 5; Ackroyd, *Shakespeare*, 466–467; Holland in Shakespeare, *Tempest* (Pelican), xi. *Tempest* elements suggest it was written for the Blackfriars: Seltzer, "Last," 128–29; Ackroyd, *Shakespeare*, 487; Dymkowski, "Production," 4; Gurr, "*Tempest*'s," 92–94; Demaray, *Spectacles*, 74.

A 1669 publication states *Tempest* previously played at the Blackfriars: Dymkowski, "Production," 5; Demaray, *Spectacles*, 11–12, 144. Early *Tempest* performances in Blackfriars and Globe may be presumed: Demaray, *Spectacles*, 75; Nagler, *Stage*, 102. No document places Strachey at a performance of *Tempest*; I have presumed he would have attended based on his interests in theater and the New World. Blackfriars description, standard 2:00 p.m. start time: Fraser, *Shake-*

speare, 207–10; R. Frye, *Life*, plates 58, 96; Gurr, *Playgoing*, 30–34, 39. Blackfriars description: Nagler, *Stage*, 93–97; Demaray, *Spectacles*, 4–5, 12, 96; Stephenson, *London*, 307. Blackfriars description, site of Henry VIII's divorce trial: Bradbrook, *Shakespeare*, 206, 250–51.

Chapter Sixteen

"Into something": 1.2.402, *ARD*, 178. "First, the *Tempest*": *TRU*, 17 (*NAR*, 367, modernized). Parallel "tempest" passages: Cawley, "Use," 690; Bristol, *Shakespeare*, 67. Word "Tempest" also in John Smith's *True Relation*: *SMI*, 1:27, 83, 85. Imagery evoked by "tempest": Cummings, "Alchemical," 131–40. "A tempestuous noise": stage direction before 1.1.1, *ARD*, 143. Stage directions are by Shakespeare or later editor: *ARD*, 127, 141–43. "Gape at widest": 1.1.59, *ARD*, 148. "Glut of water": *PIL*, 4:1735 (*NAR*, 385). Parallel "glut" passages: Cawley, "Use," 692, 699; Gayley, *Shakespeare*, 55; *ARD*, 148 (Shakespeare also uses "glut" in 3.2, *Henry IV, Part 1*). "Mercy on us!": 1.1.60, *ARD*, 148. "There was not," muffled cries of passengers: *PIL*, 4:1735 (*NAR*, 385–86). "A plague upon": 1.1.35–36, *ARD*, 146. Parallel muffled cries passages: Cawley, "Use," 692–93; Gayley, *Shakespeare*, 54–55; Bullough, *Sources*, 8:240. "As leaky as": 1.1.46–47, *ARD*, 147. Parallel leaky ship passages: Gayley, *Shakespeare*, 54.

"An honest old": cast list, *ARD*, 140. "Roaring," "a hell of," "the sea swelled," "at length did": *PIL*, 4:1735 (*NAR*, 384–85). "Put the wild," "stinking pitch," "the sea, mounting," "dashes the fire": 1.2.2–5, *ARD*, 149. Parallel stormy sky passages: Bullough, *Sources*, 8:240; Cawley, "Use," 691; Gayley, *Shakespeare*, 56. Blackfriars stage effects: Gurr, "*Tempest*'s," 95; Nagler, *Stage*, 97. Shakespeare's "sulphurous" and "stinking pitch" lines evoke stage effects: *ARD*, 149, 163. Strachey uses "amazement": *PIL*, 4:1735–37 (*NAR*, 384, 386, 389). Shakespeare uses "amazement": 1.2.14, 1.2.198, 5.1.104, *ARD*, 150, 163, 270. Parallel "amazement" passages: Gayley, *Shakespeare*, 54; Cawley, "Use," 692; Bullough, *Sources*, 8:240. Ariel's likely costume: Egan, "Costume," 63; Law, "Produced," 161–62; Saenger, "Costumes"; Demaray, *Spectacles*, 71, 78.

"I boarded," "all but mariners": 1.2.196–201, 210–15, *ARD*, 162–64. "Make many constructions," "an apparition": *PIL*, 4:1737 (*NAR*, 388–89). Parallel St. Elmo's fire/Ariel passages: Bullough, *Sources*, 8:240; Brockbank, "Conventions," 187; Bailey, "Founders," 9; Brown, *Republic*, 114. Science of St. Elmo's fire: Schonland, *Thunderbolts*, 44–48, 61, 92, 146; Barry, *Weather*, 355. Nautical maneuvers in *Tempest*: Allen, "Shakespeare's." "Safely in harbour": 1.2.226–29, *ARD*, 165. Analysis of *Tempest* Bermuda reference: Vaughan and Vaughan, *ARD*, 165; Bullough, *Sources*, 8:266; Gayley, *Shakespeare*, 59; Kathman, "Dating." Interpretation of Ariel's line to mean *Tempest* ship is hidden in a place *from which* Ariel was sent to Bermuda and not one *on* Bermuda: Stoll, "Fallacies," 487; Knapp, *Empire*, 220–21.

Bermuda's reputation as a Devil's Isle influenced crafting of *Tempest*: Gayley, *Shakespeare*, 54; Kathman, "Dating." Word "devil" used a dozen times in *Tempest*: Kathman, "Dating." Parallel enchanted island passages: Gayley, *Shakespeare*, 54; Bullough, *Sources*, 8:240, 243; Cawley, "Use," 696–98, 705; Vaughan and Vaughan in *ARD*, 41–42; Brockbank, "Conventions," 184–85, 189–90. "Shut up hatches": *PIL*, 4:1737 (*NAR*, 390). "They were so overwearied," "fallen asleep": Jourdain, *DIS*, 6 (*VOY*, 106–7). "The mariners all," "to the King's ship," "we were dead": 1.2.230–32, 5.1.97–99, 5.1.230–31, *ARD*, 165, 269, 278. Parallel sleepy mariner passages: Bullough, *Sources*, 8:240; Brockbank, "Conventions," 189; Cawley, "Use," 695–96. "The rest o'th' fleet": 1.2.232–37, *ARD*, 165–66. Parallel fleet unification passages: Salingar, "World," 213–14; Kathman, "Dating." "Sadly up the river": *PIL*, 4:1748 (*NAR*, 419).

"A savage": cast list, *ARD*, 140. Caliban's likely costume: Saenger, "Costumes"; Demaray, *Spectacles*, 71. Terms used to describe Caliban in *Tempest*: *ARD*, 216, 225–26, 280–83. "Tortoise": 1.2.317, *ARD*, 172; "a man or a fish": 2.2.24–25, 208; "half a fish": 3.2.28, 226; "legged like a man": 2.2.32–33, 208–9; "mooncalf": 2.2.105, 109, 132–33 and 3.2.20–21, 213, 214, 226. "A kind of meat," "feeding upon seagrass": *PIL*, 4:1741 (*NAR*, 400). Parallel sea turtle and moon passages: Gayley, *Shakespeare*, 60; Cawley, "Use," 717; Kathman, "Dating." "Wouldst give me": 1.2.334–35, *ARD*, 173. "The berries whereof": *PIL*, 4:1739 (*NAR*, 395). Parallel berry drink passages: Gayley, *Shakespeare*, 60; Cawley, "Use," 709; Bullough, *Sources*, 8:240; Kathman, "Dating." "Upon the coast": *PIL*, 4:1735 (*NAR*, 386). Strachey's voyage to Turkey: Culliford, *Strachey*, 68–70. Sycorax's banishment from Algiers: 1.2.260–66, *ARD*, 167–68. Parallel Algiers passages: Gayley, *Shakespeare*, 58.

"Powhatan, understanding," "most trusty messenger": *SMI*, 1:93–95 ("nonpareil" repeated: *SMI*, 1:274). "And that most deeply": 3.2.98–103, *ARD*, 230; "a savage": cast list, 140. Parallel "nonpareil" and Rawhunt passages: Luce in Shakespeare, *Tempest* (1901), 159–60; Knapp, *Empire*, 337–38; Vaughan and Vaughan, *ARD*, 230. Bullough, *Sources*, 8:241, rejects link between Pocahontas and Miranda. Cooke in his 1885 novel *My Lady Pocahontas* has a fictionalized Pocahontas attend a performance of *The Tempest* at the Globe (there is no evidence that she actually did so), see Mossiker, *Pocahontas*, 266–67. "No more dams": 2.2.176, *ARD*, 217 (a footnote cautions that weirs were also used in England). Analysis of Caliban's statement on dams: Kupperman, *Project*, 249–50. "When they will not," "were I in England": 2.2.27–29, 31–32, *ARD*, 208 (a footnote cautions that Trinculo may also have meant he would have an advertising sign painted). Analysis of Caliban as New World man: Hamlin, "Inde," 23–26, 36–37. Ferdinando Weynman mentioned: *PIL*, 4:1752, 1754 (*NAR*, 427, 433). Parallel Ferdinand/Ferdinando names: Frey, "Tempest," 38. "Wooden slavery," "for your sake": 3.1.62, 3.1.66–67, *ARD*, 222–23. "To fell, carry": *PIL*, 4:1743 (*NAR*, 404).

"Full fathom five": 1.2.397–402, *ARD*, 178. Parallel undersea passages: Salingar, "World," 210: Hayward, *Bermuda*, 119.

Chapter Seventeen

"Such stuff": 4.1.156–57, *ARD*, 254. Remora story: *PIL*, 4:1736 (*NAR*, 388). "What strange fish": 2.1.113–14, *ARD*, 191. Franciso suggests Ferdinand survived: 2.1.114–23, *ARD*, 191–92; "have more widows": 2.1.133–35, 192; "uninhabitable": 2.1.40, 188. Parallel "inaccessible" and "uninhabitable" passages: Cawley, "Use," 702; Kathman, "Dating." "Some monster": 2.2.64–65, *ARD*, 211; "pied ninny," "scurvy patch": 3.2.61, 228. Background on Trinculo descriptions: *ARD*, 140, 142, 228. Parallel Stephen/Stephano names: Gayley, *Shakespeare*, 63–65; Cawley, "Use," 715; Kennedy, *Isle*, 62. "Many a butt": *PIL*, 4:1737 (*NAR*, 389) (the *Sea Venture* casks were emptied over the side while the *Tempest* casks went overboard whole). "I escaped upon": 2.2.118–20, *ARD*, 213–14. Parallel cask passages: Bullough, *Sources*, 8:267; Gayley, *Shakespeare*, 61; Cawley, "Use," 690.

"Get thee young": 2.2.168–69, *ARD*, 217. "Sea-mew": *PIL*, 4:1740 (*NAR*, 398). "Scamel" possible misprint of "seamel": Holland in Shakespeare, *Tempest* (Pelican), 45. *Tempest* only known use of the word "scamel" (with the exception of "doubtful" 1866 reference): *Oxford English Dictionary*. Parallel "sea-mews"/"scamels" passages: Gayley, *Shakespeare*, 60; Cawley, "Use," 711; Bullough, *Sources*, 8:240. "Bat-fowling": 2.1.185, *ARD*, 197. "Lowbelling": *PIL*, 4:1741 (*NAR*, 399). Parallel "bat-fowling"/"lowbelling" passages: Vaughan and Vaughan, *ARD*, 197; Gayley, *Shakespeare*, 60; Cawley, "Use," 711. "Hollow burst": 2.1.312–13, *ARD*, 206; "be not afeard": 3.2.135–38, 232; "strange and several": 5.1.232–34, 278.

"Bloody issues," "desire forever": *PIL*, 4:1743, 1745 (*NAR*, 404, 410). "Bloody thoughts": 4.1.220–21, *ARD*, 258; "let me live here": 4.1.122, 251; "had I plantation": 2.1.144, 193. Parallel mutineer motivations passages: Gayley, *Shakespeare*, 61; Bullough, *Sources*, 8:240; Kathman, "Dating"; Cawley, "Use," 713. Ariel similar to English indentured servants: Holland in Shakespeare, *Tempest* (Pelican), xxxi. Caliban similar to Bermuda mutineers: Brockbank, "Conventions," 196. "Had I plantation," "Golden Age," "no occupation," "everything advantageous," "true, save means," "all idle—whores": 2.1.52–53, 144, 155–57, 167, 169, *ARD*, 188, 193, 195, 196. Shakespeare's use of Montaigne: Vaughan and Vaughan in *ARD*, 193; Bullough, *Sources*, 8:243, 255; Ebner, "Ideal," 161, 164–68, 173. Parallels between Gonzalo's speech (and his mocking colleagues) and Virginia Company's publications (and the company's critics): Marx, *Machine*, 36–66; Vaughan and Vaughan, *ARD*, 4–5; Holland in Shakespeare, *Tempest* (Pelican), xxix–xxx; Cheyfitz, *Poetics*, 67–68; Knapp, *Empire*, 221–22; Gillies, "Masque," 682–83; Hamlin, *Image*, 118–24.

Prospero and Caliban threaten to force others to drink brine: 1.2.463, 3.2.64–65, *ARD*, 182, 228. "Fens, marshes": *PIL*, 4:1740 (*NAR*, 398). "All the infections":

2.2.1–3, *ARD*, 207; "filthy-mantled": 4.1.182, 256; "I do smell": 4.1.199, 257. Parallel contaminated water passages: Gillies, "Masque," 684, 691; Gayley, *Shakespeare*, 59–60; Cawley, "Use," 702, 708; Kathman, "Dating." "A low level": *PIL*, 4:1752 (*NAR*, 428–29). *Tempest* debate on Queen Dido: 2.1.77–102, *ARD*, 189–91. Parallel Dido passages: Cawley, "Use," 706; Kathman, "Dating"; Salingar, "World," 209–10.

Musical instruments used during Shakespeare's plays: Lindley, *Music*, 235–39. "Strange and solemn," "several strange," "gentle actions": stage directions before 3.3.18, *ARD*, 235; harpy scene: 3.3.53–82, 238–40. Levitation machines and trick tables, "a bucket into": Demaray, *Spectacles*, 66, 76–91, 97–98, 155, 160–61. *Tempest* goddesses section: 4.1.60–138, *ARD*, 246–53; Jonson on "sitting in a throne": 68; "Juno descends": stage direction before 4.1.73, 248; "sunburned sicklemen": 4.1.134, 252; "reapers properly," "to a strange hollow": stage directions after 4.1.138, 253; "glistering apparel": stage direction after 4.1.193, 257. Spangled costumes likely used: Demaray, *Spectacles*, 78. "Two suits of apparel": *PIL*, 4:1745 (*NAR*, 410). Parallel two suits passages: Gayley, *Shakespeare*, 61–62; Kathman, "Dating." "The murmuring": *PIL*, 4:1746 (*NAR*, 411). "A noise of hunters": stage direction before 4.1.255, *ARD*, 261; "you sty me": 1.2.343, 174. Parallel hogs/"sty" passages: Bristol, *Shakespeare*, 88. *Tempest* chess scene: 5.1.172–77, *ARD*, 274–75.

Parallel Gates/Prospero passages: Marx, *Machine*, 34–36; Bullough, *Sources*, 8:242, 272, 273; Cheyfitz, *Poetics*, 67; Fulton, "Pamphlets," 5–7; Brockbank, "Conventions," 186–87. Gates's reaction to Blunt killing: *PIL*, 4:1755 (*NAR*, 434–35). Parallel between Gates's reaction to Blunt and Prospero interaction with Caliban: Mowat in Shakespeare, *Tempest* (New Folger Library), 193–94; Kathman, "Dating"; Berger, "Miraculous," 261–62. "Thou most lying": 1.2.345–49, *ARD*, 174. Parallel between Shakespeare's biography and Prospero's speech: McGinn, *Philosophy*, 143–46, 150; Greenblatt, *Will*, 372–73. "The solemn temples": 4.1.153–56, *ARD*, 254. "I have both in": Strachey, *For the Colony* (1612), v (1969 edition, 3).

Chapter Eighteen

"Our revels": 4.1.148, *ARD*, 253. Strachey's attempts to find a patron: Barbour, *Three*, 302. Strachey's literary debt to John Smith: Barbour in *SMI*, 1:124–25. Strachey biography, "this last dismal," "my hour is come": Culliford, *Strachey*, 128, 130, 133, 140–41. Additional Strachey biography: Wright in *VOY*, xvii; Haile in *NAR*, 62–63. Performance of *Tempest* at Princess Elizabeth's wedding: Law, "Produced," 164; Bullough, *Sources*, 8:237; Demaray, *Spectacles*, 80. "The malicious": Johnson, *Life*, 4. Analysis of Johnson's statement: Salingar, "World," 210–11; Nuzum, "Company," 17. Contemporary audiences would have recognized New World theme of *Tempest*: Lee, "Visits," 342; Lindley in Shakespeare, *Tempest* (New Cambridge) [43].

Shakespeare's life during *Tempest* period: Greenblatt, *Will*, 373, 378–79; Chute, *Shakespeare*, 298–99; Gurr, "*Tempest*'s," 93–94. "Gentlemanlike": Chute,

Shakespeare, 298. Shakespeare's purchase of Blackfriars gatehouse: Greenblatt, *Will*, 379; Chute, *Shakespeare*, 306; Bradbrook, *Shakespeare*, 226; Fraser, *Shakespeare*, 250. Globe fire description, "some of the paper," marriages of Shakespeare's daughters: Greenblatt, *Will*, 379–80; Bradbrook, *Shakespeare*, 222–23, 225. Parallels between Shakespeare and daughters and Prospero and Miranda: McGinn, *Philosophy*, 145, 147; Bradbrook, *Shakespeare*, 224–25. Shakespeare's will and death, "Shakespeare, [poet Michael] Drayton": Greenblatt, *Will*, 384–88. Importance of the First Folio: Demaray, *Spectacles*, 1–3. "He was not of": Jonson in Shakespeare, *Mr. William Shakespeares* (First Folio) [vi].

Chapman's Virginia play: Gillies, "Masque," 673–74; Demaray, *Spectacles*, 94, 112–16. "If there be never," "he is loth to": Jonson in *ARD*, 7–8. "O, I, mooncalves!": Jonson in Demaray, *Spectacles*, 119–20. Fletcher's *Sea Voyage*, Taylor the Water Poet: McMullan, *Unease*, 197–99, 240–43; Kennedy, "Significance," 28–32, 35. Analysis of Taylor's poetry, "Epitaph in the Barmooda," "Epitaph in the Utopian," "Caleb Quishquash": Malcolm, *Origins*, 19, 140–41.

Matthew Somers's return to England with body of uncle: *SMI*, 1:277–78, 2:350–52; Burrage, *Lost*, 5; Craven, "Hughes," 76. Parish register says Somers's body buried June 4, 1611 (suggesting his nephew reached port in late May): Malone, *Account*, 20. George Somers stopped on the coast north of Jamestown before crossing to Bermuda: *SMI*, 1:277, 2:350; Oldmixon, *Empire*, 441. Ring purported to bear Somers coat of arms found on Connecticut beach in 1924: Kennedy, *Isle*, 57. Two men previously left on Bermuda join Somers on arrival: *BER*, 15. Somers's death by food poisoning: Stow, *Annales* (1615), 944, and (1632), 1018; *SMI*, 1:277. Pig-bel probably killed Somers: Puntis, "Pig-bel." Symptoms of pig-bel: Merck & Co., "Clostridial." Somers died November 9, 1611: Sainsbury, *State Papers: Colonial*, 1:10; Green, *State Papers: Domestic*, 2:268. Notice of Somers's death: *SMI*, 2:350–51; Burrage, *Lost*, 5; *REL*, 252; Craven, "Hughes," 76; *BER*, 15. "A surfeit": Stow, *Annales* (1632), 1018.

Somers's body buried England and heart buried Bermuda: *SMI*, 2:351, 378. Heart burial mentioned on 1620, 1876, 1959 memorials: Darrell, *Links*, 8, 9, 13. Heart burial site in or near the modern Somers Garden in St. George's: editor Lefroy in *BER*, 305–8. Alternatively, heart burial site near campsite of castaways: Zuill, "Cast Away," 66. Embalming methods, hearts routinely buried separately: Guibert, *Physitian*, 143–47. History of ceremonial heart burial, salt common preservative when bodies sent home: Bradford, *Heart*, 38, 40–42, 45, 47, 51–52, 54–58, 169–72, 177–78. Dual practical and ceremonial purposes for removing heart: Chamberlain and Pearson, *Earthly*, 26–28. Somers's body transported in cedar chest, "his heart and bowels" (Butler's claim that sailors were unaware body was on board is not credible): *BER*, 15–16.

Somers's men defied his wishes, sailed for England, left three men on Bermuda: Burrage, *Lost*, 5; Craven, "Hughes," 76; *BER*, 16; *SMI*, 2:351. "His body by":

SMI, 1:277–78, 2:351. Parish register says Somers buried June 4, 1611: Malone, *Account*, 20. Somers's burial lost during church restoration: editor Lefroy in *BER*, 307–8. New monument dedicated 1980: Ware, "Journey," 22. Settlement of Somers's estate July 26, 1611: Sainsbury, *State Papers: Colonial*, 1:10; Green, *State Papers: Domestic*, 2:268. Somers's will details: Broadley, "Will." "Sir George Somers": *NAR*, 709. Renaming of Bermuda as the Somers Islands: Neill, *History*, 64–65; Stow, *Annales* (1615), 945. "In the year 1611": *SMI*, 2:378. Bermuda monuments to Somers: *BER*, 15–16, 305–6; Darrell, *Links*, 8–10; Jones, *Bermuda*, 28–29. "Riotous and disorderly": Pope, "Somers," 31.

Return of *Starr*: *HIS*, 130 (*NAR*, 686); Brown, *Republic*, 157, 162–63; Barbour in *SMI*, 1:130. "He hath sent his": Neill, *History*, 52. Gates's biography: *NAR*, 46–47; Sheehan, "Gates"; *GEN*, 2:894–96. Gates's use of Bermuda limestone in Jamestown house: Kelso, *Buried*, 23, 107, 109; Lounsbury, *Church*, 2; D'Alto, "Hurricane," 62. Gates's death: Sainsbury, "Death"; Morey, *Gates*, 15. Pierce biographies: Dorman, *Purse*, 1:30, 31, 2:797–800, 3:24; Bernhard, "Men," 616–17. "Mistress Pierce": *SMI*, 3:218. Clark biography: *REL*, 260, 274; *SMI*, 2:254–55; *NAR*, 44–45, 49–50; Wright, "Spanish," 455–57. Hopkins biography: Johnson, "Origin," 165–69; Dorman, *Purse*, 2:355–56. Clark's and Hopkins's *Mayflower* history: Philbrick, *Mayflower*, 24–26, 38–39, 70; Anderson, *Pilgrim*, 111, 271–75.

Epilogue

Uranus's moons: Jet Propulsion Laboratory, "Planetary." Early essays on parallels between Jamestown chronicles and *Tempest*: Vaughan, *Caliban*, 118–20; Marshall, "Imperium," 381–82; Culliford, *Strachey*, 1–2. Shakespeare's late plays: Lytton Strachey, *Books*, 51–69. Lytton Strachey's descent from William Strachey: Sanders, *Family*, 53, 65, 108–9.

Recent essays on *Tempest* as colonial-themed play: Vaughan, *Caliban*, 118–71; Hulme and Sherman, *Travels*, 171–78; McDonald, "Reading," 15–17; Fiedler, *Stranger*, 208–9; Gillies, *Geography*, 153–55; Griffiths, "Colonialism"; Brotton, "Contesting," 25–31. Recent essays that downplay the colonial interpretation of *Tempest*: Bate, "Humanist," 6; Bloom in Shakespeare, *Tempest* (Riverhead), 3–4; N. Frye, "*Tempest*," 49; Hadfield, *Literature*, 242–45. "A prologue": Marx, *Machine*, 72. "A kaleidoscope": H. Smith, *Interpretations*, 1. "A complex Rorschach blot": Hamlin, *Image*, 118. Shakespeare authorship question: Looney, *Identified*; Baron, *De Vere*; Farina, *De Vere*; Michell, *Who Wrote*; McCrea, *Case*; Stritmatter and Kositsky, "Revisited."

"Magnificent—it has some," "notably good": Jones and Walcutt, *Literature*, 58, 65. Strachey's documentation of the Powhatans: Porter, *Inconstant*, 325–38. "One of the finest": Quinn in *NEW*, 288. "The large Strachey vocabulary": Barbour, *Three*, 299. "Could trace," "Sea Vulture," "bitter feud," "a complete schism" "the three kings": Irving, *Wolfert's*, 62–71, 315. Kipling on *Sea Venture* and *Tempest*:

Kipling, *How Shakespeare*, and *"Tempest"*; Stamers-Smith, "Kipling"; Franssen, "Bard." "Seven months among mermaids": Kipling, *Limits*, 169–70. "The *Sea Venture*": Joyce, *Ulysses*, 1:439. Background on Joyce allusion: Thornton, *Allusions*, 197. Strachey in *Dark Lady*: O'Neal, *Dark*, 5, 9, 11, 21–22, 34–35, 80–81, 186, 211, 219, 222–25, 228, 242–43, 252–53, 257, 294–303, 306–13. Césaire's *Une Tempête* analyzed, "unmasking the brutality," "In *Une Tempête*": Sarnecki, "Mastering," 276, 280. Durham's Caliban masks, "one time Prospero": Hulme and Sherman: *Travels*, 175–79.

Hogs became scarce on Bermuda: Hughes, *Letter* [7]. Early regulations to protect cahow: *BER*, 4; *SMI*, 2:342–43. Colonists' uses of Bermuda plants, early regulations to protect plants: Bernhard, "Bermuda," 61; Stamers-Smith, "Flora," 116–17; Collett, *Plants*, 56–57, 78, 83. Introduction of foreign crops: Stamers-Smith, "Flora," 120–24; Phillips-Watlington, *Botanical*, 114. Count of native and introduced flora: Phillips-Watlington, *Botanical*, 15–18. Cedar epidemic of 1940: Stamers-Smith, "Flora," 117; Phillips-Watlington, *Botanical*, 15. Impact of habitat reduction on birds: Amos, *Birds*, 21. Rediscovery of the cahow in 1951: Murphy and Mowbray, "Cahow"; Bowen and Andrews, "Starving," 63; Amos, *Birds*, 39–40; Kennedy, *Isle*, 261. Commercial use of island cavern as "Prospero's Cave": Stamers-Smith, "Kipling," 104. Cave creatures named for Prospero and Somers: Sterrer and Iliffe, *"Mesonerilla,"* 509–10, 512; Hart and Manning, "Cavernicolous," 441–42.

Celebration of Somers' Day: Emanuel, *Divine*, 51. Plaques commemorating Somers, 1984 statue of Somers: Darrell, *Links*, 8–15; Fountain, "Statue." Somers's legacy as a mariner: Haile in *NAR*, 61–62, 445. Discovery of ring that may have belonged to Somers: Kennedy, *Isle*, 57. Raising of guns from *Sea Venture*, "to make a discovery": *BER*, 26, 290; *SMI*, 2:355, 387. "Arguably the most": Armitage, "Victuals," 8. Discovery of wreck and artifacts: Wingood, "Report" (1982), 333–34, 337, 341–45. Further details on wreck discovery: Jones, *Bermuda*, 26; Kennedy, *Isle*, 260; Wright, *Story*, 22. Jamestown archaeological dig, discovery of ring that may have belonged to Strachey: Kelso, *Buried*, 44–55, 89–93, 111–15, 126–39, 141–60, 170, and "Shakespearean," 187–89.

BIBLIOGRAPHY

Aberth, John. *From the Brink of the Apocalypse: Confronting Famine, War, Plague, and Death in the Later Middle Ages.* New York: Routledge, 2001.

Ackroyd, Peter. *Shakespeare: The Biography.* New York: Doubleday, 2005.

Adams, Jonathan. "*Sea Venture*: A Second Interim Report—Part 1." *International Journal of Nautical Archaeology and Underwater Exploration* 14, no. 4 (November 1985): 275–99.

Adams, Stephen. *The Best and Worst Country in the World: Perspectives on the Early Virginia Landscape.* Charlottesville: University Press of Virginia, 2001.

Allen, Harold B. "Shakespeare's 'Lay Her A-hold.'" *Modern Language Notes* 52, no. 2 (February 1937): 96–100.

Amos, Eric J. R. *A Guide to the Birds of Bermuda.* Warwick, Bermuda: Eric J. R. Amos, 1991.

Ancient Planters. "A Breife Declaration of the Plantation of Virginia During the First Twelve Yeares." In *Journals of the House of Burgesses of Virginia 1619–1658/59*, edited by H. R. McIlwaine. Richmond, VA: Colonial Press, 1915.

Anderson, Robert Charles. *The Pilgrim Migration: Immigrants to Plymouth Colony 1620–1633.* Boston: New England Historic Genealogical Society, 2004.

Andrews, K. R. "Christopher Newport of Limehouse, Mariner." *William and Mary Quarterly*, 3rd ser., 11, no. 1 (January 1954): 28–41.

Armitage, Philip L. "Ship Rats, Salted Meat and Tortoises: Selected Aspects of Maritime Life in the 'Great Age of Sail' (1500–1800s)." *Bermuda Journal of Archaeology and Maritime History* 1 (1989): 143–59.

———. "Victuals and Vermin: Life on Board the *Sea Venture* in 1609." *Bulletin of the Institute of Maritime History and Archaeology* 10 (December 1987): 8-10.

Ashe, Geoffrey. "William Strachey." *Notes and Queries* 195, no. 24 (November 25, 1950): 508–11.

Bailey, James H. "Shakespeare and the Founders of Virginia." *Virginia Cavalcade* 1, no. 3 (Winter 1951): 9–10.

Baker, Thomas H. *Records of the Seasons, Prices of Agricultural Produce, and Phenomena Observed in the British Isles.* London: Simpkin, Marshall & Company, 1911.

Baker, William A. *The Mayflower and Other Colonial Vessels.* Annapolis, MD: Naval Institute Press, 1983.

Barbour, Philip L. "The Honorable George Percy, Premier Chronicler of the First Virginia Voyage." *Early American Literature* 6, no. 1 (Spring 1971): 7–17.

———, ed. *The Jamestown Voyages Under the First Charter, 1606–1609.* 2 vols. London: Cambridge University Press for the Hakluyt Society, 1969.

———. *Pocahontas and Her World.* Boston: Houghton Mifflin, 1970.

———. *The Three Worlds of Captain John Smith.* Boston: Houghton Mifflin, 1964.

Baron, Dennis. *De Vere Is Shakespeare: Evidence from the Biography and Wordplay.* New York: Oleander Press, 1997.

Barry, Roger G. *Mountain Weather and Climate.* 2nd ed. New York: Routledge, 1992.

Bate, Jonathan. "The Humanist *Tempest*." In *Shakespeare* La Tempête: *Etudes critiques*, edited by Claude Peltrault. Besançon, Fr.: Université de Franche-Comté, 1994.

Bender, John B. "The Day of the Tempest" *ELH: English Literary History* 47, no. 2 (Summer 1980): 235–58.

Berger, Harry, Jr. "Miraculous Harp: A Reading of Shakespeare's Tempest." *Shakespeare Studies* 5 (1969): 253–83.

Bergeron, David M. *Shakespeare's Romances and the Royal Family.* Lawrence, KS: University Press of Kansas, 1985.

Bermuda Maritime Museum. "The Wreck of the *Sea Venture*." Exhibit sponsored by Bank of Bermuda, Treasure House, Bermuda Maritime Museum, Sandys, Bermuda, c. 1991.

Bermuda Turtle Project. "Bermuda Sea Turtle Species." Bermuda Aquarium, Museum and Zoo and Caribbean Conservation Corporation. http://cccturtle.org/bermuda/index2.htm.

Bernhard, Virginia. "Bermuda and Virginia in the Seventeenth Century: A Comparative View." *Journal of Social History* 19, no. 1 (Fall 1985): 57–70.

———. "'Men, Women and Children' at Jamestown: Population and Gender in Early Virginia, 1607–1610." *Journal of Southern History* 58, no. 4 (November 1992): 599–618.

———. "A Response: The Forest and the Trees: Thomas Camfield and the History of Early Virginia." *Journal of Southern History* 60, no. 4 (November 1994): 663–70.

Beverly, Robert. *The History and Present State of Virginia.* Edited by Louis B. Wright. 1705. Reprint, Chapel Hill: University of North Carolina Press, 1947.

Blackburn, Bonnie, and Leofranc Holford-Strevens. *The Oxford Book of Days.* New York: Oxford University Press, 2000.

Blanton, Dennis B. "Drought as a Factor in the Jamestown Colony, 1607–1612." *Historical Archaeology* 34, no. 4 (Winter 2000): 74–81.

Blanton, Wyndham B. *Medicine in Virginia in the Seventeenth Century.* Richmond, VA: William Byrd Press, 1930.

Bowen, Joanne, and Susan Trevarthen Andrews. "The Starving Time at Jamestown: Faunal Analysis of Pit 1, Pit 3, the Bulwark Ditch, Ditch 6, Ditch 7, and Midden 1." Report Submitted to Jamestown Rediscovery, Association for the Preservation of Virginia Antiquities, 2000.

Bradbrook, M. C. *Shakespeare: The Poet in His World.* New York: Columbia University Press, 1978.

Bradford, Charles Angell. *Heart Burial*. London: George Allen & Unwin, 1933.

Bristol, Frank M. *Shakespeare and America*. 1898. Reprint, New York: AMS Press, 1971.

Broadley, A. M. "Last Will & Testament." *Heritage Magazine*, 1984, 25–26.

Brockbank, Philip. "'The Tempest': Conventions of Art and Empire." In *Later Shakespeare*. London: Edward Arnold, 1966.

Brotton, Jerry. "'This Tunis, sir, was Carthage': Contesting Colonialism in *The Tempest*." In *Post-Colonial Shakespeares*, edited by Ania Loomba and Martin Orkin. New York: Routledge, 1998.

Brown, Alexander. *The First Republic in America*. Boston: Houghton Mifflin, 1898.

———, ed. *The Genesis of the United States*. 2 vols. Boston: Houghton Mifflin, 1890.

Brown, Paul. "'This Thing of Darkness I Acknowledge Mine': *The Tempest* and the Discourse of Colonialism." In *Political Shakespeare: Essays in Cultural Materialism*, edited by Jonathan Dollimore and Alan Sinfield. 2nd ed. Ithaca: Cornell University Press, 1994.

Bullough, Geoffrey, ed. *Narrative and Dramatic Sources of Shakespeare*. 8 vols. New York: Columbia University Press, 1957–75.

Burrage, Champlin. *John Pory's Lost Description of Plymouth Colony in the Earliest Days of the Pilgrim Fathers Together with Contemporary Accounts of English Colonization Elsewhere in New England and in the Bermudas*. Boston: Houghton Mifflin, 1918.

Butler, Nathaniel. *Boteler's Dialogues*. Edited by W. G. Perrin. London: Navy Records Society, 1929.

———. *The Historye of the Bermudaes or Summer Islands*. Edited by J. Henry Lefroy. London: Hakluyt Society, 1882.

Camfield, Thomas M. "A Can or Two of Worms: Virginia Bernhard and the Historiography of Early Virginia, 1607–1610." *Journal of Southern History* 60, no. 4 (November 1994): 649–62.

Canny, Nicolas. "The Permissive Frontier: The Problem of Social Control in English Settlements in Ireland and Virginia 1550–1650." In *The Westward Enterprise: English Activities in Ireland, the Atlantic, and America, 1480–1650*, edited by K. R. Andrews, N. P. Canny, and P. E. H. Hair. Liverpool, UK: Liverpool University Press, 1978.

Cawley, Robert Ralston. "Shakspere's Use of the Voyagers in *The Tempest*." *Publications of the Modern Language Association of America* 41, no. 3 (September 1926): 688–726.

———. *Unpathed Waters: Studies in the Influence of the Voyagers on Elizabethan Literature*. Princeton, NJ: Princeton University Press, 1940.

———. *The Voyagers and Elizabethan Drama*. Modern Language Association of American Monograph Series 8. Boston: D. C. Heath, 1938.

Chalmers, George. *Another Account of the Incidents from which the Title and a Part of the Story of Shakespeare's Tempest Were Derived*. 1815. Reprint, New York: AMS Press, 1975.

Chamberlain, Andrew T., and Michael Parker Pearson. *Earthly Remains: The History and Science of Preserved Human Bodies*. New York: Oxford University Press, 2001.

Chambers, E. K. *William Shakespeare: A Study of Facts and Problems*. 1930. Reprint, New York: Oxford University Press, 1988.

Chambers, R. *Chambers's Book of Days: A Miscellany of Popular Antiquities in Connection with the Calendar*. 2 vols. Philadelphia: J. B. Lippincott, 1891.

Chapman, George. *An Epicede or Funerall Song: On the Most Disastrous Death, of the High-borne Prince of Men, Henry Prince of Wales*. London: John Budge, 1612 [1613 new style].

Chapman, George, Ben Jonson, and John Marston. *Eastward Hoe, As It Was Playd in the Black-friers by the Children of Her Majesties Revels*. London: William Aspley, 1605.

Cheyfitz, Eric. *The Poetics of Imperialism: Translation and Colonization from The Tempest to Tarzan*. Oxford and New York: Oxford University Press, 1991.

Chorley, E. Clowes. "The Planting of the Church in Virginia." *William and Mary Quarterly*, 2nd ser., 10, no. 3 (July 1930): 191–213.

Christensen, Ernest Martin. "The Probable Parentage of Stephen Hopkins of the *Mayflower*." *The American Genealogist* 79, no. 4 (October 2004): 241–49.

Chute, Marchette. *Shakespeare of London*. New York: E. P. Dutton, 1964.

Cichoke, Anthony. *Secrets of Native American Herbal Remedies*. New York: Avery, 2001.

Collett, Jill. *Bermuda: Her Plants and Gardens 1609–1850*. London: Macmillan, 1987.

Connor, Seymour V. "Sir Samuel Argall: A Biographical Sketch." *Virginia Magazine of History and Biography* 59, no. 2 (April 1951): 162–75.

Cooper, Harold. "John Donne and Virginia in 1610." *Modern Language Notes* 57, no. 8 (December 1942): 661–63.

Crashaw, William. *A Sermon Preached in London Before the Right Honorable the Lord Lawarre, Lord Governour and Captaine Generall of Virginea . . . Febr. 21. 1609* [1610 new style]. London: William Welby, 1610.

Craven, Wesley Frank. "An Introduction to the History of Bermuda." *William and Mary Quarterly*, 2nd ser., 17, no. 2 (April 1937): 176–215; no. 3 (July 1937): 317–62; no. 4 (October 1937): 437–65; 18, no. 1 (January 1938): 13–63.

———. "Lewis Hughes' 'Plaine and Trve Relation of the Goodnes of God Towards the Sommer Ilands.'" *William and Mary Quarterly*, 2nd ser., 17, no. 1 (January 1937): 56–89.

Culliford, S. G. *William Strachey, 1572–1621*. Charlottesville, VA: University Press of Virginia, 1965.

Cummings, Peter. "The Alchemical Storm: Etymology, Wordplay, and New World *Kairos* in Shakespeare's *The Tempest*." *The Upstart Crow: A Shakespeare Journal* 12 (1992): 127–40.

Cunningham, Peter, ed. *Extracts from the Accounts of the Revels at Court, in the Reigns of Queen Elizabeth and King James I*. London: Shakespeare Society, 1842.

D'Alto, Nick. "The Hurricane that Saved America." *American History* 41, no. 4 (October 2006): 56–62.

Darrell, Owen H. "Admiral Sir George Somers." *Heritage Magazine*, 1984, 19–20.

———. *Sir George Somers Links Bermuda with Lyme Regis*. Hamilton, Bermuda: Print Express, 1997.

Davenport, Frances Gardiner, ed. *European Treaties Bearing on the History of the*

United States and Its Dependencies to 1648. 1917. Reprint, Gloucester, MA: Peter Smith, 1967.

Deacon, John, and John Walker. *Dialogicall Discourses of Spirits and Divels.* London: George Bishop, 1601.

Dean, Bashford. "On American Polearms, Especially Those in the Metropolitan Museum of Art." *Journal of the American Military History Foundation* 1, no. 3 (Autumn 1937): 108–21.

Demaray, John G. *Shakespeare and the Spectacles of Strangeness:* The Tempest *and the Transformation of Renaissance Theatrical Forms.* Pittsburgh: Duquesne University Press, 1998.

Doherty, Kieran. Sea Venture: *Shipwreck, Survival, and the Salvation of the First English Colony in the New World.* New York: St. Martin's Press, 2007.

Donne, John. *John Donne: The Complete English Poems.* Edited by A. J. Smith. Rev. ed. New York: Penguin, 1976.

Dorman, John Frederick, ed. *Adventurers of Purse and Person, Virginia, 1607–1624/5.* 4th rev. ed. 3 vols. Baltimore: Genealogical Publishing Company, 2004–2007.

Dymkowski, Christine, ed. *The Tempest.* Shakespeare in Production. New York: Cambridge University Press, 2000.

Earle, Carville V. "Environment, Disease, and Mortality in Early Virginia." In *The Chesapeake in the Seventeenth Century: Essays on Anglo-American Society,* edited by Thad W. Tate and David L. Ammerman. Chapel Hill: University of North Carolina Press, 1979.

Eaton, Dorothy S. "A Voyage of 'ffisshinge and Discovvery.'" *The Library of Congress Quarterly Journal of Current Acquisitions* 10, no. 4 (August 1953): 181–84.

Ebner, Dean. "The Tempest: Rebellion and the Ideal State." *Shakespeare Quarterly* 16, no. 2 (Spring 1965): 161–73.

Egan, Gabriel. "Ariel's Costume in the Original Staging of *The Tempest.*" *Theatre Notebook* 51, no. 2 (1997): 62–72.

Elsner, James B. *Hurricanes of the North Atlantic: Climate and Society.* New York: Oxford University Press, 1999.

Elze, Karl. "The Date of *The Tempest.*" In *Essays on Shakespeare,* translated by L. Dora Schmitz. London: Macmillan, 1874.

Emanuel, Kerry. *Divine Wind: The History and Science of Hurricanes.* New York: Oxford University Press, 2005.

Evans, Cerinda W. *Some Notes on Shipbuilding and Shipping in Colonial Virginia.* Williamsburg, VA: Virginia 350th Anniversary Celebration Corporation, 1957.

Fagan, Brian. *The Little Ice Age: How Climate Made History 1300–1850.* New York: Basic Books, 2000.

Farina, William. *De Vere as Shakespeare: An Oxfordian Reading of the Canon.* Jefferson, NC: McFarland & Company, 2006.

Fausz, J. Frederick. "An 'Abundance of Blood Shed on Both Sides': England's First Indian War, 1609–1614." *Virginia Magazine of History and Biography* 98, no. 1 (January 1990): 3–56.

———. "Middlemen in Peace and War: Virginia's Earliest Indian Interpreters, 1608–1632." *Virginia Magazine of History and Biography* 95, no.1 (January 1987): 41–64.

———. "Powhatan." In *American National Biography*, edited by John A. Garraty and Mark C. Carnes. 24 vols. New York: Oxford University Press, 1999.

———. "Samuel Argall." In *American National Biography*, edited by John A. Garraty and Mark C. Carnes. 24 vols. New York: Oxford University Press, 1999.

Fiedler, Leslie A. *The Stranger in Shakespeare*. New York: Stein and Day, 1972.

Fitzmaurice, Andrew. "'Every Man, That Prints, Adventures': The Rhetoric of the Virginia Company Sermons." In *The English Sermon Revised*, edited by Lori Anne Ferrell and Peter McCullough. New York: Manchester University Press, 2000.

———. *Humanism and America: An Intellectual History of English Colonisation, 1500–1625*. New York: Cambridge University Press, 2003.

Foster, Donald W. *Elegy by W. S.: A Study in Attribution*. Newark, DE: University of Delaware Press, 1989.

Fountain, Miranda. "A Statue of Sir George Somers." *Heritage Magazine*, 1984, 26.

Franssen, Paul. "The Bard, the Bible, and the Desert Island." In *The Author as Character: Representing Historical Writers in Western Literature*, edited by Paul Franssen and Ton Hoenselaars. Madison, NJ: Fairleigh Dickinson University Press, 1999.

Fraser, Russell. *Shakespeare: The Later Years*. New York: Columbia University Press, 1992.

Frey, Charles. "*The Tempest* and the New World." *Shakespeare Quarterly* 30, no. 1 (Winter 1979): 29–41.

Frye, Northrop. "Shakespeare's *The Tempest*." *Shenandoah* 42, no. 4 (Winter 1992): 36–50.

Frye, Roland Mushat. *Shakespeare's Life and Times: A Pictorial Record*. Princeton, NJ: Princeton University Press, 1967.

Fuller, Mary C. *Voyages in Print: English Travel to America, 1576–1624*. Cambridge, UK: Cambridge University Press, 1995.

Fuller, Thomas. *The History of the Worthies of England*. London: Thomas Williams, 1662.

Fulton, Robert C. "*The Tempest* and the Bermuda Pamphlets: Source and Thematic Intention." *Interpretations* 10, no. 1 (Fall 1978): 1–10.

Gayley, Charles Mills. *Shakespeare and the Founders of Liberty in America*. New York: Macmillan, 1917.

Gill, Crispin. *Plymouth: A New History, Ice Age to the Elizabethans*. 2nd rev. ed. North Pomfret, VT: David and Charles, 1979.

———. *Plymouth: A New History, 1603 to the Present Day*. North Pomfret, VT: David and Charles, 1979.

Gillies, John. *Shakespeare and the Geography of Difference*. Cambridge, UK: Cambridge University Press, 1994.

———. "Shakespeare's Virginian Masque." *ELH: English Literary History* 53, no. 4 (Winter 1986): 673–707.

Glover, Lorri, and Daniel Blake Smith. *The Shipwreck That Saved Jamestown: The Sea Venture Castaways and the Fate of America*. New York: Henry Holt and Company, 2008.

Gray, Robert. *A Good Speed to Virginia*. London: William Welby, 1609.

Green, Mary Anne Everett, ed. *Calendar of State Papers: Domestic Series, of the Reign of James I.* 4 vols. London: Longman, Brown, Green, Longmans, and Roberts, 1857–59.

Green, Nina. "False Parallels in David Kathman's 'Dating *The Tempest*.'" *The Oxford Authorship Site.* http://www.oxford-shakespeare.com/new_files_july_22_05/Kathman_refutation.pdf.

Greenblatt, Stephen. "*King Lear.*" In *The Norton Shakespeare*, edited by Stephen Greenblatt. New York: W. W. Norton, 1997.

———. *Shakespearean Negotiations: The Circulation of Social Energy in Renaissance England.* Oxford, UK: Clarendon Press, 1990.

———. *Will in the World: How Shakespeare Became Shakespeare.* New York: W. W. Norton, 2004.

Griffiths, Trevor R. "'This Island's Mine': Caliban and Colonialism." *The Yearbook of English Studies* 13 (1983): 159–80.

Guibert, Philbert. *The Charitable Physitian with the Charitable Apothecary.* London: Lawrence Chapman, 1639.

Gurr, Andrew. *Playgoing in Shakespeare's London.* 3rd ed. Cambridge, UK: Cambridge University Press, 2004.

———. "The *Tempest's* Tempest at Blackfriars." *Shakespeare Survey* 41 (1988): 91–102.

Hadfield, Andrew. *Literature, Travel, and Colonial Writing in the English Renaissance 1545–1625.* New York: Oxford University Press, 2007.

Haile, Edward Wright, ed. *Jamestown Narratives: Eyewitness Accounts of the Virginia Colony, The First Decade: 1607–1617.* Champlain, VA: Roundhouse, 1998.

Hakluyt, Richard, ed. *The Principal Navigations, Voyages, Traffiques and Discoveries of the English Nation.* 3 vols. London: George Bishop, Ralph Newberie, and Robert Barker, 1598–1600.

Hamlin, William M. *The Image of America in Montaigne, Spenser, and Shakespeare: Renaissance Ethnography and Literary Reflection.* London: Macmillan, 1995.

———. "Men of Inde: Renaissance Ethnography and *The Tempest.*" *Shakespeare Studies* 22 (1994): 15–44.

Hamor, Ralph. *A True Discourse of the Present Estate of Virginia, and the Successe of the Affaires There Till the 18 of June 1614.* London: William Welby, 1615.

Hardy, John. *Description of the Last Voyage to Bermudas, in the Ship* Marygold. London: Rowland Reynald, 1671.

Harland, John. *Seamanship in the Age of Sail.* Annapolis, MD: Naval Institute Press, 1984.

Harrington, J. C. *Glassmaking at Jamestown: America's First Industry.* Richmond: Dietz Press, 1952.

Hart, C. W., Jr., and Raymond B. Manning. "The Cavernicolous Caridean Shrimps of Bermuda." *Journal of Crustacean Biology* 1, no. 3 (August 1981): 441–56.

Hart, Jonathan. *Columbus, Shakespeare and the Interpretation of the New World.* New York: Palgrave Macmillan, 2003.

Hayward, Walter Brownell. *Bermuda Past and Present: A Descriptive and Historical Account of the Somers Islands.* New York: Dodd, Mead, 1911.

Horn, James. *A Land As God Made It: Jamestown and the Birth of America.* New York: Basic Books, 2005.

Hotson, Leslie. *I, William Shakespeare.* London: Jonathan Cape, 1937.

Hughes, Lewis. *A Letter, Sent into England from the Summer Ilands.* London: William Welby, 1615.

Hulme, Peter. *Colonial Encounters: Europe and the Native Caribbean, 1492–1797.* 1986. Reprint, New York: Routledge, 1992.

——. "Hurricanes in the Caribbees: The Constitution of the Discourse of English Colonialism." In *1642: Literature and Power in the Seventeenth Century*, edited by Francis Barker et al. Proceedings of the Essex Conference on the Sociology of Literature, July 1980. Colchester, UK: University of Essex, 1981.

Hulme, Peter, and William H. Sherman, eds. The Tempest *and Its Travels.* London: Reaktion, 2000.

Hunter, Joseph. *A Disquisition on the Scene, Origin, Date, etc. etc. of Shakespeare's* Tempest. London: C. Whittingham, 1839.

Irving, Washington. *Wolfert's Roost.* Edited by Roberta Rosenberg. Boston: Twayne, 1979.

James, D. G. *The Dream of Prospero.* Oxford, UK: Clarendon Press, 1967.

Jet Propulsion Laboratory, California Institute of Technology, Pasadena, California. "Planetary Satellite Discovery Circumstances." *Solar System Dynamics.* Donald K. Yeomans et al. http://ssd.jpl.nasa.gov/?sat_discovery.

Johnson, Caleb. "The True Origin of Stephen Hopkins of the *Mayflower* with Evidence of His Earlier Presence in Virginia." *The American Genealogist* 73, no. 3 (July 1998): 161–71.

Johnson, Robert. *A New Life of Virginea.* In *Tracts and Other Papers, Relating Principally to the Origin, Settlement, and Progress of the Colonies in North America from the Discovery of the Country to the Year 1776*, edited by Peter Force. 4 vols. 1835. Reprint, Gloucester, MA: Peter Smith, 1963. First published 1612 by W. Welby.

——. *Nova Britannia: Offering Most Excellent Fruites by Planting in Virginia.* London: Samuel Macham, 1609.

Jones, Howard Mumford, and Sue Bonner Walcutt. *The Literature of Virginia in the Seventeenth Century.* 2nd. ed. Charlottesville: University Press of Virginia, 1968.

Jones, Rosemary. *Bermuda: Five Centuries.* Bermuda: Panatel VDS, 2004.

Jonson, Ben. *Sejanus: His Fall.* London: Thomas Thorpe, 1605.

Jourdain, Silvester. *A Discovery of the Barmudas, Otherwise Called the Ile of Divels.* London: Roger Barnes, 1610.

——. *A Plaine Description of the Barmudas, Now Called Sommer Ilands.* In *Tracts and Other Papers, Relating Principally to the Origin, Settlement, and Progress of the Colonies in North America from the Discovery of the Country to the Year 1776*, edited by Peter Force. 4 vols. 1836. Reprint, New York: Peter Smith, 1947. First published 1613 by W. Welby.

Joyce, James. *Ulysses: A Critical and Synoptic Edition.* Edited by Hans Walter Gabler et al. 3 vols. New York: Garland Publishing, 1984.

Karwoski, Gail Langer. *Miracle: The True Story of the Wreck of the* Sea Venture. Plain City, OH: Darby Creek Publishing, 2004.

Kathman, David. "Dating *The Tempest.*" *The Shakespeare Authorship Page.* David

Kathman and Terry Ross. http://shakespeareauthorship.com/tempest.html.

Kelso, William M. *Jamestown: The Buried Truth.* Charlottesville: University of Virginia Press, 2006.

———. "Shakespearean Americans." *Jamestown Rediscovery* 3 (1997): 8–10.

Kennedy, Jean. *Isle of Devils: Bermuda under the Somers Island Company 1609–1685.* London: Collins, 1971.

Kennedy, Neil. "The Significance of *Tempest* Allusions in the Work of John Taylor the Water Poet." *Bermuda Journal of Archaeology and Maritime History* 11 (1999): 25–38.

Kermode, Frank. "*King Lear.*" In *The Riverside Shakespeare*, edited by G. Blakemore Evans et al. 2nd ed. Boston: Houghton Mifflin, 1997.

Kingsbury, Susan Myra, ed. *The Records of the Virginia Company of London.* 4 vols. Washington, DC: United States Government Printing Office, 1906–35.

Kipling, Rudyard. *How Shakspere Came to Write The Tempest.* Papers on Playmaking 1. New York: Dramatic Museum of Columbia University, 1916.

———. "Kipling and *The Tempest.*" *Kipling Journal* 59 (March 1985): 56–60.

———. *Limits and Renewals.* Garden City, NY: Doubleday, Doran & Company, 1932.

Knapp, Jeffrey. *An Empire Nowhere: England, America, and Literature from Utopia to The Tempest.* Berkeley: University of California Press, 1992.

Knowles, Richard. "How Shakespeare Knew *King Leir.*" *Shakespeare Survey* 55 (2002): 12–35.

Kolb, Avery. "The Tempest." *American Heritage* 34, no. 3 (April/May 1983): 26–35.

Kuhl, E. P. "Shakespeare and the Founders of America: *The Tempest.*" *Philological Quarterly* 41, no. 1 (January 1962): 123–46.

Kupperman, Karen Ordahl. "Apathy and Death in Early Jamestown." *Journal of American History* 66, no. 1 (June 1979): 24–40.

———. "Fear of Hot Climates in the Anglo-American Colonial Experience." *William and Mary Quarterly*, 3rd ser., 41, no. 2 (April 1984): 213–40.

———. *The Jamestown Project.* Cambridge, MA: Harvard University Press, 2007.

Laird, Matthew R. "'In the Hollow Lotos-Land': Discord, Order, and the Emergence of Stability in Early Bermuda, 1609–1623." Master's thesis, College of William and Mary, 1991.

Lavery, Brian. *The Colonial Merchantman Susan Constant 1605.* The Anatomy of the Ship Series. Annapolis, MD: Naval Institute Press, 1988.

Law, Ernest. "Shakespeare's *Tempest* as Originally Produced at Court." In The Tempest: *Critical Essays*, edited by Patrick M. Murphy. New York: Routledge, 2001.

Lawson, Lesley. *Out of the Shadows: The Life of Lucy, Countess of Bedford.* New York: Hambledon Continuum, 2007.

LeConte, John. *How to Make Salt from Sea-Water.* Columbia, SC: Charles P. Pelham, 1862.

Lee, Sidney. "Caliban's Visits to England." *Cornhill Magazine* 34 (1913): 333–45.

Lefroy, J. H. *Memorials of the Discovery and Early Settlement of the Bermudas or Somers Islands 1515–1685.* 2 vols. London: Longmans, Green, and Company, 1877–79.

Lindley, David. *Shakespeare and Music.* The Arden Critical Companions. London: Thomson Learning, 2006.

Linebaugh, Peter, and Marcus Rediker. *The Many-Headed Hydra: Sailors, Slaves, Commoners, and the Hidden History of the Revolutionary Atlantic*. Boston: Beacon Press, 2000.

Linschoten, Jan Huygen van. *His Discours of Voyages into the Easte and West Indies*. London: John Wolfe, 1598.

Lloyd, Bertram. " 'Scamels' in *The Tempest*." *Modern Language Review* 19, no. 1 (January 1924): 102–3.

Looney, J. Thomas. *"Shakespeare" Identified in Edward De Vere, the Seventeenth Earl of Oxford*. New York: Duell, Sloan and Pearce, 1949.

Lounsbury, Carl. *The Early Church at Jamestown: A History and Precedents for Its Design and Reconstruction*. Williamsburg, VA: Colonial Williamsburg Foundation, 2004.

Mainwaring, Henry. *The Seaman's Dictionary*. In *The Life and Works of Sir Henry Mainwaring*, edited by G. E. Mainwaring and W. G. Perrin. 2 vols. London: Navy Records Society, 1920–22.

Malcolm, Noel. *The Origins of English Nonsense*. London: HarperCollins, 1997.

Malone, Edmond. *An Account of the Incidents from Which the Title and Part of the Story of Shakspeare's* Tempest *Were Derived*. London: C. and R. Baldwin, 1808.

Mancall, Peter. *Hakluyt's Promise: An Elizabethan's Obsession for an English America*. New Haven, CT: Yale University Press, 2007.

Mardis, A., Jr. Sea Venture: *The Downing Wreck Revisited*. San Marino, CA: Fathom Eight, 1981.

Marienstras, Richard. "Elizabethan Travel Literature and Shakespeare's *The Tempest*." In *New Perspectives on the Shakespearean World*, translated by Janet Lloyd. New York: Cambridge University Press, 1985.

Marsden, R. G. "English Ships in the Reign of James I." *Transactions of the Royal Historical Society*, n.s., 19 (1905): 309–37.

Marshall, Tristan. "*The Tempest* and the British Imperium in 1611." *The Historical Journal* 41, no. 2 (June 1998): 375–400.

Martin, R. Aidan. "Biology of the Common Thresher (*Alopias vulpinus*)." In "Biology of Sharks and Rays." ReefQuest Centre for Shark Research. http://elasmo-research .org/education/shark_profiles/a_vulpinus.htm.

Marx, Leo. *The Machine in the Garden: Technology and the Pastoral Ideal in America*. New York: Oxford University Press, 1964.

Masaki, Tsuneo. "Shakespeare's Use of the New World in *The Tempest*." *Studies in English Literature* (1993): 3–13.

Mason, F. van Wyck. *The Sea 'Venture*. Garden City, NY: Doubleday, 1961.

Mathew, Frank. *An Image of Shakespeare*. London: Jonathan Cape, 1922.

McCrea, Scott. *The Case for Shakespeare: The End of the Authorship Question*. Westport, CT: Praeger, 2005.

McDonald, Russ. "Reading *The Tempest*." *Shakespeare Survey* 43 (1991): 15–28.

McGinn, Colin. *Shakespeare's Philosophy: Discovering the Meaning Behind the Plays*. New York: HarperCollins, 2006.

McMullan, Gordon. *The Politics of Unease in the Plays of John Fletcher*. Amherst: University of Massachusetts Press, 1994.

Merck & Co., Inc. "Clostridial Necrotizing Enteritis." In *The Merck Manuals Online Medical Library: The Merck Manual for Healthcare Professionals*, edited by Robert S. Porter et al. Whitehouse Station, NJ: Merck & Co., 2005-. http://www.merck.com/mmpe.

Michell, John. *Who Wrote Shakespeare?* New York: Thames and Hudson, 1996.

Monger, George P. *Marriage Customs of the World: From Henna to Honeymoons*. Santa Barbara, CA: ABC-CLIO, 2004.

Moore, Peter. "*The Tempest* and the Bermuda Shipwreck of 1609." *Shakespeare Oxford Newsletter* 32, no. 3 (Summer 1996): 6.

Morey, Dennis A. J. *Sir Thomas Gates: Governor of Virginia*. Chesterfield, VA: Henricus Foundation, 1998.

Mossiker, Frances. *Pocahontas: The Life and the Legend*. New York: Knopf, 1976.

Mountford, K. "Storms: A Long Perspective from History." In *Hurricane Isabel in Perspective: Proceedings of a Conference Convened 15-17 November 2004 at The Maritime Institute*, edited by Kevin G. Sellner and Nina Fisher. Edgewater, MD: Chesapeake Research Consortium, 2005.

Murphy, Robert Cushman, and Louis S. Mowbray. "New Light on the Cahow, *Pterodroma Cahow*." *The Auk* 68 (July 1951): 266-80.

Nagler, A. M. *Shakespeare's Stage*. Enlarged ed. New Haven, CT: Yale University Press, 1981.

Najmuddin, Shahzad Z. *Shakespeare's* The Tempest, *Its Political Implications and the First Colonists of Virginia*. Islamabad, Pakistan: Leo Book, 2005.

Neill, Edward D. *History of the Virginia Company of London*. Albany, NY: Joel Munsell, 1869.

Nicholls, Mark. "George Percy's 'Trewe Relacyon': A Primary Source for the Jamestown Settlement." *Virginia Magazine of History and Biography* 113, no. 3 (2005): 212-75.

Noël Hume, Ivor. *Here Lies Virginia: An Archaeologist's View of Colonial Life and History*. New ed. Charlottesville: University Press of Virginia, 1994.

———. "The Mystery of Sir George Somers and His Bermuda Triangle." *Colonial Williamsburg* 29, no. 3 (Summer 2007): 34-40.

———. *The Virginia Adventure*. New York: Knopf, 1994.

———. "William Strachey's Unrecorded First Draft of his *Sea Venture* Saga." *Avalon Chronicles* 6 (2001): 57-87.

Nosworthy, J. M. "The Narrative Sources of *The Tempest*." *Review of English Studies* 24 (October 1948): 281-94.

Nuzum, David G. "The London Company and *The Tempest*." *West Virginia University Bulletin Philological Papers*, ser. 60, 12, no. 5-1 (November 1959): 12-23.

Officer, Lawrence H. "Purchasing Power of British Pounds from 1264 to 2007." MeasuringWorth. http://www.measuringworth.com/ppoweruk/.

Oldmixon, John. *The British Empire in America*. 2 vols. 1741. Reprint, New York: Augustus M. Kelley Publishers, 1969.

O'Neal, Cothburn. *The Dark Lady: A Novel*. New York: Crown Publishers, 1954.

Oxford University Press. *Oxford English Dictionary*. Edited by John Simpson et al. 3rd ed. Oxford: Oxford University Press, 1999-. http://www.oed.com/.

Parker, John. *Van Meteren's Virginia 1607–1612.* Minneapolis: University of Minnesota Press, 1961.

Payne, Robert. *By Me, William Shakespeare.* New York: Everest House, 1980.

Peterson, M. L. R. "The *Sea Venture.*" *Mariners Mirror* 74, no. 1 (Feb. 1988): 37–48.

Philbrick, Nathaniel. Mayflower: *A Story of Courage, Community, and War.* New York: Viking, 2006.

Phillips-Watlington, Christine. *Bermuda's Botanical Wonderland: A Field Guide.* London: Macmillan Education, 1996.

Picard, Liza. *Elizabeth's London: Everyday Life in Elizabethan London.* London: Weidenfeld and Nicolson, 2003.

Pope, F. J. "Sir George Somers and His Family." *Proceedings of the Dorset Natural History and Antiquarian Field Club* 32 (1911): 26–32.

Porter, H. C. *The Inconstant Savage: England and the North American Indian 1500–1660.* London: Gerald Duckworth and Company, 1979.

Price, Daniel. *Sauls Prohibition Staide or The Apprehension, and Examination of Saule.* London: Matthew Law, 1609.

Price, David A. *Love and Hate in Jamestown: John Smith, Pocahontas, and the Start of a New Nation.* New York: Vintage Books, 2003.

Prince, John. *Danmonii Orientales Illustres: or The Worthies of Devon.* London: Rees and Curtis, 1810.

Puntis, John. "Pig-bel (Necrotizing Enteritis) in the Americas?" *Journal of Pediatric Gastroenterology and Nutrition* 34, no. 3 (March 2002): 323.

Purchas, Samuel, ed. *Purchas His Pilgrimes.* 4 vols. London: Henrie Fetherstone, 1625.

Quinn, David B. "Bermuda in the Age of Exploration and Early Settlement." *Bermuda Journal of Archaeology and Maritime History* 1 (1989): 1–23.

———. "Christopher Newport in 1590." *North Carolina Historical Review* 29, no. 3 (July 1952): 305–16.

———, ed. *New American World: A Documentary History of North America to 1612.* 5 vols. New York: Arno Press, 1979.

———. "Notes by a Pious Colonial Investor, 1608-1610." *William and Mary Quarterly,* 3rd ser., 16, no. 4 (October 1959): 551–55.

Raine, David F. *Shakespeare, an Island and a Storm (The Bermuda Connection).* St. George's, Bermuda: Pompano Publications, 2000.

———. *Sir George Somers: A Man and His Times.* St. George's, Bermuda: Pompano Publications, 1984.

Ransome, David R. "Christopher Newport." In *American National Biography,* edited by John A. Garraty and Mark C. Carnes. 24 vols. New York: Oxford University Press, 1999.

Rich, Richard. *Newes from Virginia: The Lost Flocke Triumphant.* London: Edward Allde, 1610.

Rountree, Helen C. *Pocahontas, Powhatan, Opechancanough: Three Indian Lives Changed by Jamestown.* Charlottesville: University of Virginia Press, 2005.

———. *The Powhatan Indians of Virginia: Their Traditional Culture.* Norman: University of Oklahoma Press, 1989.

Rountree, Helen C., and E. Randolph Turner III. *Before and After Jamestown: Virginia's Powhatans and Their Predecessors.* Gainesville: University Press of Florida, 2002.

Rowse, A. L. *Shakespeare's Southampton: Patron of Virginia.* New York: Harper and Row, 1965.

Rutman, Darrett B. "The Historian and the Marshal: A Note on the Background of Sir Thomas Dale." *Virginia Magazine of History and Biography* 68, no. 3 (July 1960): 284–94.

Rutman, Darrett B., and Anita H. Rutman. "Of Agues and Fevers: Malaria in the Early Chesapeake." *William and Mary Quarterly,* 3rd ser., 33, no. 1 (January 1976): 31–60.

Saenger, Michael Baird. "The Costumes of Caliban and Ariel Qua Sea-Nymph." *Notes and Queries,* n.s., 42, no. 3 (September 1995): 334–36.

Sainsbury, W. Noel et al., eds., *Calendar of State Papers: Colonial Series.* 44 vols. and addenda. London: Longman, Brown, Green, Longmans, & Roberts et al., 1860–1969.

———. "Death of Sir Thomas Gates." *Virginia Magazine of History and Biography* 6, no. 4 (April 1899): 371.

Salingar, Leo. "The New World in 'The Tempest.'" In *Travel and Drama in Shakespeare's Time,* edited by Jean-Pierre Maquerlot and Michele Willems. New York: Cambridge University Press, 1996.

Sams, Conway Whittle. *The Conquest of Virginia: The Second Attempt.* Norfolk, VA: Keyser-Doherty Printing Corporation, 1929.

Sanders, Charles Richard. *The Strachey Family 1588–1932: Their Writings and Literary Associations.* Durham, NC: Duke University Press, 1953.

———. "William Strachey, the Virginia Colony, and Shakespeare." *Virginia Magazine of History and Biography* 57, no. 2 (April 1949): 115–32.

Sarnecki, Judith Holland. "Mastering the Masters: Aimé Césaire's Creolization of Shakespeare's The Tempest." *The French Review* 74, no. 2 (December 2000): 276–86.

Schmidgall, Gary. "*The Tempest* and *Primaleon*: A New Source." *Shakespeare Quarterly* 37, no. 4 (Winter 1986): 423–39.

Schonland, B. F. J. *The Flight of Thunderbolts.* Oxford, UK: Clarendon Press, 1950.

Scull, G. D. *The Evelyns in America.* Oxford, UK: Parker and Company, 1881.

Seltzer, Daniel. "The Staging of the Last Plays." In *Later Shakespeare.* London: Edward Arnold, 1966.

Sermon, William. *The Ladies Companion, or the English Midwife.* London: Edward Thomas, 1671.

Shakespeare, William. *The History of King Lear.* The Oxford Shakespeare. Edited by Stanley Wells. New York: Oxford University Press, 2000.

———. *King Lear.* The Arden Shakespeare. Edited by Kenneth Muir. London: Methuen and Company, 1972.

———. *King Lear.* The Arden Shakespeare. Edited by R. A. Foakes. London: Thomson Learning, 2001.

———. *Mr. William Shakespeares Comedies, Histories, & Tragedies, Published According to the True Originall Copies* (First Folio). London: Isaac Iaggard and Ed. Blount, 1623.

———. "The Tempest." In *The Riverside Shakespeare*, edited by G. Blakemore Evans et al. 2nd ed. Boston: Houghton Mifflin, 1997.

———. *The Tempest*. Edited by Harold Bloom. New York: Riverhead Books, 2005.

———. *The Tempest*. The Pelican Shakespeare. Edited by Peter Holland. New York: Penguin, 1999.

———. *The Tempest*. The New Cambridge Shakespeare. Edited by David Lindley. New York: Cambridge University Press, 2002.

———. *The Tempest*. The Works of Shakespeare. Edited by Morton Luce. London: Methuen, 1901.

———. *The Tempest*. The New Folger Library Shakespeare. Edited by Barbara A. Mowat and Paul Werstine. New York: Washington Square Press, 1994.

———. *The Tempest*. The Oxford Shakespeare. Edited by Stephen Orgel. New York: Oxford University Press, 1987.

———. *The Tempest*. The Arden Shakespeare. Edited by Virginia Mason Vaughan and Alden T. Vaughan. London: Thomson Learning, 1999.

———. *The Tempest*. The Arden Shakespeare. Edited by Frank Kermode. 6th ed. Cambridge, MA: Harvard University Press, 1958.

Sheehan, Bernard W. "Sir Thomas Gates." In *American National Biography*, edited by John A. Garraty and Mark C. Carnes. 24 vols. New York: Oxford University Press, 1999.

———. "William Strachey." In *American National Biography*, edited by John A. Garraty and Mark C. Carnes. 24 vols. New York: Oxford University Press, 1999.

Sievers, Julie Ann. "Evidence of Wonders: Writing American Identity in the Early Modern Transatlantic World." PhD diss., University of Texas at Austin, 2004.

Skura, Meredith Anne. "Discourse and the Individual: The Case of Colonialism in *The Tempest*." *Shakespeare Quarterly* 40, no. 1 (Spring 1989): 42–69.

Smith, Cyril H. "Was This the Course the *Sea Venture* Really Took?" *Royal Gazette* (Bermuda), March 24, 1971.

Smith, Hallett, ed. *Twentieth Century Interpretations of* The Tempest. Englewood Cliffs, NJ: Prentice-Hall, 1969.

Smith, John. *The Complete Works of Captain John Smith (1580–1631)*. Edited by Philip L. Barbour. 3 vols. Chapel Hill: University of North Carolina Press, 1986.

Srigley, Michael. *Images of Regeneration: A Study of Shakespeare's* The Tempest *and Its Cultural Background*. Uppsala, Swed.: Academia Upsaliensis, 1985.

Stahle, David W., et al. "The Lost Colony and Jamestown Droughts." *Science* 280 (April 24, 1998): 564–67.

Stamers-Smith, Eileen. "Kipling and Bermuda." *Bermuda Journal of Archaeology and Maritime History* 8 (1996): 100–114.

———. "Reflections on the Bermuda Flora." *Garden History* 8, no. 3 (Winter 1980): 115–27.

Stationers' Company. *A Transcript of the Registers of the Company of Stationers of London: 1554–1640 A.D.* Edited by Edward Arber. 5 vols. London: Stationers' Company, 1875–94.

Stephenson, Henry Thew. *Shakespeare's London*. New York: Henry Holt and Company, 1905.

Stern, Virginia F. *Sir Stephen Powle of Court and Country.* Selinsgrove, PA: Susquehanna University Press, 1992.

Sterrer, Wolfgang, and A. Ralph Cavaliere. *Bermuda's Seashore Plants and Seaweeds.* Bermuda: Bermuda Natural History Museum and Bermuda Zoological Society, 1998.

Sterrer, Wolfgang, and Thomas M. Iliffe. "*Mesonerilla Prospera*, A New Archiannelid from Marine Caves in Bermuda." *Proceedings of the Biological Society of Washington* 95, no. 3 (October 5, 1982): 509–14.

Stoll, Elmer Edgar. "Certain Fallacies and Irrelevancies in the Literary Scholarship of the Day." *Studies in Philology* 24, no. 4 (October 1927): 485–508.

Stow, John. *The Annales, or a Generall Chronicle of England, Begun First by Maister John Stow, and After Him Continued and Augmented with Matters Forreyne, and Domestique, Auncient and Moderne, Unto the End of This Present Yeere 1614.* London: Thomas Adams, 1615.

———. *Annales, or a Generall Chronicle of England, Begun by John Stow, Continued and Augmented with Matters Forraigne and Domestique, Ancient and Moderne, Unto the End of This Present Yeere 1631.* London: Richard Meighen, 1632.

Strachey, Lytton. *Books and Characters: French & English.* New York: Harcourt, Brace and Company, 1922.

Strachey, William. *A Dictionary of Powhatan.* Southampton, PA: Evolution Publishing, 1999.

———. *For the Colony in Virginea Britannia, Lawes Divine, Morall and Martiall, &c.* London: Walter Burre, 1612.

———. *For the Colony in Virginea Britannia, Lawes Divine, Morall and Martiall, Etc.* Edited by David H. Flaherty. Charlottesville: Association for the Preservation of Virginia Antiquities by the University Press of Virginia, 1969.

———. *The Historie of Travaile into Virginia Britannia.* Edited by R. H. Major. London: Hakluyt Society, 1849.

———. *The Historie of Travell into Virginia Britania.* Edited by Louis B. Wright and Virginia Freund. London: Hakluyt Society, 1953.

———. "A True Reportory of the Wracke, and Redemption of Sir Thomas Gates Knight." In *Purchas His Pilgrimes,* edited by Samuel Purchas. Vol. 4. London: Henrie Fetherstone, 1625.

Stritmatter, Roger, and Lynne Kositsky. "Shakespeare and the Voyagers Revisited." *Review of English Studies,* n.s., 58 (September 2007): 447–72.

Stubbs, John. *John Donne: The Reformed Soul.* New York: W. W. Norton, 2007.

Sturgess, Keith. *Jacobean Private Theatre.* New York: Routledge and Kegan Paul, 1987.

Symonds, William. *A Sermon Preached at White-Chappel, in the Presence of Many, Honourable and Worshipfull, the Adventurers and Planters for Virginia.* London: Eleazer Edgar and William Welby, 1609.

Taylor, Gary. "A New Source and an Old Date for King Lear." *Review of English Studies,* n.s., 133 (November 1982): 396–413.

Thomson, P. "John Donne and the Countess of Bedford." *Modern Language Review* 44, no. 3 (July 1949): 329–40.

Thornton, Weldon. *Allusions in Ulysses: An Annotated List.* Chapel Hill: University of North Carolina Press, 1968.

Thurley, Simon. *Whitehall Palace: An Architectural History of the Royal Apartments, 1240–1698*. New Haven, CT: Yale University Press, 1999.

Townsend, Camilla. *Pocahontas and the Powhatan Dilemma*. New York: Hill and Wang, 2004.

Tucker, Terry. *Bermuda—Unintended Destination 1609–1610*. Bermuda: Island Press, 1978.

———. *Bermuda Today and Yesterday: 1503–1980s*. 3rd ed. London: Robert Hale Limited, 1983.

Turman, Nora Miller. "The *Sea Venture* in History and Fiction." *Virginia Record* 81, no. 10 (October 1959): 12–13; no. 12 (December 1959): 24–25, 50.

Vaughan, Alden T. "Powhatans Abroad: Virginia Indians in England." In *Envisioning an English Empire: Jamestown and the Making of the North Atlantic World*, edited by Robert Appelbaum and John Wood Sweet. Philadelphia: University of Pennsylvania Press, 2005.

———. "Shakespeare's Indian: The Americanization of Caliban." *Shakespeare Quarterly* 39, no. 2 (Summer 1988): 137–53.

———. *Transatlantic Encounters: American Indians in Britain, 1500–1776*. New York: Cambridge University Press, 2006.

———. "Trinculo's Indian: American Natives in Shakespeare's England." In *The Tempest and Its Travels*, edited by Peter Hulme and William H. Sherman. London: Reaktion, 2000.

———. "William Strachey's 'True Reportory' and Shakespeare: A Closer Look at the Evidence." *Shakespeare Quarterly* 59, no. 3 (Fall 2008): 245–73.

Vaughan, Virginia Mason, and Alden T. Vaughan. *Critical Essays on Shakespeare's The Tempest*. New York: G. K. Hall and Company, 1998.

———. *Shakespeare's Caliban: A Cultural History*. New York: Cambridge University Press, 1991.

Verrill, Addison E. *The Bermuda Islands: An Account of Their Scenery, Climate, Productions, Physiography, Natural History and Geology*. New Haven, CT: Addison E. Verrill, 1902.

Virginia Company of London. *A Publication by the Counsell of Virginia, Touching the Plantation There*. London: William Welby, 1610.

———. *A True and Sincere Declaration of the Purpose and Ends of the Plantation Begun in Virginia*. London: J. Stepneth, 1610.

———. *A True Declaration of the Estate of the Colonie in Virginia*. London: William Barret, 1610.

Ward, A. W. *Shakespeare and the Makers of Virginia*. London: Oxford University Press, 1919.

Ware, Sylvia. "A Journey to Dorset." *Heritage Magazine*, 1981, 20–22.

Waters, David W. *The Art of Navigation in England in Elizabethan and Early Stuart Times*. 2nd rev. ed. 3 vols. Greenwich, UK: Trustees of the National Maritime Museum, 1978.

Weinreb, Ben, and Christopher Hibbert, eds. *The London Encyclopaedia*. London: Macmillan, 1983.

Wilbraham, Roger. *The Journal of Sir Roger Wilbraham, Solicitor-General in Ireland and Master of Requests, for the Years 1593–1616.* Edited by Harold Spencer Scott. London: Royal Historical Society, 1902.

Wilkinson, Henry C. *The Adventurers of Bermuda: A History of the Island from Its Discovery until the Dissolution of the Somers Island Company in 1684.* 2nd ed. New York: Oxford University Press, 1958.

Willes, Richard, ed. *The History of Travayle in the West and East Indies.* London: Richard Jugge, 1577.

Willis, Deborah. "Shakespeare's *Tempest* and the Discourse of Colonialism." In *William Shakespeare, The Tempest: A Case Study in Critical Controversy,* edited by Gerald Graff and James Phelan. New York: Bedford/St. Martin's, 2000.

Wingood, Allan J. "*Sea Venture.* An Interim Report on an Early 17th Century Shipwreck Lost in 1609." *International Journal of Nautical Archaeology and Underwater Exploration* 11, no. 4 (November 1982): 333–47.

———. "*Sea Venture* Second Interim Report—Part 2: The Artefacts." *International Journal of Nautical Archaeology and Underwater Exploration* 15, no. 2 (May 1986): 149–59.

Wingood, Allan J., and Peggy Wingood. "*Sea Venture*: The Adventure that Started 375 Years Ago." *Heritage Magazine,* 1984, 21–24.

Wingood, Allan J., Peggy Wingood, and Jonathan Adams. Sea Venture: *The Tempest Wreck.* Bermuda: Island Press Ltd., 1986.

Wood, Betty. "William Strachey." In *Oxford Dictionary of National Biography,* edited by H. C. G. Matthew and Brian Harrison. New York: Oxford University Press, 2004.

Wood, Michael. *In Search of Shakespeare.* London: BBC Books, 2003.

Wright, Irene A. "Spanish Policy Toward Virginia, 1606–1612: Jamestown, Ecija, and John Clark of the *Mayflower.*" *American Historical Review* 25, no. 3 (Apr. 1920): 448–79.

Wright, Louis B. *Religion and Empire: The Alliance Between Piety and Commerce in English Expansion 1558–1625.* Chapel Hill: University of North Carolina Press, 1943.

———, ed. *A Voyage to Virginia in 1609, Two Narratives: Strachey's "True Reportory" and Jourdain's "Discovery of the Bermudas."* Charlottesville: Association for the Preservation of Virginia Antiquities by the University Press of Virginia, 1964.

Wright, P. M. *The Sea Venture Story.* Bermuda: Bermuda Press, 1960.

Zuill, William S. "Cast Away on Bermuda." *Bermuda Historical Quarterly* 16, no. 2 (Summer 1959): 49–67.

———. "'A Lamb on Land; A Lion at Sea.'" *Heritage Magazine,* 1984, 27–31.

———. "Sir George Somers: The Sailor and the Man." *The Bermudian* (December 1982): 37, 74–81; (January 1983): 23, 41–45; (February 1983): 19, 41–45; (March 1983): 21, 35–40.

———. *The Story of Bermuda and Her People.* 3rd ed. London: Macmillan Education, 1999.

INDEX

on Bermuda, 51–53, 55, 56, 58, 64,
    66, 75, 77, 79, 80, 91, 93, 145
and Blackfriars Theater, 155
and class prejudices, 19, 60, 62,
    69, 78
death of, 181–82
and Delaware, 115, 116, 131
family background of, 1–2
financial problems of, 3, 4, 146–47,
    181
*Historie of Travaile into Virginia
    Britannia*, 193, 206
and hurricane, 38–39, 42, 43
and Indian attacks, 119, 122, 124
Indian life studied by, 17, 70, 127–28,
    193
influence on literature, 193–95
and Jamestown's desperate straits,
    102, 103, 104
landing at Bermuda, 48
and land sighting, 46, 47
leaving Bermuda, 96, 98
marriage of, 2
"On Sejanus" (sonnet) by, 2, 4
patronage sought by, 7, 95, 116, 121,
    131, 146–47, 154–55, 181
Powhatans seen in England by, 6
preparations to leave England, 9–10
return to England, 143–44, 145–47
ring of, 199
and St. Elmo's fire, 43–44
schooling of, 2
on *Sea Venture*, 29
and Shakespeare's *Tempest*, 155–56,
    157–68, 169–80, 182
travel narratives read by, 5, 7
True Repertory, 193
and Turkish assignment, 3–4, 7, 165
as Virginia chronicler, 8–9, 17, 70,
    95, 102, 107, 116, 118, 121, 125–26,
    131, 132, 145–46, 180, 181, 192–93
Strachey, William (father), 2

Strachey, William (grandfather), 2
Strachey, William Jr. (son), 2, 10, 145, 181
Stratford-upon-Avon, England, 149,
    182–83
Swallow:
    arrival at Jamestown, 104
    disappearance in hurricane, 33
    leaving England, 21, 22
    return to England, 124–25
Swift, James, 90
Symonds, Rev. William, 15, 16

Tackonekintaco (Indian leader), 121
Tangoit (Indian), 121
Taylor, John, the Water Poet, 185–86
Tempest, The (Shakespeare), 147, 148
    Ariel in, 160–63
    at Blackfriars Theater, 155–56, 157
    Caliban in, 163–67, 185, 192, 194, 195
    endurance of, 191
    "Full Fathom Five," 182
    influence of, 184–85, 194–95, 196
    language of, 157, 171
    popularity of, 182, 184
    production of, 157–68, 169–80
    publication of, 184
    putting the story together, 152–56
    sources of ideas for, 149–52, 154–55,
        157, 182, 191
    "Where the Bee Sucks," 182
Thomas, William, *Historye of Italye*,
    149
Tien, Jasper, 4, 146
Torrid Zone, 31
Tsenacomoco, Powhatans in, 5–6,
    69, 151

Unity:
    arrival at Jamestown, 104, 127
    births at sea, 31
    disappearance in hurricane, 33
    leaving England, 12